Building
Media
Relationships

Building Media Relationships

How to Establish, Maintain, and Develop
Long-term Relationships with the Media

SECOND EDITION

by
Susan Sommers

OXFORD
UNIVERSITY PRESS

OXFORD
UNIVERSITY PRESS

70 Wynford Drive, Don Mills, Ontario M3C 1J9
www.oupcanada.com

Oxford University Press is a department of the University of Oxford.
It furthers the University's objective of excellence in research, scholarship,
and education by publishing worldwide in

Oxford New York
Auckland Cape Town Dar es Salaam Hong Kong Karachi
Kuala Lumpur Madrid Melbourne Mexico City Nairobi
New Delhi Shanghai Taipei Toronto

With offices in
Argentina Austria Brazil Chile Czech Republic France Greece
Guatemala Hungary Italy Japan Poland Portugal Singapore
South Korea Switzerland Thailand Turkey Ukraine Vietnam

Oxford is a trade mark of Oxford University Press
in the UK and in certain other countries

Published in Canada
by Oxford University Press

Copyright © Oxford University Press Canada 2009

The DVD accompanying this text is © Media Skills & Diversity Support
Group, 2006. Used with permission. www.mediaskillsanddiversity.com

The moral rights of the author have been asserted

Database right Oxford University Press (maker)

First published 2009

All rights reserved. No part of this publication may be reproduced,
stored in a retrieval system, or transmitted, in any form or by any means,
without the prior permission in writing of Oxford University Press,
or as expressly permitted by law, or under terms agreed with the appropriate
reprographics rights organization. Enquiries concerning reproduction
outside the scope of the above should be sent to the Rights Department,
Oxford University Press, at the address above.

You must not circulate this book in any other binding or cover
and you must impose this same condition on any acquirer.

Library and Archives Canada Cataloguing in Publication

Sommers, Susan
Building media relationships : how to establish, maintain & develop
long-term relationships with the media / Susan Sommers. — 2nd ed.

Includes bibliographical references.
ISBN 978-0-19-542695-3

1. Public relations—Canada. 2. Mass media and business—Canada.
3. Industrial publicity—Canada. I. Title.

HD59.S64 2008   659.2'0971   C2008-902371-4

1 2 3 4 - 12 11 10 09
This book is printed on permanent (acid-free) paper ∞.
Printed in Canada

Contents

Acknowledgements   vii

Credits   vii

Introduction   ix

About the Author   xi

Part 1   **Understanding Media Relations   1**
Chapter 1   The Role of Media Relations   3
Chapter 2   Understanding the Media   10
Chapter 3   Media Relations in Practice   21

Part 2   **Developing a Media Relations Program   33**
Chapter 4   Conducting Research   35
Chapter 5   Analyze: Problems, Goals, and Strategies   43

Part 3   **Executing a Media Relations Program   67**
Chapter 6   Developing a Media Database   69
Chapter 7   Creating a Media Kit   83
Chapter 8   Contacting the Media   129
Chapter 9   Managing Media Interviews   147
Chapter 10   Staging Media Events   157
Chapter 11   Monitoring the Media, and Measuring
and Evaluating Success   169

Part 4   **Issues Management and Crisis Communications   185**
Chapter 12   Defining Your Issues and Creating a Plan   187
Chapter 13   Avoiding/Preparing for a Crisis and
Creating a Plan   199
Chapter 14   Crisis Communication and Management
(with contributions from Kim Taylor Galway,
Perfect 10 Communications)   210

Appendix   Media Relations Past and Present   225

Resources   Media Organizations and Associations   232
Media Relations Online Resources   233
PR/Media Relations Blogs   233
Canadian Public Relations Society Accreditation Reading List   235

Index   239

Acknowledgements

Many people have contributed directly and indirectly to this book.

Thanks to Katherine Skene, Jennifer Charlton, and Oxford University Press, who recognized the opportunity for a new edition of *Building Media Relationships* and remained committed to my vision.

Thanks to my mentor, Ruth Hammond, who taught me well and has always been an inspiration to me—you are a clear example of how someone can be ethical, honest, and passionate in this industry.

Thanks to my colleagues—to all the people who I have worked with, and for, over the years, for helping me to understand Canadian media: Melanie Kurzuk, Kim Taylor Galway, Sue Davidson, Allison Baird, Lee MacTavish, Yvonne Burnside, Beverly Bowen, Jane O'Hare, Edna Levitt, Marcia McClung, Anne Sarsfield, and Lorraine Hunter.

A special thanks to the following companies for graciously sharing the experiences, tools, and techniques of their successful media relations campaigns, for permitting me to reproduce examples of their work, and for contributing to this book: Canadian Public Relations Society, International Association of Business Communicators, Aids Committee of Toronto (ACT), Argyle Communications, BC Housing, Blue Nose International Marathon, Carl Friesen, City of Edmonton (Marcomm Works), CNW Group, Gill Research, Hill & Knowlton Canada, Kim Taylor Galway, MT&L Public Relations, Nestle Purina PetCare, Purolator Courier Ltd., Teresa Donia, *The Toronto Star*, Virgin Mobile Canada, and Weber Shandwick Worldwide (Toronto).

Thanks to my students, who have participated in my workshops and courses over the past 15 years, shared their successes and problems, and provided their insights. I have learned as much as I have taught. Thanks for supporting, encouraging, and challenging me over the years.

Thanks to my family—to my mother, Lee Sommers, who at 93 continues to inspire me; to my husband Peter, for his encouragement and commitment; to my two daughters, Andrea and Danielle; and to my brother, Howard.

And finally, thanks to my readers. I hope that this book will be a constant resource to you, and I welcome your comments, suggestions, and additions. Please contact me at susan@susansommers.ca

Enjoy this book and good luck in building long-term media relationships.

Credits

Introduction

Over the years, the media has always fascinated me: I wrote for the media, pitched to the media, talked about the media, and taught media relations. I had my minutes of fame—and I had hours of anonymity. I wrote articles ranging from how to select the most gorgeous handmade porcelain vase to how to find the best mattress. My media relations clients praised me for the front-page coverage they received and rejected me when the media didn't turn up at their special events.

So, why did I write this book? Over the past 30 years, I have seen a great deal of the mistrust and misunderstanding that exists between the people who seek media coverage and the writers and producers who fill the available time and space. Reporters and producers explain that they are just trying to do their jobs—to present 'news' that is relevant to their audience; the public feels that the media only want to sensationalize and distort the truth. Most of the current books about media relations reinforce this adversarial image, with aggressive words such as 'managing', 'controlling' and 'confronting' in the titles.

With this in mind, I decided to write a book on how to work both professionally and productively with the media. I was lucky enough to gain the support of high-profile Canadian companies and organizations willing to share the details of their award-winning media relations campaigns. This book is designed for anyone responsible for generating media understanding and coverage for any corporation, organization, non-profit, or small business, regardless of size or scope. It provides tips, information, and exercises on all aspects of a media relations campaign, from research through to evaluation, in order to help ensure your success.

The second edition of *Building Media Relationships* was updated and expanded as a way to distill my 30-year career of working with the Canadian media as a journalist, a public relations consultant, a trainer, and a teacher. I believe that there is nothing more exciting and rewarding for an organization or company than building solid, on-going relationships with the media. Those are, after all, the only kind that matter.

Susan Sommers, 2008
Toronto, Canada

About the Author

Susan Sommers is an award-winning journalist, speaker, trainer, marketing consultant, educator, and coach with 40 years of experience in business communications. She is one of Canada's leading experts in marketing and media relations consulting and training.

Susan was born and raised in New Jersey and earned a Masters Degree from Columbia University and a Bachelor of Science Degree from Syracuse University. After moving to Toronto, she received a Public Relations Certificate from the University of Toronto.

In 1982, Susan founded her own agency, susan sommers + associates, which has designed marketing and publicity programs for hundreds of companies and organizations in the private and public sectors in Canada and in the United States.

Susan is the author of four books: *Handmade in Ontario* (Van Nostrand Reinhold, 1976); *Building Media Relationships* (Irwin Publishing, 2002); *media wise* (United Way of York Region, 2002); and *Building Media Relationships, Second edition* (Oxford University Press, 2008). She has also written weekly columns for *The Globe and Mail* and *The Toronto Star*, as well as monthly columns for *Toronto Life Magazine* and PR Canada's online newsletter.

Susan has developed credit courses in Marketing and Media Relations for Schulich School of Business (York University), University of Western Ontario, Ryerson Polytechnic University, George Brown College, and Sheridan College. She currently teaches through the University of Toronto (Continuing Studies), Sprott School of Business (Carleton University), Humber College, and Canadian Fundraiser.

For over 15 years, Susan has also designed and delivered hundreds of workshops, presentations, and in-house training programs for corporations, retailers, small business owners, sales professionals, associations, non-profit groups, and government agencies. She is a popular keynote speaker and workshop leader for associations, Boards of Trade, and Chambers of Commerce throughout North America.

Susan's newest inspirational workshop—Achieve It!—is based on her experiences while training for and completing marathons in 2005 and 2007.

Part 1

Understanding Media Relations

Chapter 1

The Role of Media Relations

There is no single definition of media relations. This is largely because the practice of media relations has such a broad range of applications. Media relations, for example, can be part of a promotional campaign to increase awareness of a new product or service. Media relations can also be defensive, for example, to help a company maintain a positive public image. In this chapter, we'll examine these diverse roles.

Chapter Summary

By the end of Chapter 1, you will be able to:

- understand media relations in the context of marketing and promotion,
- define media relations,
- determine the advantages and disadvantages to publicity and advertising,
- understand the role of media relations and the communications process, and
- outline the top ten reasons for setting up a media relations program.

Marketing, Promotion, and Media Relations

Media relations programs are most often undertaken as part of a larger campaign to achieve a specific objective. For example, let's say that a snack-food company's main objective is increased sales, and it determines that the introduction of a new product will achieve this goal. Current market research points to increased consumer demand for healthier foods, so the company develops a new line of potato chips that have less fat but plenty of flavour. To enhance consumer acceptance, the chips are sold at the same price as higher-fat brands. To ensure widespread availability, the company sets up distribution channels to all major retailers. Finally, to ensure customer awareness, the new chips must be promoted and, ideally, customers must be prompted to purchase the product. This combination—product (or service), price, distribution, and promotion—is defined as the **marketing mix**.

Media Relations

Ask someone to define media relations and you'll get a wide variety of answers. Here are a few of the most useful descriptions.

- The development and maintenance of effective communication with representatives of the print and broadcast media in order to facilitate the flow of information to the public by explaining programs and activities; answering media inquiries; and supplying feature, background, and current information.
- Communicating the right message to the right audience through the right medium at the right time.
- Providing the media with your Key Messages.
- Establishing and maintaining relationships with reporters who cover stories relevant to an organization and the business it performs. Examples include political reporters, health reporters, or financial reporters. The objective of media relations is to communicate information about the organization and its goals to educate the public and foster positive public perception.
- Putting a positive spin on an unfavourable event.

Marketing

Marketing activities include 'inbound marketing', such as market research, and 'outbound marketing', which includes promotions, public relations and publicity, advertising, and sales.

Promotions

While all components of the marketing mix are important, **promotion** is vital to the success of a new product or service because consumers must almost always be given a reason to buy something unfamiliar. Indeed, since companies and organizations are constantly competing for consumer attention, promotion is also very important to the ongoing viability of established products and services.

Public relations, publicity, and media relations

While the terms **public relations**, **publicity**, and **media relations** are often used interchangeably, and while they can involve similar goals and methods, public relations and publicity are nevertheless different types of promotion.

   Public relations is generally more closely identified with a company or organization's management than its marketing department, and it typically involves the development and execution of communications strategies designed to influence the attitudes of specific groups (or '**publics**') toward the organization. These publics may include current and prospective customers (in which case the communication is promotional in the traditional sense), but can also extend to employees, shareholders, regulatory authorities, and the community in which the organization operates. Public relations efforts are generally intended to create or support a positive image, and they often achieve this through activities such as the sponsorship of cultural or sporting events, or the provision of information that is (or is perceived to be) in the public interest. The effectiveness of these activities does not necessarily depend on media coverage, although positive coverage is always helpful.

The PR Practitioner's View

What is public relations? Here's how two PR organizations define it.

- *From the Canadian Public Relations Society (CPRS)*: 'The management function which provides the leadership and expertise to evaluate public attitudes; identifies the policies and procedures of an individual or organization with the public interest; and plans and executes a program of action to earn public understanding and acceptance.'
- *From the International Association of Business Communicators (IABC)*: 'Public relations explains an organization's actions and policies in a focused, consistent and credible manner, to both employees and publics outside of the organization. The result is an informed and motivated workforce, a well recognized brand name and a favourable public image.'

Publicity, unlike public relations, is entirely focused on getting a specific message about a company and/or its products and services into the media. In this sense, publicity is similar to advertising; the difference is that the company or organization does not pay for publicity messages. Also, since the message is typically presented as a news story, it is often perceived as having more credibility than advertising. Publicity does have its drawbacks, however. For example, the message is much harder to control when it's unpaid. This is one of the primary challenges that confront the media relations practitioner.

Advertising

Advertising—perhaps the most widely recognized form of mass promotion—communicates a company's message through a variety of media, including traditional print (newspapers and magazines) and broadcast (radio and television) media, as well as outdoor and transit ads, and, more recently, interactive banner ads on websites. Advertising is distinguished from other types of media promotion in that the advertiser, who is identified as such in the advertisement itself, pays it for. The message appears exactly as the advertiser created it, in a space or at a time selected by the advertiser.

Advertorial

An advertorial combines advertising and editorial into one article or within the scope of a publication. Advertorials are a growing trend that many reporters and writers feel compromises their ability to report what is 'newsworthy'. Advertorials are fueled by the competition that exists both between and within media outlets.

Direct selling

Direct selling involves one-on-one communication between a company or organization's representative (salesperson) and the prospective buyer of its products or services, either by face-to-face contact or by other means, such as the telephone or email. Although it is less efficient than the mass media in terms of communicating a promotional message, and therefore it is more costly, direct selling can be highly effective—if only because the message is harder to ignore.

Sales promotion

Sales promotion is a catch-all category that includes coupons, in-store demonstrations, free samples, point-of-sale (POS) displays, and other promotional events, all of which are designed to enhance consumer awareness of a product or service. Where such promotions are intended to attract media attention, they will often involve the services of a media relations practitioner.

Publicity or Advertising?

Publicity offers a number of advantages over advertising, but it is not without its drawbacks. Consider the following pros and cons and you'll understand why the advertising business is still going strong.

Pros

- *Lower cost.* Publicity is essentially free—although a media relations program isn't (as we'll see later in the book). Still, even the most elaborate program, if successful, is substantially less expensive than an advertising campaign.
- *Higher impact.* People pay more attention to news than to advertising, much of which they automatically 'tune out'. Messages presented in the context of news have a much greater impact.
- *More credibility.* News stories are generally considered to be objective, and therefore more believable than paid advertising.
- *More detail.* Advertising must communicate its message within a limited space or time. A news story can provide much more detail about a company and its products or services.
- *Potentially greater reach.* If a news story is carried by a national news service or broadcast network, it will be read, seen, or heard by significantly more people than an advertisement (unless it is part of a multimillion-dollar media campaign).

Cons

- *No guarantee of coverage.* A media relations practitioner can provide compelling, newsworthy media releases to every media outlet in the country, and still not be assured any coverage—particularly if a major news story breaks on the same day. An advertisement, on the other hand, is guaranteed to appear in the space or time purchased.
- *No control over the message.* While the subject of a media release may capture the media's attention, the resulting story will not necessarily be positive or presented with any meaningful level of detail. Reporters have credibility because they are generally free to present their stories as they see fit. Advertisers, on the other hand, have complete control over their messages.
- *Potentially limited reach.* Publicity is dependent on timing. If a story is not picked up while it is still fresh (or if it is carried by only a few small media outlets), the chance to convey a company's message cannot be recovered. An advertisement can reach as many people and can be repeated as many times as the advertiser's budget allows.

Media Relations and the Communications Process

The various activities that make up the marketing mix all involve some form of communication. Understanding the communications process—and how to maximize its effectiveness—is essential for the media relations practitioner. Fundamentally, communications can be broken down into four elements:

- the message to be communicated;
- the source or sender of the message;
- the medium or distribution channel of the message, and
- the receiver of the message.

At first glance, this would appear to be a simple one-way transaction, requiring only the transfer of information from sender to receiver. But successful communication is a two-way process. A message that is perfectly clear and meaningful to the sender may not register with the receiver. This is why the sender's message must be constructed with the receiver's concerns, ideas, and perceptions in mind. This construction process, often referred to as 'encoding', selects symbols (words and/or pictures) that will be meaningful to the receiver, often by appealing to the receiver's self-interest. The communication is successful when the sender's message creates a desired response (such as a change in attitude or opinion) from the receiver.

Consider, for example, a large multinational corporation that is perceived by the public as being more interested in profits than in the environmental effects of its operations. The company has just implemented a major recycling program and wants to convey the message 'We care about the environment,' to the public. Using paid advertising, the company could simply state the message directly. But such a claim would be unlikely to have much credibility with a skeptical public. Instead, the company's media relations person creates a media release announcing the recycling program, supplying impressive figures about how much waste will be reduced and outlining the positive impact this will have on overburdened landfill sites. The media release, accompanied by a photo of the company president surrounded by massive recycling bins, is distributed to the media, and results in a number of favourable news stories.

In this example the message, although not stated overtly, is nevertheless communicated effectively because it is 'encoded' in a way that is meaningful to the concerns of the receiver.

The Top 10 Reasons to Set Up a Media Relations Program

1. To enhance a company or organization's sales and profits, attract financial support, and raise funds
2. To educate the public on how to choose, buy, or use products and services, motivating them to take action
3. To raise awareness and credibility for a company or organization and its products and services
4. To help a company and its spokesperson become an acknowledged expert in its industry—to be the one the media call when they want a quote
5. To test-market a new idea, launch a new product or service, or diversify a business
6. To build a new image
7. To generate goodwill, prestige, trust, and approval from key markets, which will then attract new employees, clients, members, donors, shareholders, sponsors, and volunteers
8. To overcome resistance or counteract misconceptions
9. To help to insulate an organization or company during a crisis
10. To support other aspects of a company's marketing program, such as advertising and sales promotion

Exercises

1. Media relations has no single definition. Should it have one? Should practitioners be licensed?
2. Michael Levine, author of *Guerilla PR*, talks about a state of 'data smog' in which consumers are walking around utterly overwhelmed by the amount of messages they receive. Discuss this statement.

Chapter 2

Understanding the Media

A media relations practitioner must fully understand the media, be able to think like an advertiser *and* like a reporter, and appreciate the needs of both. In this chapter, we'll examine the most common types of media and what they need.

Chapter Summary

By the end of Chapter 2, you will be able to:

- see the media from the perspectives of an advertiser and a reporter;
- determine the advantages and disadvantages of various forms of print media, including newspapers, newswire services, magazines, zines, inserts, bulletins, and newsletters;
- determine the advantages and disadvantages of watching television and listening to the radio;
- determine the advantages and disadvantages of the Internet;
- think like a reporter;
- understand the types of information that are considered 'news'; and
- appreciate the history of the newswire in Canada.

Seeing Both Sides of the Media

In Chapter 1, we saw how publicity and advertising often share a common goal—to build public awareness of a company or organization and its products/services. But publicity and advertising each achieve this goal through different means.

Advertising involves crafting a message, choosing the media that will most effectively convey that message to the target audience, and purchasing space or time in those media. This is a simple business transaction between the advertiser (or its agency) and the medium's advertising department; there is no evaluation—apart from issues of decency or taste—as to whether the medium's audience will find the message of interest or value.

Advertorials, as discussed in Chapter 1, are a combination of advertising and editorial coverage of a company or organization within a publication. The company or organization buys an advertisement and, in addition, receives editorial coverage. Today, as competition grows between media outlets—and even within media conglomerates—more and more media combine advertising and editorial coverage.

Publicity, on the other hand, is not paid for. It involves the editorial department, and its integrity is measured by its independence from advertising. Editorial decision-makers, such as a magazine editor or a television news director, must consider the interests of their audience first. As a result, publicity must be presented as something newsworthy or valuable to the audience.

A successful publicity campaign requires an understanding of both sides of the media. It means thinking like a reporter in terms of the message and thinking like an advertiser in terms of choosing the media that will be most effective in conveying that message. Later in this chapter we'll examine what reporters look for in a story; however, it is worthwhile to first consider the different types of media that act as vehicles for publicity.

Print Media

For centuries, the printed word has ruled supreme. And while electronic media has significantly eroded this supremacy over the last century, print remains a powerful force in the world of mass communications.

Newspapers

Although they offer less immediacy than radio and television, newspapers still provide a significant amount of timeliness and flexibility. With advances in production technology, newspapers now require very little lead-time and satellite transmission allows national newspapers to be printed locally and distributed in major markets throughout the country. In recent years, newspapers have responded to competition from other media by becoming more reader-friendly; they have redesigned their formats, increased the use of colour, and added special sections and themed supplements.

Newspapers vary in a number of ways. The frequency of newspaper publication can be daily, weekly, or monthly, and the reach of any given newspaper varies in terms of a national, regional, or local/community audience. As more and more readers turn to their local communities for a sense of belonging, community newspapers have grown in both size and popularity. The market focus is also an element of variability. In addition to general-audience publications, newspapers are often targeted to specific audiences, including trade and business groups, ethnic and linguistic groups, and universities and colleges, as well as 'underground' and 'alternative' readers.

Most newspapers also have extensive websites that allow readers to view current stories or search for archived stories relating to a particular subject. This enhances the papers' timeliness and provides stories with a life beyond the print editions.

Newspapers

Pros

- *Flexibility*. The distribution, variety, and location of a newspaper makes it easy to target a specific audience.
- *Depth of coverage*. Newspapers typically provide greater detail than broadcast media. In addition, regional or community papers will often give extended coverage to local events that other media will not.
- *Reader loyalty*. Daily newspapers provide day-to-day continuity, create intimacy with readers, and inspire loyalty and confidence. Locally-produced community newspapers also enjoy a loyal readership.
- *Convenience*. An audience can choose when to read newspapers, whereas broadcast news must be seen or heard at a specific time.

Cons

- *Incomplete readership*. Few people have time to read an entire newspaper and so many stories will be missed.
- *Greater potential for inaccuracy*. Newspaper stories are usually written quickly, which can potentially lead to inaccuracies and/or superficial coverage.
- *Headline spin*. Newspaper reporters do not write the headlines to their own stories; the editors do. As a result, headlines can be sensational and/or unrepresentative of the story's content.

On the Wire

Newswire services are privately owned organizations that function like a large newspaper, complete with reporters, editors, bureau chiefs, and photographers, but don't publish as one. Instead, they offer their resources to other papers (as well as television and radio stations) that pay a fee for the service. This category includes Canadian Press (CP), Associated Press (AP), United Press International (UPI), Southam News Service, Dow Jones Canada, Reuters Canada, Bloomberg News Wire, Bridge News, Canadian University Press, Sterling News, Agence France Press (AFP), Press Canadienne, and Telemedia. In the UK, the Press Association (PA) is the sole editorial newswire.

The largest Canadian newswire service is Canadian Press (CP), which has print and broadcast divisions; their head office is in Toronto, while their French-language operations—La Presse Canadienne (PC) and Nouvelles Télé-Radio (NTR)—are directed from Montreal. Editorial offices in Canada are located in St John's, Halifax, Fredericton, Quebec City, Montreal, Ottawa, Toronto, Winnipeg, Regina, Edmonton, Calgary, Vancouver, and Victoria. Editors to contact include sports, business, arts and lifestyles, picture services, foreign news, and features.

For the media relations practitioner, newswire services offer a large advantage: they provide instantaneous stories and widespread distribution across the country, including distribution to many smaller papers and stations that rely on the service as a primary news source. However, even if a story gets picked up, media relations practitioners have virtually no control over where it will be published and how it will be presented.

Magazines

Magazines are generally more targeted than newspapers to specific audiences with shared interests or affiliations. Published in a variety of formats—most often in full colour and on glossy stock—magazines typically have higher production values than newspapers. They are produced with various frequencies, ranging from biweekly to monthly to annually. Magazines can be consumer-oriented (designed for mass circulation of general interest) or trade-related (designed for people in a specific business or industry).

Other types of magazine publications include newsmagazines and business and finance magazines. Some magazines, such as those for college and university alumni or those for professional associations, have very limited—although sometimes influential—audiences. The best resource for information about Canadian-produced magazines is the Canadian Magazine Publishers Association (CMPA). This national, non-profit organization represents more than 300 Canadian consumer magazines, both large and small, and is the public voice of the Canadian magazine publishing industry.

Magazines

Pros

- *Attentive readership*. Magazines are generally read more completely than newspapers. They provide stories with greater focus and visibility, and they typically cover a topic, organization, or issue in great depth.
- *Well-defined audience*. Magazines enable you to reach a specific market directly with stories that are of particular interest to their readership.
- *Receptive to publicity-oriented stories*. Magazine editors are always looking for well-written feature articles that will be of interest to their readers. Business magazines, for example, will often run executive profiles or stories about successful products.

Con

- *Long lead times*. Magazines usually require stories three to four months before publication. This may be too long for time-sensitive publicity.

Other print media
Zines

As might be inferred from their abbreviated name (a contraction of 'magazine' or 'fanzine'), zines are a highly specialized subset of the magazine category, often focusing on a single topic or, in the case of 'fanzines', a particular celebrity or musical group. Zines are produced by one person or a small group of people, often created for fun or personal reasons, and tend to be irreverent, bizarre, and/or esoteric. Zines are not 'mainstream' publications—they generally do not contain advertisements (except, sometimes, advertisements for other zines), are not intended for a mass audience, and are not usually produced to make a profit. An 'e-zine' is a zine that is distributed online. Unlike their print counterparts, many e-zines have a wide readership and cover topics ranging from politics to science fiction.

Newsletters, inserts, and bulletins

Newsletters, inserts, and bulletins are produced for a wide variety of specific markets. Published on a monthly, bimonthly, quarterly, or semi-annual basis, they are sometimes sold by subscription but more often are distributed free of charge. These types of publications are created both for and by special interest groups and clubs, business groups (such as Rotary or a local Chamber of Commerce), church members, company employees, university students and alumni, government agencies, and retailers. The content of a typical newsletter, insert, or bulletin includes feature profiles, trends, problems and solutions, new products and services, and upcoming events.

Broadcast Media

The CBC—Canada's public broadcaster—is the oldest broadcasting service in Canada; it was first established in its present form on 2 November 1936.

The **Canadian Association of Broadcasters (CAB)** is the national voice of Canada's private broadcasters, representing the vast majority of Canadian programming services, including private radio and television stations, networks, specialty channels, and pay-per-view services.

Television

A powerful medium in terms of its immediacy and impact (providing both visual and sound information), television is now supplied by conventional transmission, by cable (analog and digital), and by satellite. As a result, individual television stations can be seen almost anywhere; they are no longer limited to their immediate broadcast area, and their reach can now equal that which was once available only through the major networks.

With the number of television channels expanding each year, audiences are becoming increasingly fragmented—so much so that the 'broadcasting' is often replaced by 'narrow casting'. While this makes reaching a mass audience more difficult for the media relations professional, it also makes it easier to target a specific market.

All types of television stations, including commercial, community, and multilingual stations, provide opportunities for publicity.

Commercial stations

Commercial stations produce news stories and features, documentaries, talk shows, and call-in shows. Advertising sponsors most shows, although stations may also provide both unpaid public service announcements and non-commercial programming of interest to the local community. Many stations provide 'community information message wheels'. The 'message wheels' enable non-profits to promote their special events at no cost through the station.

Community stations

Community programming emphasizes local content and production. Its role is to facilitate self-expression by members of the community.

Multilingual stations

Meeting the needs of Canada's ethnically diverse population (particularly in major urban centres), multilingual stations target specific linguistic groups. OMNI TV is Canada's first multi-lingual television system. OMNI-TV features programming in more than 18 languages and reflects 20 different cultures. It produces more than 22 hours of original programming each week, including newscasts in Portuguese, Italian, and Chinese.

Television

Pros

- *Timeliness.* Television provides virtually as-it-happens coverage of news stories.
- *Reach.* While the increasing number of channels is fragmenting television audiences, television remains the best way to reach the largest number of people.
- *Impact and persuasiveness.* The power of television to persuade an audience is unparalleled by any other medium.
- *Range of opportunities for publicity.* Television stations provide airtime for public service announcements. Cable stations are also a very important source of publicity.

Cons

- *Cost.* Supplying stories with video content can be very expensive.
- *Lack of focus.* While viewer profiles for some specialty channels are reasonably well defined, the audiences for most channels vary considerably by program and time of day.

Radio

From the peak of its popularity in the 1930s and 1940s, radio has declined sharply as a mass medium. At one time it was expected that television would displace radio completely; however, radio has since found its niche alongside television, reaching audiences that television can't and providing defined formats that appeal to specific demographics. Radio also provides opportunities for in-depth interviews and in-depth coverage of issues and themes.

Categories of radio include network, local, multilingual, and university/college. CHIN—the pioneer in multicultural radio broadcasting—was the first multicultural/ multilingual station to be established in Ontario. The contribution of CHIN to the cause of multiculturalism and to achieving understanding and tolerance between people of many national, racial, and religious origins has been recognized and acknowledged throughout Canada.

Radio stations run public service announcements for non-profit public interest groups, as well as political, educational, and public affairs programs. These announcements can be a good source of coverage, but there is no guarantee they will be aired.

Radio

Pros

- *Immediacy*. Whether jogging or driving, radio can be (and is) taken along.
- *Intimacy*. Radio is far less intrusive than television and requires less concentration than newspapers. It is a subtle, powerful persuader.
- *Seasonal advantage*. Radio is often called 'the summer medium'—as outdoor activities increase, television viewing drops off and radio listening increases.

Con

- *Less impact*. Because it delivers only an audio message, radio's impact is inherently limited. Furthermore, because radio is often used as background sound, audience attention can be uncertain.

Internet

The Internet provides text and visual information that can be viewed by anyone with a computer and a connection, whether that connection is via a modem, cable, or a wireless router. The growth of high-speed connections (cable, digital subscriber lines, and satellite), has allowed the Internet to develop into a medium for transmitting both audio and video content.

As discussed earlier, many print and broadcast outlets now supply their traditional offerings on complementary websites; there are also a number of media outlets that are Internet-only. Many journalists also maintain their own blogs on the Internet.

Internet

Pros

- *Reach*. Internet users can reach a given site from anywhere in the world.
- *Immediacy*. Websites can be updated with new information almost instantly.

Con

- *Credibility*. Unlike other types of media, there are few entry barriers for 'publishing' online. Anyone can post whatever they like on a website, whether it's accurate or not. New media—blogs, social media sites, and RRS feeds, for example—mean that organizations and companies need to continuously monitor and evaluate what people are saying about them online.

Understanding the Needs of the Media

A large part of a media relations practitioner's job is to reconcile two sets of objectives: those of the client—to obtain publicity for a company or organization and its products or services—and those of the media—to provide as much important and interesting information as possible to their viewers, listeners, and readers. Ultimately, the client's objectives can only be achieved by understanding—and meeting—the media's needs.

Is It News?

Before approaching a media representative with a story, ask yourself whether what you are offering has a 'news hook' or 'angle'. To determine if your story has a hook, consider the following points:

- Is the information timely? Can it be tied to a current major story, a national or international event, an issue, a personality in the news, or an industry trend?
- Is the story tied into an issue that is currently 'hot', such as fraud, unemployment, the environment, the impact of technology, government deficits and debt, employment equity, training and education, or corporate contributions to local communities?
- What's 'new' about the development or product/service described in your news story? Is it the first? The last? The latest? The biggest?
- Is the story of benefit to the audience? Does it provide how-to information on choosing, buying, or using products or services?
- Is your story about people? Does it concern success stories or the winning of awards and scholarships by employees, volunteers, or customers?
- Is the story accurate, truthful, and complete? Can it be easily checked out and confirmed?
- Do you have a credible spokesperson or third-party source who can be interviewed and quoted? Can you provide back-up in the form of great anecdotes, quotes, and/or statistics?
- Is the story visually-interesting for a television interview?
- Does the story have 'legs'? In other words, is it strong enough to warrant on-going coverage or follow-up coverage in the future?
- Finally, is the information blatantly self-serving? Does it sound like an advertisement for the company or organization? If it sounds that way to you, it certainly will to an editor.

Thinking like a Reporter

In general, reporters are ordinary people trying to do a job; they must report news-worthy events and issues. Reporters try to be objective and to get as many sides of a story as possible; however, the realities of the job—which include the pressures of deadlines and the need to fill a certain number of inches of print or so many minutes of air time—often make absolute fairness impossible to achieve. When a reporter has been assigned to cover an event, he or she must prepare a story with or without input from everyone involved. Consequently, your delay or refusal to provide needed information won't kill the story but will instead result in an inaccurate or one-sided version being published—and that will please neither you nor the reporter. In the end, news is what the editor thinks it is. If the editor thinks you have a problem, then you do.

A History of Newswire in Canada

Mankind's desire to know what is happening around him has been responsible for a myriad of technological changes in the nearly 160 years since Paul Julius Reuter used carrier pigeons in 1849 to deliver stock market information from Brussels to Aachen, Germany.

But the rise of the Internet and personal computers as a staple in nearly every Canadian's daily life has done nothing to quench the thirst for timely informa-tion. It is in this rapidly changing world that CNW Group has firmly positioned itself as a leader in the provision of communication services to thousands of pub-lic corporations, governments, and private organizations.

CNW Group, formerly Canada NewsWire, was founded in 1960 and depended on copper wire and teletype printers to move news releases from clients to the media. That changed in the 1970s when computer-to-computer delivery became possible with the introduction of satellite delivery.

But Canadians continued to demand more information and they wanted it faster. They wanted much more than just plain text; they demanded photos, graphs, charts, video and audio clips. And they wanted to receive it on the plat-form of their choice.

To meet this insatiable appetite for information, CNW Group moved to lead-ing edge IP-based technology in 2005 to distribute all types of content—be it photos, audio, plain text or video—to thousands of points in the media and financial community. This Internet-based technology is flexible enough to meet all of the requirements of our hundreds of drop points but also robust enough to satisfy the increasing demand for multimedia content.

continued

But improving delivery is only one part of the equation. CNW Group has also introduced a new editorial system that is resulting in dramatically increased accuracy and significant declines in turnaround times. The editorial system is fully integrated into a new service fulfillment system that streamlines and consolidates all processing from the minute a draft news release is received at one of our News Centres to distribution and through to invoicing.

In early 2007, Access CNW, a full-service client portal was introduced that allows clients to control their interactions with CNW from their own desktop in a totally secure and easy to use environment.

In continuing to strive to be Canada's full-service communications services provider, CNW Group has added an in-house photo unit that provides a full suite of photo assignment, distribution, and archive services; a translation unit capable of handling a wide variety of translation needs in a number of languages; and MediaVantage, Canada's most comprehensive media monitoring service.

Article by Joe Freeman, Director, News, Wire & Distribution Products, CNW Group, July 2007

Exercises

1. Tabloid journalism, which focuses on celebrities, gossip, and scandal, has become increasingly pervasive. What does this mean to 'news', media relations, and publicity?
2. How have social media and citizen journalism changed our perceptions of the media and media outlets?
3. Discuss the validity of the following statements:
   a. Journalists write for journalists.
   b. The public sees journalists and politicians as being on the same side.
   c. Journalists worry about what their competitors are doing, not what their readers are doing.

Chapter 3

Media Relations in Practice

Thus far, Part 1 of this book has been devoted mainly to defining the context of media relations, and to examining its theoretical basis within the broader fields of public relations and marketing. In this chapter, we provide the groundwork for the remainder of the text, putting theory into practice, learning the essential elements of a media relations campaign, and observing the successes of real-life practitioners.

Chapter Summary

By the end of Chapter 3, you will be able to:

- develop and execute a media relations program using the RACE formula (Research, Analyze, Communicate, and Evaluate),
- understand the basic elements involved in a number of professional, award-winning case studies,
- define the possible roles and responsibilities of a media relations firm,
- see the 'big picture' in media relations practice, and
- know what to look for when hiring a media relations firm.

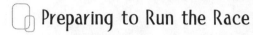 Preparing to Run the Race

In their book *Effective Public Relations* (Englewood, NJ: Prentice Hall, 1952), Scott M. Cutlip and Alan H. Centeras outline a four-step approach—known by its acronym, RACE—that is still used today in the media relations process. By following these steps in a methodical way, you can identify issues, solve problems, and achieve tangible results. In this chapter the RACE formula will be described briefly; it will be examined in greater detail in the following chapters.

Research

The research step asks the question: '**Where are we now?**' This is the fact-finding stage; your goal is to get to know your organization or company, and then describe it. This stage is a chance to listen to your key publics and provide an objective look at your company or organization. The research you do at this stage will also indicate trouble spots, problems, and potential crises. Steps in this process can include the following tasks:

- Reviewing existing research: sources can include studies and polls
- Identifying and describing all of your "publics": assess the importance of each and prioritize these markets
- Conducting employee and customer research: determine attitudes, opinions, and reactions of key publics to your company or organization; methodologies can include mailed questionnaires, telephone surveys, comment cards, focus groups, and correspondence analysis, as well as personal contacts
- Performing a media audit: examine attitudes, awareness, and behaviour through media questionnaires, reports, and media content analysis. Typical elements of a media audit include:
    - assessing current media lists;
    - reviewing past media contacts and coverage received, noting its type, extent, placement, and tone;
    - examining past advertising; and
    - analyzing the company's competitors and looking at their past and current advertising, publicity, promotions, and events.

Analyze

This step of the RACE process asks the question: '**Where are we going?**' Using research data collected in the previous step, the analysis phase involves:

- understanding your organization's reputation with key publics;
- developing objectives and goals, as well as a plan to measure results;
- determining strategies and designing your Key Messages; and
- assessing your potential partners.

At this developmental stage, you can propose a media relations program for your company or organization, as well as a preliminary budget and a critical path/timetable with dates and assigned responsibilities.

Communicate

After determining where your company or organization wants to go, it is time to ask the question: '**How do we get there?**' This is the execution phase of a media relations program and involves using a variety of tactics or tools to accomplish the program's objectives. These tools, described in Part 3 (Chapters 7 to 11), include:

* developing a media list,
* preparing a Media Kit and an Internet Media Room,
* designing Key Messages,
* contacting and following up with key media,
* arranging and managing media interviews and appearances,
* organizing media previews and on-site media rooms/tables, and
* staging media events.

Evaluate

Once the media relations program has been executed, you should then ask the question: '**How did we do?**' There are a number of techniques you can use to measure and evaluate the program and make adjustments as required. Specific elements of the evaluation phase will ultimately depend on the type of media relations program involved, but you will typically find that you need to:

* arrange a wrap-up meeting;
* report media follow-up and monitor media coverage;
* create a media report that analyzes media coverage and content;
* conduct research with your key internal and external audiences;
* assess the effectiveness of your media tools;
* evaluate the program against stated, written objectives;
* document your media materials, media coverage, and media reports; and
* build for the future.

The measuring and evaluation phase, discussed in Part 3 (Chapter 11), provides important information for the next RACE formula.

How the Pros Do It

While this book will equip you with the tools and techniques necessary to become an accomplished media relations practitioner, there's no substitute for experience. For this reason, we will examine a number of award-winning case studies that demonstrate how the RACE process works in real life. First, we will briefly outline the scenario surrounding each example, and then we will discuss how it was achieved. As we discuss the RACE process in the following chapters, we will draw upon these case studies for further analysis.

CASE STUDY

Fashion Cares 2005, M.A.C. *VIVA GLAM* Bollywood Cowboy
Who: Lisa Bednarski, Weber Shandwick Worldwide (Toronto) for the AIDS Committee of Toronto
When: March–July 2005
Winner: 2006 IABC Ovation Award of Excellence, Media Relations up to $50,00.00

Need/Opportunity
In 2005, Fashion Cares, Canada's largest AIDS fundraising event, celebrated its 19th year in support of the AIDS Committee of Toronto (ACT). Fashion Cares is ACT's most important fundraising event generating more than 57% of ACT's fundraising revenues—money which finances the programs and services ACT directly and indirectly provides people living with HIV, including education, advocacy and emotional support.

   With more than 6,000 patrons, 200 accredited media and a list of celebrity performers, Fashion Cares enjoys international recognition as one of the premier charity benefits and is one of lead sponsor, M·A·C Cosmetics', highest-profile marketing events of the year. Although the event's roots are in HIV/AIDS awareness and fundraising, and its brand image is still provocative and outrageous, Fashion Cares has become a mainstream entertainment event of Torontonians. The evening features a Gala dinner, a Fashion Boutique including high-end items for home and fashion at dramatically reduced prices, on-site entertainment in a number of lounges and bars, capped off with a high-end fashion and entertainment show featuring internationally-recognized designers, models and entertainers.

CASE STUDY

The Purina Walk for Dog Guides
Who: **Daniel Tisch, APR, and Alison George, Argyle Communications**
When: **2005**
Winner: 2006 CPRS National Award of Excellence, Media Relations

Need/Opportunity

Nestlé Purina PetCare, a leading pet product company, is an active supporter of Lions Foundation of Canada Dog Guides—an Oakville-based organization that trains and provides dog guides to Canadians with visual, hearing, medical or physical disabilities, at no cost to the individual. In 2005, Purina became the title sponsor of Lions Foundation's most important annual fundraising event—the Purina Walk for Dog Guides.

CASE STUDY

The Launch of Virgin Mobile Canada

Who: Virgin Mobile PR Team

When: November 2004–March 2005, with the official launch days occurring on 1 March 2005 in Toronto, 2 March 2005 in Montreal, and 3 March 2005 in Vancouver.

Winner: 2006 IABC Gold Quill Award of Excellence

Need/Opportunity

In early 2005, Virgin Mobile Canada entered Canada's mobile phone service sector, which was heavily dominated by four established players. Virgin Mobile's much-anticipated entry into the pre-paid mobile phone sector—targeted to young Canadians frustrated by long-term contracts, confusing rates, and services catering to their parents' needs—required a comprehensive media relations program featuring its well-known Chairman, Sir Richard Branson, to support its launch into the Canadian market.

CASE STUDY

Purolator Tackle Hunger 2006

Who: Andrew Bryden and Tim Maloney, Purolator, and Hill & Knowlton

When: 17 June–21 October 2006

Winner: 2006 CPRS National Award of Merit, Community Relations

Need/Opportunity

As part of Purolator's larger commitment to drive away hunger in Canada, Purolator Tackle Hunger aims to increase food donations for local food banks in cities across Canada. Developed in partnership with the Canadian Football League and the Canadian Association of Food Banks, the program is comprised of game day food drives in CFL hometown cities, Grey Cup photo opportunities for the public and Purolator employees and customers, as well as a sack tally program in which Purolator donates the equivalent of a sacked quarterback's weight in food to the hometown region food bank.

Why Go Outside?

Many companies and organizations are large enough to develop and manage a media relations program themselves, yet it often makes more sense to hire outside media relations specialists. The most common reasons?

- They lack the expertise internally.
- They do not have the staff or time to spare.
- Media relations specialists have better contacts with specific media.
- Media relations specialists are able to be more realistic about budgeting than internal staff.
- Internal office politics are avoided by hiring an outside firm.
- The company or organization may want an outside firm that has national or international affiliations.
- An outside firm can provide or liaise with other services; for example, advertising, sales promotion, special events planning, etc.

Roles and Responsibilities of a Media Relations Firm or Consultant

The services offered by a media relations firm or consultant will vary depending on the client, the project, or the position. As we'll see as we discuss some of the previously mentioned case studies, the roles and responsibilities can include some, or all, of the following elements:

- Research:
  - designing, conducting, and evaluating communications audits of key markets, both internal (management and staff) and external (all other markets)
  - designing, conducting, and evaluating a media audit; creating surveys and questionnaires
- Strategic planning:
  - developing a PR needs analysis
  - examining objectives, long-term and short-term
  - developing overall strategy (long-term and short-term)
  - creating Key Messages and Q & As
  - preparing spokespeople for media interviews
  - developing employee communications

- researching and writing media materials, including Media Kit inserts and information for the Internet Media Room
  - organizing media campaigns and events
  - developing a budget and timetable; providing on-going strategic counsel
- Supervision and execution of campaign:
  - securing client input and all approvals
  - organizing on-going reporting and information meetings
  - providing the final report to measure and evaluate success of program
  - organizing staffing
  - developing checklists

CASE STUDY

Fashion Cares 2005, M.A.C. *VIVA GLAM* Bollywood Cowboy

Fashion Cares is planned, organized and executed by a volunteer Steering Committee of approximately 20 members, each managing their own sub-committee of volunteers to help in their respective areas. There are representatives from the event's main sponsors (M·A·C Cosmetics, the Bay and BMO Financial Group) as well as two full-time ACT staff members who also sit on the Steering Committee to act as liaison between ACT and the event organizers. Weber Shandwick was engaged to support the event as a media relations partner, providing human and office resources to the public relations committee led by Lisa Bednarski, co-chair of public relations on the Fashion Cares Steering Committee and vice president, consumer, for Weber Shandwick Worldwide's Toronto office.

CASE STUDY

The Purina Walk for Dog Guides

Purina engaged Argyle Communications to raise awareness of the walk in general—and Purina's involvement in particular.

CASE STUDY

The Launch of Virgin Mobile Canada

Virgin Mobile engaged Hill & Knowlton Canada as the PR Agency of Record for the launch of Virgin Mobile Canada. Virgin Mobile and Hill & Knowlton worked in a partnership to execute and manage all PR activities in advance, during and following the launch of Virgin Mobile. Responsibilities included:

- PR needs analysis
- Preparation of media materials: media advisory, media alert, news release, Q&A, product/service backgrounders, bios, key messages, VIP and media invitations

- Media relations pre-, during and post-launch day events
- Controlling media access to Richard Branson and Andrew Black at stunts, news conferences, and evening VIP events
- Prepping spokespeople for media interviews
- Launch day PR strategy and logistics
- PR rollout across Canada
- Responding to competitor and analyst criticism
- Ongoing liaison with affiliated agencies (i.e. advertising and event logistics)

CASE STUDY

Purolator Tackle Hunger 2006

While Purolator Tackle Hunger has raised a steady amount of food and cash donations for local food banks on game days since its inception in 2003, the program was not well known to audiences outside football circles. With 2006 marking the fourth year of the program, Purolator enlisted the help of Hill & Knowlton for the second year in a row to help raise the program's visibility in every community in hopes of increasing food and cash donations and positioning Purolator as a responsible corporate citizen committed to driving away hunger in Canada.

Reaching Strategic Goals Through Publishing Articles

by Carl Friesen, MBA, CMC

Contributed articles in magazines and newspapers can be a wonderful way to put one's message in front of a target market. These are articles written by an authoritative expert, providing useful information to readers. Generally contributed on a no-money basis—the author does not pay for coverage, and the publication pays no writer's fee—they can show the writer's ability to obtain results on behalf of the reader.

They are most relevant for a business-to-business professional such as an accountant, actuary, architect, consultant, engineer or lawyer. They can also work for a professional who sells to consumers, such as a personal financial planner, a physiotherapist or a lawyer who specializes in divorces, as well as a vendor of complex industrial products where the vendor's expertise is a big part of the relationship's success.

It is less available to business-to-consumer manufacturers, unless the goods in question are what marketers call 'high involvement'—which the customer buys only after significant research and planning. If the buyer feels the need to research the product before buying a product such as a sailboat, she or he will be

continued

willing to read an informative article about it such as 'Avoiding the ten most common errors in buying a racing yacht.' Contributed articles can have tremendous advantages from a media relations perspective.

Many media relations professionals have worked hard to arrange an interview between their client and the media—and are disappointed to find that the resulting coverage barely mentions the client, or even worse, makes the client look bad. A contributed article, by contrast, generally gets published pretty much exactly as written, meaning more dependable coverage.

Compared to advertising, contributed articles are low-cost. Consider a 1,500-word article that covers a double-page spread in a trade magazine—to buy an ad that would cover this much space might easily be $10,000 or more. Generally, the article will be more effective as a marketing tool—an interested potential customer or client will take the time to read it, and may clip it and/or send it to others, while the same person would just flip past an ad with barely a glance.

Despite the advantages, many media relations professionals seem reluctant to support their clients in getting published. The reasons often have to do with a lack of understanding of how to increase chances that the article will actually get written, and how to make it more likely to be accepted by the magazine editor.

Only a few businesspeople or professionals will actually take the time to write an article, and get it done in time to meet the editor's deadline. Even if they do, it may be badly written, too long and too self-promotional.

It is much better to separate the two tasks—the 'author' who is named in the by-line and whose ideas are expressed in the article, and the 'writer' who does the actual writing, possibly a freelance journalist, who interviews the author and ghost-writes the article for that person's by-line. A good journalist can conduct the interview in half an hour, ghost-write the article in three, and all that the author needs to do is review the manuscript and correct any errors. As a bonus, the article is likely to be readable, informative—and acceptable to the editor.

The second 'how' aspect comes in ensuring that the editor will accept the article, through getting the editor's buy-in ahead of time. This is through what journalists call a 'query letter'—a mini-proposal—to present the idea before writing. The query should have four points: the proposed article's topic, reasons why the readers of the magazine will be interested in it, some points to be covered, and the writer's qualifications.

Editors much prefer to receive queries first, rather than having to wade through a 2,000 word article only to find that in the end, it is not suitable. With a query, the editor is able to fine-tune the idea: 'It sounds like a good article idea, but it would be better if you could discuss how the new XYZ legislation affects the issue.'

continued

In choosing a topic, many businesspeople want to write a sales pitch for their product or service, thinking that the publication will accept this. Some publications will, but most of them are not worth pursuing, because they are generally not considered credible or read thoroughly. The readers know a promotional 'puff piece' when they see it. Rather, the article needs to contain genuinely useful information.

Another common idea is the 'how-to' article—setting out the steps to achieve an outcome, which demonstrates the author's grasp of the topic. Be sure that the topic will actually be of interest to the reader, however. Rather than writing about the steps in conducting an audit of a company's production processes, for example, it may be better to write about how to present the audit's findings to company management in a way that will result in positive action.

The most effective kind of article to write, from a marketing perspective, is the 'trend' article, which discusses a situation and how it is changing—where it has come from, the current situation, how it can be expected to develop, and what the reader should do as a result. This type of article is interesting and also shows the writer's grasp of the issues affecting readers.

A good article-writing campaign can help an organization move into new territory. That might be geographical territory, contributing articles to magazines circulating in another country. It can mean a new industry, through that industry's magazines. By showing the organization's abilities to meet the needs of a new market, the writer can get a chance to meet those needs—profitably.

Carl Friesen has a background in journalism and 15 years of experience in media relations, currently Manager of Media Relations for the Canadian part of the international environmental and geotechnical firm, Golder Associates Ltd. He can be reached at 905.567.4444 or cfriesen@golder.com.

What to Look for in a Media Relations Firm

- *Flexibility.* The firm should be able to work on either a single project or on a long-term basis.
- *Full-service.* Can the firm provide copywriting, event management, strategic counselling, publicity, and community affairs? Can they advise on advertising? Can they handle national, international, and Internet programs? Do they have affiliates?
- *Talent at the top.* Check the professional backgrounds of the principals. Find out who will be working on your account. Do their qualifications, special training, and background relate to your needs?
- *Relevant experience.* Find out what experience the firm has related to your business or organization. Ask for a list of current clients and find out how the firm has served them.
- *Reputation.* What is the general reputation of the firm? Are its integrity and professional standing above reproach? Ask current and past clients about their relationships with the firm.

Exercise

1. Describe the ways in which you could use the RACE formula to develop a media relations strategy and program for your organization or company.

Part 2

Developing a Media Relations Program

Chapter 4

Conducting Research

In Chapter 3, we defined media-relations research as the activity that answers the question: 'Where are we now?' But where do you turn for the answer? As we'll see in this chapter, the answer comes from a number of audiences, each of whom may have a different perception. Research helps us to understand these perceptions objectively, as well as serving as the basis for developing a media relations strategy.

Chapter Summary

By the end of Chapter 4, you will be able to:

- understand the goals of primary and secondary research,
- determine a company or organization's 'voice',
- define and prioritize key internal and external audiences,
- use research tools to conduct a communications' audit of key audiences, and
- conduct a media audit.

Just the Facts

The goal of any media relations program is to, ultimately, communicate a company or organization's Key Messages to its intended audiences. But if that communication is to be effective, we must first be able to define those audiences—both in terms of who they are, and how they are likely to respond to a given message. This is why research is the first element of the RACE sequence.

Research is essentially a fact-finding exercise in which we start with the most general and easily accessible types of information (such as company reports) and, using a variety of research tools, continue to look for more challenging data (such as how the company or organization is perceived by its key audiences).

The Goals of Research

- Provide a methodical and systematic way to assess your organization or company.
- Obtain an objective perspective; a public viewpoint.
- Track trends and understand issues.
- Identify and qualify groups both inside and outside an organization or company.
- Determine and measure the groups' current attitudes and understanding of your organization or company.
- Isolate the factors that determine these attitudes.
- Identify the issues that may alter these attitudes.
- Determine how a media relations program may affect issues and influence attitudes.
- Identify a problem or opportunity.
- Shape and pre-test Key Messages.
- Evaluate and measure changes in perception.

Where to Start

To develop a successful media relations program you must first discover everything you can about your company or organization's history, current status, divisions, practices, policies, products and services, goals and objectives, communication patterns, problems and issues, achievements, awards, strategic advantages, weaknesses, and competition. This is no small task! Sources for this information may include:

- annual reports, company policy, mission statements, and history;
- surveys, statistics, and reports on national trends in your company or organization's industry or field;

- competitors' annual reports, advertising, and editorial coverage;
- testimonials and letters of complaint;
- websites, blogs, and chat rooms;
- trade and consumer shows;
- books and magazines;
- associations affiliated with your company or organization; and
- studies and reports.

Defining and Qualifying Your Key Audiences

Your organization or company communicates with a variety of internal and external audiences on a continuing basis. Understanding who these audiences are—and defining which audiences are the most important—is essential for choosing the media that will most efficiently communicate your messages to them.

Once the key audiences have been identified, the next phase of your research should focus on qualifying each audience—who they are (for example, age, occupation, national origin, income, sex, education, family life-cycle stage, affiliations, hobbies, and interests), where they are (geographical location), and what their attitudes are towards your company or organization.

Keep in mind, too, that you may be trying to reach different target audiences during different phases of your media campaign. For example, in the first phase, your target audience might include employees, current clients, people and organizations within the industry, as well as trade media. The next phase might enlarge the audience to include potential clients and general-interest media. The final phase could expand to include the local, national, and international communities.

Finding Your Voice

In order to communicate effectively, your organization or company must have a single 'voice'—in other words, there must be a consistent message, derived from an understanding of your audiences.

Consistency is the key. One voice must be used in all lines of communications—business cards, brochures, newsletters, postcards, annual report, sales and Media Kits, advertising, and websites. How do you find that voice? Start by describing (in 20 words or less), the organization or company, what it does, and how it differs from the competition. For example:

continued

- The Back Chiropractic Centre offers an integrated health care approach by combining chiropractic services with registered massage therapy.
- Street Smart Developments is a builder of high-quality town homes and condominiums in the Greater Toronto area servicing all home-buying markets.
- Carnival Communications is a full-service public relations and marketing company that specializes in the development and marketing of events for ethnic markets.
- Green Earth Stage Company, a registered not-for-profit organization, produces events, celebrations, and education programs to promote awareness of our interdependence on a healthy planet.

Try it yourself:

_____is a _____ that offers _____to _____

_____.

Finding Your Audience

Who are your key audiences? Consider the following:

- Employees/staff
- Current clients or customers
- Past clients
- Potential clients
- Donors
- Referral partners
- Suppliers
- Colleagues
- Competitors
- Shareholders or members
- Board of Directors
- Influencers
- Associations
- Government agencies (federal, provincial, and municipal)

- Sponsors/partners
- Retailers
- Visitors/tourists
- Educators
- Multicultural groups
- Students
- Special interest groups
- Media
- Volunteers
- The local community
- The general public
- International
- The online community

Key Audiences and Media Channels

CASE STUDY

Fashion Cares 2005, M.A.C *VIVA GLAM* Bollywood Cowboy

Past and potential event patrons:

- 18–34; male/female 60/40; gay/straight 60/40
- Vanguard social influencers—those who are at the hot events to see and be seen in the Toronto social calendar, including:
  - "Friends" of the event who buy tickets each year
  - Those who have attended and likely will again but, as patron surveys showed, want to know the event theme, entertainment line-up and shopping opportunities before committing
  - Those who have not attended in the past, but fit the profile of those likely to attend
  - Event sponsors: corporations and individuals who sponsor the event as part of marketing or charitable-giving plans and have a vested interest in its success and profile
  - Media, as a conduit to reach these audiences: fashion, lifestyle, social scene, gay community, and entertainment reporters and editors at print, broadcast and online outlets primarily in Toronto, but some national outlets given the event's profile.

CASE STUDY

The Purina Walk For Dog Guides

- General public in 110 communities hosting walks across Canada—to attract walkers, volunteers and donors;
- Participants in 110 walks across the country—principally dog owners and critical targets for Purina; and
- Media—reporters for local and national mainstream TV, radio and print outlets—the best conduit to all our audiences.

CASE STUDY

Launch of Virgin Mobile Canada

Canadians aged 12 to 34. Virgin Mobile's research found that 3.5 million youth would enter the mobile market by 2011, representing 50% of total growth. Furthermore, many Canadian youth felt that mobile phone service providers provided poor, overpriced service, took youth for granted and ignored their demographic.

Purolator Tackle Hunger 2006
Male sports fans between the ages of 21 and 54 and fathers with young children in nine cities: Halifax (exhibition game), Winnipeg, Calgary, Edmonton, Regina, Vancouver, Ottawa, Toronto and Hamilton.

What Are They Saying?

Once you have defined your key audience(s), it is important to understand their attitudes toward your company or organization. This phase of the research, called a **communications audit**, requires the use of more sophisticated research tools, including:

- *Surveys.* Conducted as telephone or personal interviews, or as written questionnaires, surveys are an excellent tool to use before or after an event or campaign. Survey results allow you to assess your reputation and the effectiveness of the media campaign, both immediately after the campaign has concluded, as well as on an annual basis.
- *Comment cards.* Comment cards can be used to collect the most recent information on your programs and services on an on-going basis. Improvements and changes can be made based on the responses and suggestions. Comment cards provide general information which often leads to more formalized studies.
- *Focus groups.* This type of research generally involves groups of eight to ten people who are invited to attend a one-hour session with you or with a facilitator, to assess your company or organization's strengths and weaknesses, uncover problems, and discuss products and services. Focus groups can target current customers, potential customers, and past customers (people who are no longer buying from you, volunteering with you, etc.). Participants are usually rewarded with a gift certificate, a discount, or a fee.

Using these tools, as well as other research tools, will help you to understand your audiences and develop effective Key Messages to be used in a media relations campaign. They are also useful for conducting research on an annual basis to measure a company's reputation or to assess changes to that reputation resulting from a campaign.

Don't Forget to Look Inside

While communications audits are most often directed at key external audiences, it's equally important to understand the attitudes of people inside your company or organization. In fact, before starting any media relations program, it is essential that you spend time researching how management, staff, even the Board of Directors, feel about the company. Unhappiness in any of these quarters can ultimately sabotage your relationships with the media.

Do the Media Like Us?

Given that the media are the principal vehicles for conveying your message to your key audiences, it's important to understand the attitudes, awareness, and behaviour of the media as they relate specifically to your organization or company. This type of research, called a **media audit**, provides answers to a number of questions:

- How comprehensive and up-to-date is your current media list?
- What is the current reputation of your organization or company with the media?
- Do the media contact your spokesperson when they are looking for a quote or comment on an issue or problem in your industry?
- How recently, and how often, have the media been contacted?
- Has the organization or company tracked media coverage in the past? If so, how accurately?
- What types of media coverage have been received in the past? Review the type, extent, tone, and dollar value of previous media coverage.
- Has there been advertising in the past? If so, on what occasions (for example, special events, launch of products or services, or to explain a position or an issue)? Has the company or organization been involved in media sponsorships or partnerships? Have they used advertorials? What has worked? What hasn't worked?
- Where, when, and how often do your competitors advertise? What types of editorial coverage have they received?

In some cases—for example, where the company or its products/services are new—there is no media coverage to audit. A similar situation may exist for a company or organization that has never developed a comprehensive media campaign. In these circumstances, it is often beneficial for you to try to assess your competitors.

Research Findings

The Purina Walk For Dog Guides

The Argyle team conducted interviews with four different sources: Purina managers and employees; staff of the Lions Foundation; beneficiaries of dog guides; and local walk organizers. We gained a thorough understanding of the event's history, past and current public relations and marketing efforts, and event goals and objectives.

The research yielded several insights. (1) While Purina had been supporting the Lions Foundation by providing food for dog guides in training, there was very little consumer awareness of the company's involvement. We needed strategies to attract attention to the Purina brand. (2) Since there were 110 walks from coast to coast—and a budget of only $75,000—media relations would be the best conduit to raise awareness of both the walk and Purina's involvement. (3) Since we could not hope to be at every location, we had to equip local organizers with stronger media relations capabilities. (4) Since media coverage had not been recorded in the past, we had no benchmark; that meant developing a system of qualitative evaluation based on the media coverage received to assist Purina in determining its return on investment for public relations.

Putting it all Together

With the results of your general research, your communications audits (internal and external), and your media audit, you should be ready to move forward to the next step in developing a media relations program: analyzing the information in order to provide Key Messages, as well as to develop the campaign's strategies and goals. We will examine these elements in the next chapter.

Exercises

1. Define and prioritize the key audiences for a media relations program for your organization or company. Explain your reasons.
2. Describe the best primary and secondary research tools you could use to gain an understanding of your company or organization. What kinds of information do you hope to gain from the research?
3. How can you find out what your key media know about your company or organization, as well as any misconceptions they might have?

Chapter 5

Analyze: Problems, Goals, and Strategies

With the benefit of the research data gathered in Chapter 4, we are now in a position to answer the question, 'Where are we going?' We will identify a company's strengths and weaknesses, set goals and objectives, and develop strategies to meet those goals. This is also the stage where we get down to business—presenting the client, company, or organization with a proposal and selling our ideas.

Chapter Summary

By the end of Chapter 5, you will be able to:

• assess research data,
• identify limitations and challenges,
• define the goals of a media relations program,
• design Key Messages,
• develop strategies to achieve program goals,
• identify partnerships and sponsorships,
• create a proposal and 'sell the solution', and
• sign the contract.

What It All Means

While research is essential to the development of a successful media relations campaign, it is of limited value on its own. It is, after all, what we *learn* from the data that allows us to focus on critical issues, to create Key Messages, and to develop strategies that will achieve a company or organization's goals.

For example, research will often reveal both strengths and weaknesses. In the analysis phase, we determine how best to capitalize on the strengths and overcome the weaknesses. From these determinations we develop objectives or goals and, ultimately, the strategies (including Key Messages) that we intend to use to meet those goals. It is also at this stage that you can develop a proposal for your media relations program and initiate the process of 'selling the solution' to your company or organization.

In analyzing the research, you will probably focus primarily on any weaknesses. While the success with which you promote strengths can make the difference between a good campaign and a great one, this effort can be completely derailed by a failure to both anticipate and overcome weaknesses.

Taking a SWOT at the Issues

When assessing the position of a company or organization prior to developing a media relations program, a 'SWOT' analysis will help to identify the following critical issues:

- *Strengths*. What advantages do we have now in the marketplace and over the competition?
- *Weaknesses*. What obstacles do we face now? In what areas are we vulnerable?
- *Opportunities*. What issues can be turned to our advantage in the future?
- *Threats*. What future events or developments could have a negative impact on our company or organization?

Limitations and Challenges

The discussion in this chapter of the award-winning case studies looks at some of the challenges faced by the media relations' practitioners in identifying and overcoming the challenges inherent in the campaigns.

CASE STUDY

Fashion Cares 2005, M.A.C. VIVA GLAM Bollywood Cowboy

Due to the size and nature of Fashion Cares, there is widespread interest from a cross-section of media—relevant and non-relevant—in both attending and covering the event. The primary public relations challenges are to generate pre-event coverage that drives ticket sales for an event in its 19th year and to manage the event's media accreditation effectively, ensuring that a maximum number of tickets are left available for sale. It's also important that coverage profiles sponsors and highlights the fun and outrageous nature of the event, in keeping with its brand image.

The biggest challenge for the 2005 public relations team was in finding new and unique ways to deliver these messages, particularly in the event's 19th year. Another challenge was sustaining media interest and coverage during the eight-week ticket-selling period.

There were a number of challenges that were overcome as part of the program implementation, including:

- Budget and staffing:
  - Having the team include a cross-section of professionals with varying levels of experience and in many different locations, meant the bulk of the day-to-day work fell to the committee members from Weber Shandwick Worldwide (Toronto), putting stress on the $50,000 budget (the agency's in-kind donation of time, including that of the public relations committee co-chair). An intern was hired to be the day-to-day point person to field media inquiries and execute program activities under the direction of other committee members. There are limitless story angles to pitch, but to manage the program resources effectively activities were focused on those that offer the biggest return on investment.
- Entertainment announcement:
  - Although it was expected that the headline host or entertainer could be announced at the April Launch Party, last minute details with talent were not finalized in time to include them in the Launch Party media materials or announcement. The team turned this into an opportunity—first by focusing Launch Party media relations efforts on the four designers being featured in the show and then leveraging the announcement of a host and entertainment line-up as another opportunity to generate and sustain media interest and coverage.

CASE STUDY

The Purina Walk for Dog Guides

- **Budget**: We had to promote 110 local events for fees of $75,000—which led to a decentralized approach (See Implementation, Chapter 9).
- **Balancing philanthropic and commercial interests with sensitivity**: Argyle focused primarily on the outstanding efforts of the Lions Foundation, the success stories of the dog guides and owners, and the importance of the fundraising event—though always ensuring it was referred to by its complete name: The *Purina* Walk for Dog Guides.
- **No single, national walk date**: Walks were scheduled on different days from April through October, which made mass communications very challenging. Argyle responded by meticulously keeping track of the dates, times, locations and all other pertinent details for each of the 110 walks.
- **Late start to PR campaign**: Argyle was brought to the table a few weeks before the first local walk. We worked quickly and efficiently to prepare and obtain approvals for detailed plans and our critical path.
- **Hundreds of spokespeople**: Due to budgetary and logistical restraints, it was not possible—nor realistic—to media train each potential spokesperson. To be certain spokespersons were prepared, Argyle contacted local organizers and provided coaching on interview tips and, most important, key messages to ensure the Purina brand was subtly included in the story.

CASE STUDY

The Launch of Virgin Mobile Canada

- **Confidential launch**: Virgin Mobile Canada was faced with the challenge of controlling the information that was released in advance of the launch date in order to minimize competitors' responses. To this effect, it was necessary to execute a controlled release of the launch event details.
- **Competition for coverage**: Richard Branson and the media were distracted by the Global Flyer story, which meant we had to share our coverage with this international event. Where possible, the PR team would attempt to steer Richard Branson back to the Virgin Mobile key messages.
- **Geographic separation**: Despite the geographic separation, Hill & Knowlton Toronto, Vancouver and Montreal offices became a virtual team with Toronto-based Virgin Mobile Canada through regular cross-Canada conference calls and status updates.
- **Timeframe**: The PR component of the Virgin Mobile Canada launch had a short project timeframe from December 2004 to March 2005. Teams had to quickly learn to trust each other and lean on each other for support and resources.

Toronto-specific Challenges

- **Criticism of nurse representation**: The Toronto stunt, which featured Richard Branson as a larger than life superhero, also featured models dressed as nurses. In-store displays and commercials also featured these nurses. Although the concept successfully registered with Virgin Mobile's target audience, several groups, including the Registered Nurses' Association of Ontario, engaged in a public outcry saying Virgin Mobile misrepresented Canadian nurses. Furthermore, the RNAO demanded a public apology and urged Virgin Mobile to pull its advertising. Virgin Mobile's communication team addressed the media by saying that the approach was meant to be tongue-in-cheek and they never meant to offend anyone. In the end, Virgin Mobile turned this PR challenge into an opportunity by obtaining seven million impressions in free media coverage, while simultaneously aligning itself with the target market—youth—who enjoy Virgin's fun, edgy, and irreverent marketing.
- **Weather**: The Toronto event took place outdoors on one of the snowiest days of the year. Steps had to be taken to ensure the media corral and path to the news conference were snow-free and broadcast crews could maneuver their trucks.

Montreal-specific Challenges

- **Low awareness in Montreal**: Communications efforts had to encourage buzz and interest for the launch in a region that knew little about Richard Branson or the Virgin Group. Low awareness was combated by providing essential context, such as background information on the company, key players, and service offerings.
- **French-speaking spokesperson**: In Montreal, there were limited media opportunities as media were forced to conduct interviews in English and only use one spokesperson for French quotes.

Vancouver-specific Challenges

- **Last-minute change of plans**: Richard Branson cancelled plans to attend the Vancouver launch at the last minute. As such, media interest waned. As this was the third event in as many days it made it difficult to deliver a local story in this small media market without the celebrity factor.

CASE STUDY

Purolator Tackle Hunger 2006

While Purolator Tackle Hunger has raised a steady amount of food and cash donations for local food banks on game days since its inception in 2003, the program was not well known to audiences outside football circles.

You've Gotta Have a Plan

Once you've identified the key elements of your research (that is, the most important issues identified by that research), you can start to flesh out a course of action that includes the best ways to both reach and influence your key publics. At this stage, it's important to be realistic about how much you can expect to do: ultimately, the media relations program will depend on your size, scope, and type of organization or company—for example, whether it is for-profit or nonprofit, local or international, mainstream or multicultural, new or established, product- or service-oriented, and so on. The planning document for your media relations program should answer the following questions:

- Who is the audience?
- What is the message?
- What is the desired outcome?
- How is the desired outcome going to be achieved?

Include a proposed budget and detail the ways in which you will evaluate the success of the program. Be sure to include advertising, advertorials, and promotional tie-ins with the media in your outline.

Think Online

Your media relations plan should include an Internet component with three key elements: the Internet Media Room (often called the Online Press Room, Online News Room, or Online Media Room), blogs, and optimized media releases.

Online News Rooms*

Few corporations would discount the value of positive media profiles, yet a study done by the Nielsen/Norman Group—leaders in the field of website usability—found that although they spend millions of dollars on PR, the media sections of business websites often fail to meet journalists' most basic information needs. What you need is an Online News Room.

The Norman/Nielsen study showed that 99 per cent of journalists start their research for an article by going online. Yet they could find answers to only 68 per cent of their questions across a range of business websites.

Most Online News Rooms today consist of archived media releases and outdated material. Elements of new technologies are lacking. Information is not optimized for search engines.

continued

A well-designed News Room is an excellent resource to the media. It includes communications contacts, breaking news, archives of older materials, hot links to company facts and additional information, articles, and a place where media can request information. It has a place for readers to request automatic updates, a high-resolution image gallery, elements of social media and an investor relations section.

Journalists are looking for unique content. Just as you put time and energy into customer relationship management, managing your relationships with journalists is vital to the success of your PR campaigns. They are always in a hurry to find a source for information or a quote. If you don't give them easy access to what they want—and give it to them now—they go elsewhere. They need an Online News Room where all the data they need is easily accessible to them.

Blogs and Monitoring the Blogosphere

Blogging is one of the fastest growing communication mediums of all time and it is here to stay. It can build a reputation and status for the blogger. Not only does a blog build a profile for you and your company, it also raises your visibility in the Internet search engines. A well-written blog based on a content strategy builds a 'cloud' of content on a focused subject. This will increase your presence on the Internet much faster than any other strategy. Any form of blogging will get you some results, but using a good blog platform and having a content strategy makes a remarkable difference.

Optimized Media Releases

An optimized media release can get you in the top ten results in Yahoo!News, Google News, and other news websites across the Internet. Getting your press release onto news websites does three important things for your business. It

- reaches millions of Internet users directly,
- creates quality inbound links to your website, and
- raises the search engine visibility of your website.

Journalists use the Internet when they research a story, so your online media release can get you traditional media coverage too.

When you want information, where do you go? If you answered 'the Internet', you're in good company. Most people now get their news online. Yahoo!News and Google News—known as news engines—have a larger audience than CNN or the BBC. Placing your optimized media release into these news engines reaches a huge online audience.

continued

When someone accesses your optimized press release in a news engine on a relevant keyword, you know they are interested—they asked for the topic. And the newswire services can give you a report on exactly how many people accessed your optimized release, how many clicked through to your website, and if you are running good web metrics and analytics, you can track them through your site as well.

An optimized media release will get you a page one result for your relevant keywords in the news engines and news websites, like Yahoo! News, Google News and Topix.net. This is better than a front-page story in a newspaper, because, again, it's what your readers asked for. They are interested and qualified prospects.

Optimized media releases are an integral part of a successful Internet marketing strategy.

Based on the article 'Trends in PR', written by Teresa Donia, President, iAMBIC Communications and posted in her Online News Room. Contact Teresa Donia at (905) 508-5550, teresa@iambic.ca, or at www.iambic.ca

Where Do You Want to Go?

The next step in the planning process involves deciding on the overall, long-term communications goals for your media relations program, including what it can achieve for your company or organization. Your goals could include building awareness and generating interest in your products and services, increasing sales and raising funds, enhancing the profile of your company or organization, positioning your company or organization as the leader in your industry, educating your audiences, attracting staff and volunteers, addressing misconceptions and issues, capitalizing on trends, establishing a program to ensure on-going media relationships, and supporting the current strategic marketing plan with a targeted media relations program.

Make a written list of your objectives, ensuring that each is:

- measurable;
- specific, not general;
- focused on results, not on activities;
- individual, not shared;
- realistic and achievable; and
- defined within clear time limits.

Build the measurement tools into your program at this stage, so that you can refer back to them in the evaluation process.

Setting Goals and Objectives

CASE STUDY

Fashion Cares 2005, M.A.C. *VIVA GLAM* Bollywood Cowboy

Overall, the program goal was to position Fashion Cares as the hot event of the social calendar with the ultimate aim of driving ticket sales and sponsor interest for 2005 and beyond.

Specific program objectives were to:

- Generate pre-event media coverage communicating the event theme and ticket availability
- Generate pre-event media coverage highlighting key event elements including the entertainment line-up and on-site event shopping
- Generate event night coverage highlighting the unique nature of Fashion Cares and, where possible, profiling sponsors
- Make as many 'free' passes/tickets as possible available for sale

The public relations committee also set its own goal of surpassing the previous years' media coverage (113 total hits; 25% occurring in the pre-event period).

CASE STUDY

The Purina Walk for Dog Guides

Based on client feedback and direction, we established the following objectives and measures of success:

1. Raise awareness of The Purina Walk for Dog Guides, and establish a strong link to the Purina brand.
   - Quantitative: Total number of media stories and total audience reach. (NB: No stats were available from 2004).
   - Qualitative: Specific mentions of Purina brand; interviews with our local or national spokespersons; and inclusion of photos with accompanying branding.
2. Increase participation in the walks, particularly in Canada's mid-sized cities, through a national media campaign, supplemented by a cost-effective campaign to arm local organizers with media relations tools.
   - Growth in participation and attendance numbers—a reasonable measurement as the walk was promoted principally through media relations.
3. Expose more dog owners to the Purina brand at the walks.
   - Number of walkers intercepted by the on-site Purina team at the largest walk site.
4. Increase financial support for the cause.
   - Growth in online donations and total funds raised.

The Launch of Virgin Mobile Canada

- Effectively launch Virgin Mobile Canada to Canadian media
- Educate a wide range of media on Virgin Mobile, its service offering, and competitive advantage
- Introduce Virgin Mobile President Andrew Black and set the stage for him to take a visible leadership role
- Generate coverage of Virgin Mobile in media outlets that reached its target consumers
- Blanket news coverage in three primary markets: ON, QC, BC
- Key message pick-up in outlets nation-wide
- Build brand character
- Use Chairman Richard Branson, stunts and VIP events to communicate Virgin Mobile's messages and maximize media exposure
- Establish tone/platform for future PR and marketing initiatives

Purolator Tackle Hunger 2006

Communications Objectives:

- Increase media coverage about Purolator Tackle Hunger in every CFL community
- Increase the visibility of the issue of hunger
- Raise awareness about Purolator's commitment to helping alleviate hunger across Canada

Design Your Key Messages

A Key Message is a statement of what you want to communicate, expressed in the clearest and most concise language possible so as to avoid any chance of misinterpretation by the media. A media relations campaign may have many Key Messages, or it may have just one. The important thing to remember as a media relations practitioner is that the messages need to be repeated often and consistently throughout the campaign. The case studies in Chapter 10 will provide further examples of Key Messages and their role in a media relations campaign.

Develop Your Strategies

Once you have established the objectives or goals for a media relations program, the next step is to identify the strategies that will most effectively enable you to meet those goals. The strategies you develop will ultimately be specifically related to what the program is trying to achieve, but examples could include the following:

- using one or more spokespeople to provide testimonials,
- placing stories that position a company or organization as a leader in its industry,
- building media coverage to increase the visibility of a company or organization and its spokesperson,
- using the history of a company or organization to establish credibility,
- designing promotional events and media activities to reach the identified target audiences,
- distributing dynamic promotional materials,
- contacting a wider range of media and building relationships, and/or
- creating Key Messages targeted to different media

The strategies (or tactics) you develop should be coordinated in your plan so that they are mutually supportive in helping you meet your goals.

In Part 3 of this book, we will look at the tools used to execute your strategies. For now, let's examine how strategies were developed and executed in our case studies.

Developing Strategies

CASE STUDY

Fashion Cares 2005, M.A.C. *VIVA GLAM* Bollywood Cowboy

The Fashion Cares marketing mix includes print, broadcast and out-of-home advertising, direct marketing and public relations, mostly focused on the ultimate aim of driving ticket sales and increasing Fashion Cares' brand awareness. Media relations is an integral part of the public relations activities as it provides an opportunity to communicate some of the messages that resonate with potential attendees, yet aren't easily explained with advertising or direct marketing (as identified by patron surveys).

The communications solution involved (a) leveraging a highly-visual launch party to announce the event theme and generate some pre-event buzz and excitement; (b) creating and/or pitching relevant news hooks and story angles to sustain coverage, communicate key event elements and keep Fashion Cares top-of-mind with media and potential patrons during the pre-event period, and (c) developing and implementing an accreditation protocol to manage media access.

CASE STUDY

The Purina Walk For Dog Guides

(1) We needed strategies to attract attention to the Purina brand. (2) Since there were 110 walks from coast to coast—and a budget of only $75,000—media relations would be the best conduit to raise awareness of both the walk and Purina's involvement. (3) Since we

could not hope to be at every location, we had to equip local organizers with stronger media relations capabilities. (4) Since media coverage had not been recorded in the past, we had no benchmark; that meant developing a system of qualitative evaluation based on the media coverage received to assist Purina in determining its return on investment for public relations.

1. **The Spokesperson Media Strategy**
   - **Real people, real stories**: Use real people and real stories to demonstrate how dog guides have changed lives for the better.
   - **Brand messages present, but subordinate**: Ensure Purina key messages were present in *every* interview, but *always* subordinate to messages about the event's principal philanthropic message.
   - **Focus on pet health**: Use the common denominator of 'pet health' to connect media interest in dog guides to the Purina brand.

2. **The Launch Media Strategy**
   - Select and promote a launch event in one market. The selection would be based on various factors: the success and attendance at previous walks at the location; the availability of media in that market to cover the event; and the opportunity to create a compelling Purina event area for participants. The choice: Toronto's High Park.
   - Increase significantly the number of dog-owning walkers 'touched' by Purina by developing a fun, interactive branded space through which they had to pass en route to registration. Provide dog owners with *tangible value* through both products and information about pet nutrition.
   - Facilitate on-site media coverage through the presence of local and national spokespeople (and their dogs).

3. **The Local Market Media Strategy**
   - Extend the reach of our national launch—and make Purina's PR dollars go further—by conducting aggressive media relations activities at the local level in each market holding a walk.
   - Decentralize spokesperson duties by arming local organizers with common messages and media relations tips and tools to maximize local coverage at the many walks where resources did not allow the presence of the Argyle team.

CASE STUDY

The Launch of Virgin Mobile Canada
The following solution was developed and executed for the launch of Virgin Mobile Canada:

- Generate awareness of Virgin Mobile across the country
- Reach youth, the target consumer, and reinforce the competitive advantage Virgin Mobile had over other mobile service providers

- Create an understanding of what the brand stands for to support the launch of subsequent marketing initiatives
- Balancing Richard Branson's celebrity status with Virgin Mobile's story: ensuring consumer media received the key messages
- Identify a separate strategy for Quebec to balance language and cultural differences and low awareness of the 'British' Virgin brand

CASE STUDY

Purolator Tackle Hunger 2006

After reviewing the Purolator Tackle Hunger program, Purolator and H&K identified several untapped opportunities for Purolator to work more closely with its key partners in the program—particularly the local food banks, CFL players and CFL hometown football teams. Recognizing the value of third party endorsement, H&K developed a media relations campaign in conjunction with Purolator's communications and marketing departments that focused on strengthening Purolator's relationships with its partners through joint events to attract more attention to the issue of hunger. The campaign also capitalized on Purolator's role as the official courier of the CFL by bringing the Grey Cup, an important piece of Canadian sports history, directly to media.

Over a period of six months, H&K also worked closely with Purolator general managers and employees in each region to coordinate media interviews and secure the Purolator Tackle Hunger branded delivery truck—an important visual element of the campaign.

Forging Partnerships

Whether it is to provide funding or to support the credibility of your message, partnerships are often an essential part of a media relations program. Potential partners include:

- *Corporations*. These companies can support your events and promotions, either with money, products, or promotion. Corporations carefully evaluate sponsorship requests against sponsorship criteria, as well as in relation to their existing commitments. The emphasis is on building long-term partnerships and supporting a select number of events and activities that add value to the lives of their customers and co-workers. Before approaching a corporate sponsor or preparing a proposal, use their website or visit their head office to learn about any current sponsorships and partnerships. Sponsorship criteria for corporate sponsorships include a plan to establish relationships that will be mutually beneficial to the sponsor and their sponsored organization (such as positive exposure for the sponsor's brand), to enhance the corporation's value to its customers with exclusive and 'money can't buy' opportunities, and to reach and build relationships—both short- and long-term—with targeted audiences.

- *Non-profit (or grassroots) organizations.* These organizations can team up on special events and promotions, often as part of a fundraising campaign.
- *Media.* Media partners—whether they are print, broadcast, or Internet media organizations—provide support through advertising, participation in events and promotions, and editorial coverage.
- *Third-party.* Third-party partners can include individuals (such as doctors, students, etc.) who are able to lend credibility to your message and provide media interviews.

Once you understand the wants and needs of potential sponsors, you will need to create a sponsorship form that identifies the various support sponsorship levels available for your events or activities, and the benefits that accrue to each. For example, your sponsorship categories might include the following:

- title sponsor,
- principal sponsors,
- media sponsors, and
- 'in kind' sponsors/suppliers.

Benefits to all sponsors might include the right to have their logos appear on collateral materials (including tickets, advertising, brochures, flyers, event program, posters, event signage, table signage, and the campaign website), tables or seats at the event, and a link to your website, as well as the right to exclusivity within their field of business or activity.

Category specific rights can be distributed similar to the outline below.

- **Title Sponsor (one only)**
  - Name above the event name on all printed materials
  - Featured in all advertising
  - Banners with logo prominently featured at event
  - Major profile in publicity campaign, including sponsor presence, logos, and products highlighted at news conferences
  - Mention in all media releases, Media Kits, and invitations
  - Organization of media interviews, where possible
  - Profiled on the website and online media room
  - Links to the sponsor's website
  - Keynote speaker opportunity or the opportunity to have a speaker at the event
  - Booth at the event
  - Media Kit available in the on-site Media Room

- **Principal Sponsors**
  - Sponsor show guide (where applicable)
  - Sponsor seminar series
  - Sponsor shopping bags
  - Sponsor retail, media, or product promotion
  - Inclusion of sponsors' Media Kits in the on-site media room
  - Mention in all media releases, Media Kits, and invitations
  - Organization of media interviews, where possible
  - Profiled on the website and the online Media Room
  - Link to the sponsor's website
  - Booth at the event

- **In-kind Sponsors/Suppliers**
  - Provide product(s) for your special event or launch, in lieu of money. This could include printing, graphic design, food and beverages, décor, or room rental. In exchange, the supplier is credited in all printed materials, such as program, on-site signage, advertising campaign, and acknowledged at event.

- **Media Sponsors**
  - A radio station, television station, newspaper, magazine, or Internet service provider provides advertising space and time in exchange for acknowledgement (and logo identification) in all of your printed materials, on your website, and in the media campaign, on-site signage, booth space at event, and for the ability to sell subscriptions or give out literature at the event.

Meeting of Minds

Whether you are a media relations consultant or a staff member, you should set up a preliminary or exploratory meeting to discuss the following topics before you create a media relations proposal.

- What are the products or services and what are the benefits?
- What are three Key Messages you want to give to the media about your company/organization, its programs, services, and events?
- What makes this newsworthy?
- What is the budget?
- What is the time frame?
- What are the expected results?

SPONSORSHIP CONTACT FORM

Potential sponsor

Name: _____

Address: _____

Telephone: _____ Fax: _____

E-mail: _____

Call made by: _____

Initial contact

Date: _____

Comments: _____

_____

Action required: _____

Sponsorship package sent

Date: _____

Comments: _____

_____

Follow-up meeting

Date: _____

Comments: _____

Action required: _____

Action taken: _____

Sponsorship details

Amount or products pledged: _____ Date: _____

Amount paid: _____ Date: _____

Comments: _____

_____

_____

 Developing a Proposal

At this point, you've completed your research and analysis, and you've had an exploratory meeting. Now you're ready to create a media relations proposal that will meet your company or organization's needs. This proposal will demonstrate your understanding of the situation, needs, and objectives, and will present a clearly defined plan for meeting those objectives. Your proposal should include the following elements.

Cover

The cover for your proposal should specifically state the following details: a title for the proposed media relations program, your name, the client's name, and the date.

Situation, need, and opportunity

In this section of the proposal, you should briefly describe the company or organization's current position, strengths, and weaknesses; the goals of the company/organization; and why there is a need or opportunity for a media relations program, specifically for the program you are proposing. For example:

> On *(date)*, *(your name)* met with *(client representatives)* to discuss *(subject)*. They discussed the need to create a public relations and media relations campaign to support *(planned activity)* and to generate and sustain interest in (product/service/company).

> The goal of the company or organization is *(description of goal)*.

> Based on that request, *(your name/company)* has put together a proposal to raise the profile of *(client activity/product/service)*, to create long-term benefits for *(client activity/product/service)*, and to suggest a public relations and media strategy and action plan that will enhance, support, and reinforce the marketing efforts of *(client name)*.

Objectives

In the 'Objectives' section of the proposal, you should outline the steps you plan to take in order to achieve the goals of the media relations campaign. You should state specifically which media (for example, trade, consumer, local, national, and/or online) you intend to target, identify your target audience(s), outline your strategies, tactics, and tools, describe the programs' main benefits—what you plan to achieve through the program—and explain the budget.

Who's On Your Team?

A media relations program is a collaborative effort. This means you'll need to build a team consisting of management, staff, and consultants, which can include people with expertise in technology, marketing, writing, event management, mainstream and multicultural media relations, and Internet media.

Finalizing your Proposal

When you are ready to finalize your proposal, set up a short meeting with the client to review the proposal and to make any changes. Based on that meeting (and the elements the client wants to include in the program), you will need to design a (preliminary) budget.

How should you cost out your time? In many cases it is often better to start on a project basis. This will enable you to assess the client, amount of work, payments, etc. Then, if there is enough on-going work, you can move into a retainer arrangement. Otherwise, continue on a project basis.

Fees can be billed on an hourly, project, or retainer basis, for the following activities:

- researching and writing publicity materials, including copy for the Online Media Room;
- developing the media list;
- contacting, dealing with, and following up with the media;
- preparing for media interviews/media training;
- attending meetings;
- correspondence and telephone calls;
- advising on and/or placing advertising;
- tracking media coverage; and
- preparing media reports and evaluations.

Expenses should be billed as incurred. These include:

- Media Kit covers, including design and printing;
- letterhead, paper, and envelopes;
- postage;
- photography and prints;
- media drops;
- couriers;
- room rental, food, and décor for media events;
- set-up of on-site media room for special events;

- equipment rentals;
- newswire, sending news releases and/or broadcast (VNRs/B-rolls);
- community newspaper association (sending news releases);
- media tracking service (on and off-line);
- media evaluation service;
- photos on the newswire;
- parking;
- advertising and advertorials; and
- promotional items.

Once you have reached agreement on a budget for your media relations program, develop a contract, a preliminary invoice, and a proposed critical path.

Sample Contract

To: *Name of Client*
From: *Name of PR firm*
Date:
Re: *Contract for public relations work*

This memo will serve as a contract between *NAME OF PR FIRM OR CONSULTANT* and *NAME OF CLIENT* for work PR Firm will complete in order to (*briefly describe project*).

This work will begin upon signing of this contract and be completed no later than (*state project end date*).

During this time period, PR Firm or consultant will complete the activities outlined in Attachment A (Scope of Work).

Upon completion of this work, PR Firm or consultant will have delivered to Client all items described in Attachment B (Deliverables).

If Client requests PR Firm complete additional activities not described in Attachment A or produce deliverables not described in Attachment B, PR Firm or consultant will propose an addendum to this contract and additional fees may apply.

As part of this contract, Client agrees to appoint a point person to this project who will work as PR Firm's or consultant's main contact and coordinate all communications with PR Firm. A representative from the PR Firm will attend all meetings.

continued

In exchange for services described in Attachment A, Client will compensate PR Firm a flat fee of *$XX*. Of this amount, *$XX* will be due upon signing of this agreement and commencement of work, *$XX* will be due upon completion of _____ and *$XX* will be due upon completion scope of work described in Attachment A and delivery of all items noted in Attachment B.

PR Firm will secure advanced approval from Client for any single expense not originally agreed upon.

All design material, media events and any other public relations or marketing initiatives will require approval from Client before printing or scheduling.

Should Client opt to cancel this agreement through no fault of PR Firm, Client agrees to compensate PR Firm for hours worked prior to time of termination or 50 per cent of total project fee, whichever amount is greater.

If PR Firm does not follow the agreed upon contract, PR Firm would be at fault and subject to termination before the end of the contract period with no financial compensation responsibility.

Should PR Firm opt to cancel this agreement before agreed upon services are delivered, any remaining funds will be returned to Client.

Additionally, Client agrees to work with PR Firm to complete this project within the specified timeframe by providing requested information and feedback within a timely manner to keep within the project timeline.

If delays on the part of Client staff or representatives cause the project to exceed the timeframe described in this contract, additional fees may apply.

PR Firm shall treat as confidential all information relating to this project.

PR Firm shall not, without prior consent of Client, use or disclose such information to persons not authorized by Client to receive same.

continued

All information and property records pertaining to Client are and shall remain the property of Client.

PR Firm and its designees, and their respective directors, officers, partners, employees, attorneys and agents, shall be indemnified, reimbursed, held harmless and defended from and against any and all claims, demands, causes of action, liabilities, losses and expenses (including, without limitation, the disbursements, expenses and fees of their respective attorneys) that may be imposed upon, incurred by, or asserted against any of them, or any of their respective directors, officers, partners, employees, attorneys or agents, arising out of or related directly or indirectly to this Agreement. This paragraph, insofar as it applies to work undertaken while this agreement is in effect, shall survive the termination of this agreement.

If you accept the terms described herein, please signify your agreement by signing your name below and returning this contract to: PR FIRM (include Name, Address). A signed copy of this agreement will be returned to you for your files. If you have any questions about the terms outlined herein, please contact *XXX*.

I agree to the terms described herein.

for PR FIRM _____   _____ Date

for NAME OF CLIENT _____   _____ Date

ATTACHMENT A
SCOPE OF WORK: Under the terms of the attached contract with Client, dated (*Contract date*), PR Firm to complete the following scope of work (*describe scope of work*).

ATTACHMENT B
DELIVERABLES: Upon completion of the scope of work described in Attachment A, PR Firm will have delivered the following items to Client (*list deliverables*).

Sample Critical Path/Timetable for a One-year Media Relations Plan

A critical path/timetable is a production schedule outlining when things will be done, who will be in charge of each task, and how the work will be reported.

Phase 1
- Do your research and conduct an audit of competitive products, services, companies, and organizations.
- Interview the principals of the company or organization.
- Create a local, national, or international media list of trade, consumer, and Internet media.
- Research, propose, and develop strategic plans, with tools, for all markets.
- Research and write the copy for the Media Kit, including biographies, Fact Sheets, backgrounders, and information about the services, products, and programs.
- Create the copy for Online Media Room.
- Get approval of the Media Kit copy and the Online Media Room.
- Attend meetings.

Phase 2
- Develop a media campaign for the client/product/service based on sponsorship opportunities, events, or promotional programs.
- Create media releases (and media alerts) for the event.
- Develop story ideas based on successes and advantages.
- Send media releases and story ideas, along with a background kit, to the contacts on the media list.
- Follow up with key media.
- Arrange media interviews.
- Create a media report.

Phase 3
- Attend meetings with the client (and/or spokesperson).
- Research appropriate venues and book speaking engagements.
- Research, examine, and book booths at trade and consumer shows to generate business or raise the profile of the client/product/service.

Phase 4
- Send media releases and story ideas to the contacts on the media list throughout the year to announce 'newsworthy' items, such as the company or organization's growth, success stories, new services and programs, special events, problems, trends, issues, awards, and sponsorships. Design a schedule for meetings with the client.

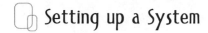

Setting up a System

With the signed contract and the first payment in hand, you can start to develop a media campaign. The best way to organize your information is to set up a filing system. As you go along, fill some (or all) of the files with information you collect, and then use this information to build your media campaign. You may find it helpful to keep files on the following items:

- Associations and networking groups
- Backgrounders on principals
- Brochures
- Business cards
- Clippings from media
- Community events and promotions
- Fact Sheets
- Industry news, trends, and problems
- Media lists
- Media Kit folders
- News releases
- Promotional ideas
- Public service announcements (PSAs)
- Publicity photographs
- Published writing
- Story ideas
- Suggested questions for media interviews
- Testimonials
- Writing opportunities

Working Within A Budget

CASE STUDY

Fashion Cares 2005, M.A.C. *VIVA GLAM* Bollywood Cowboy

Having the team include a cross-section of professionals with varying levels of experience and in many different locations, meant the bulk of the day-to-day work fell to the committee members from Weber Shandwick, putting stress on the $50,000 budget (the agency's in-kind donation of time, including that of the public relations committee co-chair).

CASE STUDY

The Purina Walk For Dog Guides
We had to promote 110 local events for fees of $75,000.

CASE STUDY

The Launch of Virgin Mobile Canada
Virgin Mobile and Hill & Knowlton executed the launch within a PR budget of approximately $180,000.

CASE STUDY

Purolator Tackle Hunger 2006
With a strict budget of $2,000 CDN in fees and out of pocket expenses for each city, H&K worked with its regional colleagues and associates in Vancouver, Calgary, Montreal, and Toronto to execute the program in all eight cities.

Exercises

1. Select the most important goals for your media relations program.
2. Describe why each goal is important to your company or organization at this time.
3. Select one media outlet that reaches your target markets and could be interested in becoming a sponsor for your company/organization and its events.
   a. Why would you be a 'good fit' for the media outlet?
   b. Who would you contact?
   c. How would you pitch the sponsorship opportunity to them?

Part 3

Executing a Media Relations Program

Chapter 6

Developing a Media Database

The third step in the execution phase of a media relations program (or the 'Communicate' element of the RACE process) is to identify the best media to reach your key audiences. Chapter 6 will build on what you learned about the media in Chapter 3 to construct a list of specific media outlets and contact names. In this way, you will provide a focus for the elements of the campaign that follows.

Chapter Summary

By the end of Chapter 6, you will be able to:

• define a media database;
• follow the seven steps necessary to create a media database;
• use media directories, including Canadian, US, and online directories;
• make use of other resources for your media database;
• store your media database;
• understand what types of information are required by the various elements of each type of media;
• identify your target audiences, including newspapers, magazines, newsletters, inserts, bulletins, television, and radio; and
• create and use a media list tracker.

Defining the Media Database

A **media database** is simply a list of key media contacts. It includes the names, addresses, telephone numbers, fax numbers, and e-mail addresses of media who would be interested in news and information about your company or organization and its events. This can include radio, television, newspapers, magazines, wire services, newsletters, bulletins, and online media. Your media database enables you to collect, track, update, and reach out to key media, while at the same time storing valuable information.

As we saw in Chapter 3, however, some types of media are better suited to certain messages than others. Magazines, for example, would not be a good choice for a fast-breaking, time-critical story, since their publication lead times are measured in months, not days. Similarly, different media attract different audiences, so it's important to ensure that your media list is constructed to reach your key audiences as effectively as possible. Before you begin to prepare your list, ask yourself the following questions:

- Who do you want to reach through your media relations program? Look at the results of your Research and Analysis phases.
- Do you want to reach a more general audience in a specific community or city, a national or international audience, or an audience with a special interest?
- Where do most of your markets get information? To answer this question it's helpful to talk to current, potential, and past clients about their media habits.
- Do they get their news from local and national newspapers, local radio and television stations, national magazines, national radio and television stations, other media (such as trade publications, specialty publications, or newsletters), or the Internet?

After you have answered these questions, take some time to study the media. Review Chapter 3 to refresh your understanding of the advantages and disadvantages of each. Look at broadcast and print media directly; analyze their formats and target markets, as well as the topics they cover. Visit their websites and analyze Internet-based media.

Where to Start

Seven steps in creating a media database

1. Review your communications goals.
Review your communication plan. Who are the people you are trying to communicate with? Where do they get their information? Where do the people who influence your target markets get their information?

2. Identify the types of media outlets.

Decide what types of media outlets you need to target, such as daily or weekly newspapers, wire services, magazines, radio, and television.

3. Look at beat codes.

Always include Assignment Editors and Producers at the top of your list, since they are often the people who 'assign' your story to a writer or producer.

For larger media outlets, find media representatives who cover the areas or issues related to your company or organization, such as business, consumers, city, environment, business and finance, technology, health and science, travel and tourism, and lifestyle.

For smaller media outlets, include Editors, News Editors or Bureau Chiefs.

4. Include pitching tips in your database.

Pitching tips are descriptions of personal preferences, methods of delivery and follow up, best times to call, and pet peeves of the key media contacts on your list.

5. Make sure you don't duplicate names on the list.

Reporters often hold multiple titles, and some Editors represent more than one publication. Send only one media release or kit to each contact.

6. Determine your delivery method.

Decide how you will send your news—by e-mail, mail, or fax—based on the preference of each media representative on your list.

7. Keep it current.

Media representatives change positions, and it is important that you address your news releases and Media Kits to the name and title of the person currently in the position. Update your media list throughout the year. Check directories or call each time you are starting a media campaign to ensure your list is current.

Sample Entry and Description for a Media Database

John James, Reporter, Toronto Daily Newspaper, Computers/Hi-Tech Desk: Covers the Internet, business technology, and e-commerce. Looking for a clear and concise description of your CEO and info about what your company does. Focuses on high-profile consumer issues, mainly covering the Internet as a business story. Writes about major trends that affect Internet business, such as advertising and e-commerce. Wants to be contacted by e-mail.

Storing Your Media Database

Always keep a printed copy of your media list, as well as a copy saved on your computer (in Excel, or a similar program). In addition, you might consider hiring a company to create *and* store your media database. There are a number of advantages to working with a professional firm. They will be able to

- create and store your database,
- customize your list to local, national, or international contacts;
- blast fax, blast email, or export a contact list;
- attach your documents and send your messages;
- include pitching tips in the database;
- provide a personal account so that you can store multiple lists and press releases (both that you have sent and that you intend to send);
- offer flexible subscription packages (or no subscription necessary);
- work with both PC and MAC formats;
- track the interaction with journalists and archive articles with reporters;
- instantly update information;
- search Editorial calendars; and
- include special sections, supplements, or special reports.

Understanding Media Directories

A good place to begin constructing your media database is with one or more of the major media directories that are published in Canada and the United States.

Who's the key contact?

When using a media directory, it's often tempting to 'go to the top' and choose the highest-ranking person within the media organization as your contact. But senior management—usually those people with titles such as Publisher, Finance Director, Production Manager, Human Resources Director, Promotions Director, Chief Engineer, Marketing Manager, or Advertising Manager—are involved in running the business of the media company; they do not generally make editorial (or content) decisions.

Canadian media directories
CCN Matthews Group

Canadian Corporate News (CCN) owns and publishes Matthews Media Directory, a comprehensive listing of Canadian media contacts. Published since 1957, it now lists about 50,000 contacts from more than 5,200 media outlets across the country. The information detailed in Matthews Media Directories is completely integrated into CCN's media lists and is updated daily.

The flagship directory, the Red Book, is published every March and September. It contains over 25,000 listings for more than 1,650 media outlets, including dailies, radio, and television stations; business and trade publications; networks/publishers; news, satellite, and wire services; syndicated features/programs, press galleries; and the Canadian Radio-television and Telecommunications Commission (CRTC). It includes listings for editorial, journalistic, production, and management departments.

The Green Book focuses on non-daily print media and lists more than 16,000 contacts from more than 2,650 media outlets, including community newspapers, consumer magazines, and ethnic and aboriginal media.

The Blue Book contains 5,000 contacts for more than 900 cable television systems, including cable system operators, multiple system operations, and specialty and pay-TV channels.

Cision (formerly Bowdens Media Directories)

Cision's comprehensive media database, available online via their MediaSource Research portal, delivers details on hundreds of thousands of journalists, editors, freelancers, analysts, and media outlets. Additionally, access to thousands of editorial calendars and a dynamic suite of tools to help build effective media lists and manage public relations activities is also available.

Cision's MediaSource Research Premium provides in-depth information about members of the media in specific industry sectors. Journalists, analysts, and media outlets are chosen by a combination of circulation rates, viewership sizes, newsstand presence, and aggregate client usage data. The premium service highlights all of the most influential media contacts that a media relations person might need to know in the following industry sectors: Business and Finance, Consumer Affairs, Health and Science, Technology, and Travel and Tourism. Detailed information, such as enhanced outlet overviews; special sections, supplements or special reports; non-disclosure agreements; art/graphic policies; ad rates; and syndicated and/or aggregated content for web outlets is also readily available and included with the premium service.

Canadian Advertising Rates and Data (CARD)

While not an editorial media directory in the same sense as Cision and Matthews, this monthly publication is nevertheless a useful source of current information for anyone who deals with the media. In addition to listing advertising rates for media in Canada, it is invaluable for finding trade and consumer magazines related to any industry or subject. CARD offers key data for over 4,300 Canadian print, broadcast, and alternative advertising options, as well as publication profiles and information about ethnic media and markets.

Community Media Canada

Community Media Canada (http://www.communitycontent.ca) is the trade name for the Canadian Community Newspaper Association, the national voice of the community press in Canada. With over 700 members, the association consists of seven affiliated member associations, representing the British Columbia and Yukon Community Newspapers Association, Alberta Weekly Newspapers Association, Saskatchewan Weekly Newspapers Association, Manitoba Community Newspapers Association, Ontario Community Newspapers Association, Quebec Community Newspapers Association, and Atlantic Community Newspapers Association.

Community Media Canada's lists are comprehensive and your message will go directly to editors across the country. The distribution network also includes daily, ethnocultural, and French-language newspapers. The service is unique: no other company emphasizes content for community newspapers. Because it is owned and operated by the Canadian Community Newspapers Association, the service also has a level of credibility with newspapers that is not seen elsewhere. News releases, mat stories ('pre-printed' feature stories—often with photos or graphics—that are presented to editors in a newspaper format that can be pasted on a page, photographed, and used as is), notices, and other information can be sent via e-mail or fax; mailing labels are also available. Customized lists can also be created to meet clients' needs. Many community organizations use the service to promote awareness weeks or special events.

US-based directories
Bacon's Media Directories

Bacon's is a Chicago-based company known for its wide range of media-related products and services, including media directories and software, comprehensive clipping services, monitoring services, and newswires for clients world-wide. It is also a major supplier of broadcast fax and mailing services and customized media lists. Bacon's has offices in New York City, Washington, and Los Angeles, and their services and publications include Premium Content, Media Calendars, and MediaSource Contact.

Burrelle's Information Services

Burrelle's products include directories for newspapers and related media, magazines and newsletters, newspapers and magazines, broadcast and related media, and a media planner.

Online directories
MediaNetCentral.ca

The CNW Group offers Canada's online media directory, MediaNetCentral.ca. This online resource provides the most current and accurate contact information on tens of thousands of media professionals at print, broadcast, and Internet outlets across Canada.

Other resources for your media database
Professional Writers Association of Canada (PWAC)

This national, non-profit organization was founded in 1976 and PWAC's membership now includes over 600 professional freelance writers, journalists, editors, and communications experts. PWAC members are professional writers who specialize in a range of topics, have been published, and freelance for a variety of newspapers and magazines. Freelance writers are an excellent source for writing stories and/or Media Kit materials (see Chapter 8), newsletters, and feature articles. In addition, they often have excellent relationships with key trade and consumer media in their areas of expertise. National magazines often work with freelancers on an on-going basis, so it is helpful to look for an established freelancer with a specialty in your industry or area. PWAC's national office has an extensive database and will provide you with the names, addresses, and telephone numbers of freelance writers who are members, according to their geographic region, skills, and areas of expertise. This free service is open to anyone looking for a freelance writer.

PWAC's online directory, Find a Professional Writer (http://www.writers.ca), was launched in the spring of 2000 and is available at no charge. It includes periodical credits, subject specialties, book titles, related skills, languages, and awards of all PWAC members.

The Canadian Press and Broadcast News

The Canadian Press and Broadcast News deliver credible, comprehensive news reporting from Canada and around the world in multiple formats, serving newspapers, broadcasters, websites, wireless carriers, magazines, government, and corporate clients. Over 250 of their journalists produce award-winning stories, photos, graphics, audio, and video. The Canadian Press, along with its French-language counterpart, La Presse Canadienne, has been Canada's bilingual, multimedia news agency for almost 90 years.

Their multimedia news is delivered around the clock and in real time to about 100 daily newspapers and more than 500 radio and television stations. All rely on news coverage from The Canadian Press when preparing their print pages, online sites, and on-air newscasts.

You should look for a reporter who specializes in your field or issues, and pitch national stories on hot topics. Stories from The Canadian Press and Broadcast News may end up getting picked up by newspapers or radio and television stations across the country.

CNW Group

CNW Group is a Canadian organization that distributes time-critical news and information. Founded in 1960, CNW is co-owned by US-based PR Newswire and UK-based PA Group; it operates its Canadian offices from coast-to-coast with 24-hour bilingual service. CNW Group's communication services facilitate the flow of news from Canadian organizations to their local, national, and global audiences in the media and financial communities.

Newswire

CNW Group's newswire is Canada's largest news release distributor and has fully bilingual news centres that operate 24/7, 365 days a year. The service gives you a dominant reach to the media and financial communities on every level, whether local, regional, provincial, national, or international. In addition, the news release is saved for two years in a searchable archive, which can be found at http://www. newswire.ca, http://www.cnxmarketlink.com, and http://www.tsx.com.

Broadcast production and distribution

The CNW Group has state-of-the-art distribution tools that can be used for everything from script-writing to video and audio production.

Broadcast-On-Demand

CNW Group has introduced Broadcast-On-Demand in response to media requests for an alternative to satellite distribution of audio and video material. The first service of its kind in Canada, Broadcast-On-Demand is a web-based media portal hosted on CNW Group's website (http://www.newswire.ca) where accredited members of the media can download broadcast-quality clips directly to their edit systems at no charge.

Microsites

CNW Group's Microsites service saves time and resources by having all CNW-issued news releases for an organization automatically posted in real-time to a page hosted by CNW Group, fully branded with your organization's look and feel. This is an efficient and cost-effective means of maintaining an up-to-date news release section of a corporate website.

Broadcast fax and e-mail

CNW Group's dedicated fax and e-mail systems enable quick and efficient delivery of information to a customized list of contacts. CNW Group's flexible systems can help deliver messages in a variety of formats designed to maximize the impact and effectiveness of a communications program. Transmission reports following distribution provide immediate confirmation of delivery and feedback.

News Canada

For over 25 years, News Canada has provided print, web, broadcast, and digital online video services to clients. They offer production and development of newsworthy content into media-ready formats, promotion and distribution of media-requested content, monitoring and reporting of news content.

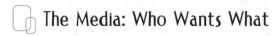 The Media: Who Wants What

In developing your media list it's essential to understand the types of material that will be of interest to different media, as well as the individuals within each media organization who are most likely to be receptive to your message. Make note of any names you see written in the newspapers under a specific category and record the names of TV reporters who could assist you. Don't forget to note any editorial/columnist names in trade publications, as well as the names of all beat reporters who are covering a particular topic or area. Visiting the websites of different organizations will also help you locate additional relevant names for your list.

Identify your target audiences

Who do you want to influence with your story? How can you communicate with this audience via the media? There are many different elements to consider.

Newspapers

As discussed earlier, there are many different types of newspapers, including weekly, daily, and monthly; national, regional, and local/community; university, community college, and private school; alumni; underground, and alternative; consumer, trade, and business; Internet; multilingual and ethnic; and supplements and special reports.

Who wants what?

Editor

The Editor is the person who edits the writing for the publication, and who usually decides on the story assignments. Trade magazines tend to have one editor who oversees all topics covered in the publication while newspapers and non-trade (such as consumer or business) publications usually have editors covering various, specific topics (such as finance or real estate). For smaller community newspapers, college and university papers, and alternative and multi-lingual papers, there is typically just one person making editorial decisions.

Managing Editor

The Managing Editor is an editor in an executive position who has supervisory charge of all editorial activities of a publication. You will rarely send information to the Managing Editor.

Assignment Editors

Assignment Editors have become very important, especially over the past few years. Most media work to tight deadlines and often don't look at information until one or two days before an event. The Assignment Editor or Photo Assignment Editor can arrange for a writer, cameraman, or photographer to 'cover' your event; they often assign the story on the day of the event.

Department Editors
Department Editors are usually the primary contacts for larger newspapers. They specialize in subject areas, such as arts, lifestyle, business, education, city, environment, health, food and beverage, foreign affairs, politics, sports, and public service announcements.

Beat reporters
Beat reporters cover one specific field, such as labour news, police news, foreign affairs, etc. They often have a background in the area they cover.

General reporters
General reporters cover all kinds of stories, ranging from local disasters to human-interest items. They may not know that much about your industry or field though, so it is important to simplify information, explain concepts, and emphasize Key Messages.

Photo editors
Photo editors are interested almost solely in stories with a visual appeal (such as human-interest stories).

Bureau reporters/editors
Many newspapers have bureaus in Vancouver, Toronto, Calgary, Edmonton, Montreal, and Ottawa. The staff will report to a Bureau Chief, who oversees the national Bureaus.

City Editor
A City Editor makes day-to-day decisions about what stories will be covered and who will do it. The person in this position will be able to refer you to the reporter who covers your beat.

Editorial Page Editor
The Editorial Page Editor writes some, or all, of a newpaper's editorials. In larger newspapers this editor will supervise any other editorial writers, as well as those responsible for selecting op-ed pieces and letters to the editor.

Deadlines to consider
Newspapers file stories the same day that a news story breaks, unless it is for a more in-depth piece. When working on a same-day news story, be sure to have all of your information—including contact numbers and key spokespeople—available for reporters immediately. Deadlines are usually around 3 pm.

Magazines
There are many types of magazines—from weekly to annually—to consider when planning a media relations campaign, including consumer- and trade-oriented publications.

Who wants what?

The best way to determine the subjects that will be of the greatest interest to a magazine is to obtain and read several issues. Do they publish stories from 'experts' in their field? Are your competitors included in the stories they carry? Be prepared to wait for a few days while they decide whether or not they are interested.

For **consumer publications**, you should query the Editor through a story outline or feature suggestion. For **trade publications**, it is helpful to look for any columns that highlight announcements, such as the introduction of new products or services, or staff appointments and changes. Submit prepared news items and feature material. You can pitch feature articles either on your own or through a freelancer who is already connected to the publication. For **entertainment guides**, you should check for lists of local events that are of interest to tourists.

Editor, Managing Editor, or Executive Editor

In magazines, the Editor, Managing Editor, or Executive Editor, will determine the overall editorial position of the publication and the general thrust of news-gathering.

Features Editor

The Feature Editor assigns, edits—and often writes—human-interest stories.

Columnists

Columnists write regular special interest articles on topics such as the outdoors, the environment, politics, and arts.

Deadlines to consider

Magazines with targeted readerships, such as women, parents, or men, have significantly longer lead times. There is very little breaking news in these magazines and they tend to spend a great deal of time researching and writing stories. Typical lead times could be between two to six months.

News magazines (weeklies) usually come out on Mondays and have Friday deadlines. This type of publication should be approached a few weeks in advance, unless the issue is particularly time-sensitive.

Newsletters, inserts, and bulletins

Who wants what?

Newsletters, inserts, and bulletins are interested in news, issues, and profiles that are directly related to their target market. You should include the Editor on your media list, as well as the writers and freelance writers.

Television

Television features or magazines usually work on a story for one or two months. Like print magazines, they also may not be able to tell you whether they are interested for a day or two. **Television news** shows that air nightly or at noon, and local or national news have a much shorter news cycle: same day for breaking news, and a few weeks for longer feature or investigative stories.

Who wants what?
Television media are interested in stories with great visuals, very short sound bites, and a human-interest or consumer angle. A great spokesperson who can easily and quickly respond to questions, as well as existing B-roll footage—video of a particular scene or event that pertains to your issue and that can be used as footage by the television reporter—will help to pique their interest in your campaign.

Executive Producer/Producer
The Executive Producer is the lead person for a particular program or a series of programs. The Producer is responsible for the overall tone and content of news programs and, on smaller stations, assigns crews to cover particular stories.

Assignment Editor
At larger stations, the Assignment Editor makes the day-to-day decisions about what to cover and who will cover it.

Station manager
A station manager, at smaller stations, will set the policies about news coverage and will supervise the overall operation.

Program Director/Public Affairs Director
The Program Director may determine content and select participants for talk shows, while the Public Affairs Director is responsible for public service announcements.

Radio
The category of radio includes network, local, college/university, and multi-lingual stations. Radio formats include call-ins, news feeds, and public service announcements. **Call-in shows** feature one or more guests and a host discussing a specific issue and include time near the end of the show for listeners to call in and voice their opinions. Should you be involved with a call-in show, it is important that you are prepared to answer a wide range of questions.

   News feeds are either written by staff or fed from a network. The local station will often enhance a story with quotes from appropriate spokespeople. PSAs are announcements made 'in the public interest', and are meant to educate or announce community events. You should call the station prior to making a PSA and find out their format requirements (for example, length of piece, 'paid for by' requirements, etc.) and the lead-time they require, which can often be several weeks before an event.

Who wants what?

Radio is most interested in news stories and features, including local issues and events, and provincial and national stories. Public service announcements and interviews, both telephone and in-studio, are common formats. It is often advantageous to a media relations program to secure sponsorship of an event by a radio station or from a radio personality.

Executive Producer/Producer

Similar to the structure at a television station, the Executive Producer is the lead person for a particular program or a series of programs. The Producer is responsible for the overall tone and content of news programs and, on smaller stations, assigns crews to cover particular stories.

Assignment Editor

At larger stations the Assignment Editor makes the day-to-day decisions about what to cover and who will cover it.

Station manager

The station manager sets the policies on news coverage and supervises overall operation at smaller radio stations.

Program Director/Public Affairs Director

The Program Director determines the content of various shows and selects the participants of talk shows, while the Public Affairs Director is primarily responsible for public service announcements.

Broadcast personality

Broadcast personalities are the on-air 'talent' one hears on the radio. It is important to consider the broadcast personality, and the demographic to which they appeal, when developing your campaign. Some on-air personalities appeal only to a specific age group or to a specific political viewpoint; you will want to work with someone who will represent the goals of your company or organization's event.

Media List Tracker

Assemble the information you need on this worksheet in order to create your media list.

- Name of publication/station/wire service
- Mailing address
- Street addresses
- Main telephone number(s), cell phone number
- Main fax number(s)
- Website address (URL)
- E-mail address
- Circulation/audience
- Geographical area
- Frequency of publication or broadcast (including date and time)
- Special supplements, if any
- Name of column/section/show
- Types of subjects covered
- Contact(s):
  - Name and title
  - Telephone number(s)
  - Fax number(s)
  - E-mail address
- Deadlines:
  - Copy
  - Photos
  - Advertising
- Special requirements (take feature articles and mat stories?)
- Follow-up required

Exercises

1. Using one or more media directories, create a media list of the important trade and consumer media for your company or organization. Include names and titles.
2. Describe *why* each of these media contacts is important to your organization.

Chapter 7

Creating a Media Kit

A media relations program is based on distributing information and the Media Kit is an essential element. The Media Kit speaks for you, providing carefully constructed messages, background information, and photos and/or broadcast clips that are designed to capture the attention of an editor or producer. Properly prepared, the Media Kit is one of your most effective communications tools.

Chapter Summary

By the end of Chapter 7, you will be able to:

- define 'Media Kit' and understand why it is necessary;
- understand the various formats in which a Media Kit can exist;
- realize the importance of keeping information up-to-date;
- recognize the components of a Media Kit;
- develop materials for the media including media releases, media advisories, fact sheets, backgrounders, story ideas, calendar listings, public service announcements, awards and statements of recognition, statistics, matt stories, product samples, annual general reports, and newsletters;
- understand the ways to use a Media Kit;
- prepare video B-rolls, video news releases, and radio news releases;
- create an Online Media Room; and
- work with outside professionals.

Defining a Media Kit

A **Media Kit** is a customized presentation that provides detailed, pertinent information to the media about a company, organization, service or product. It is often used for a special event, product launch, campaign launch, groundbreaking, etc. A Media Kit can also be defined as key information that conveys to members of the media who you are, what you do, and why they should care. It is an excellent tool for communicating important points about your company or organization to new customers and partners. A good Media Kit will explain you and your company or organization to an editor, producer, or reporter when you are not there. It should include as many different components or 'hooks' as possible, so the editorial decision-maker can select a story angle to match his or her audience's interests and needs.

Why You Need a Media Kit

Reporters and producers on tight deadlines look for the fastest and easiest way to get the information they need. The Media Kit supplies the essential information they need.

Formats
The elements of a Media Kit are supplied in hard copy, e-mail, or electronic format (for example, USB pocket drives, memory sticks, CDs, or DVDs). For broadcast media, however, Media Kits are often provided as audio or video clips. The format depends on your products, your industry's practices, and your audiences.

The information must be easily accessible in one central location (especially if it is online); furthermore, you should still print copies of your Media Kit for conferences, tradeshows, and targeted media campaigns as needed.

Keep it updated
Update key information, such as company news and online links, on a regular basis. Use focus groups, online comments from visitors, and informal surveys to track what is working within your Media Kit.

Components of a Media Kit
Depending on your organization or company, the following elements should be included in your Media Kit:

- *Kit Cover.* The inserts are generally packaged in a Media Kit Folder. These folders come in a variety of colours and some have embossing, die-cuts, extra folds, or pockets. You can customize the folder with a label on the front that matches your company identity.

- *Cover letter or 'Pitch' letter.* Your cover letter should be fairly short, introducing you (if you're the contact person), your company, and your Media Kit. Try to address the cover letter to someone specific, rather than just a title. Often you can find the appropriate names online or by calling the media outlet.
- *Media Release.* Your media release tells the media that there is something newsworthy, such as a special event, a new product or service, awards you've received, or a new partnership with another company.
- *Company or organization's mission statement and history.* Include photos, the date the business was founded, and it was founded.
- *Biographies and credentials of key personnel.* Include a biography detailing the credentials, education, and experience of your company or organization's key personnel. Include publication or production credits, patents, inventions, partnerships, or important contributions to your industry, as well as anecdotes and quotes.
- *Photos.* If you have professional photos of key personnel or products, include these in your Media Kit. Include contact information: name and title of person or name of product, company name, company contact with phone number, brief caption describing subject of photo, and copyright notice (if applicable).
- *Newsletter, written articles, or matt story.* If you produce a newsletter or have written articles or essays relevant to your industry, include copies in your Media Kit. Provide information on obtaining reprints or permission to reuse the article, so the person reading the article has proper contact information.
- *Public Service Announcement (PSA).* PSAs are particularly helpful if you're trying to call attention to an event or a time-sensitive community project. Thirty words require 30 seconds on-air. Always list the number of words in the upper-left corner of the PSA, and try to keep the announcement short.
- *CD, CD-ROM, videotape, or DVD.* Be sure to create labels and inserts for them.
- *Testimonials or product reviews.* Ask clients for testimonials; these are considered 'third party endorsement'.

In addition to the items listed above, you could also include Tip Sheets that provide industry context or surveys; upcoming calendars of events, conferences, and appearances; recent media coverage (within the past six months); copies of speeches; Frequently Asked Questions (FAQs); a list of products and/or services, and the benefits of each; and potential story ideas and case studies.

Writing for the Media

The media release

Media releases remain the most common tool for individuals and organizations to make a public statement through the news media. Every week, newsrooms receive stacks of media releases, so it's essential to make your release stand out in the crowd. To enhance the visibility and accessibility of your media releases, post them on your company's website or in your Online Media Room. Media releases are often mailed, faxed, or e-mailed to media on their own, separate from other elements of the Media Kit.

PR professionals are now using search engine optimized media releases to drive sales directly and to measure results. Social media experts are developing a new news release format for the Internet that combines text, captioned photos, audio and video on-demand, and pre-approved quotes to accommodate the needs of busy journalists filing on deadline and citizen journalists who may never actually call you for a comment.

What makes a good media release?
In order to be effective, a media release must:

- have a 'hook' or news angle that is clearly communicated in the headline and first paragraph;
- be concise, brief, and to the point;
- be written in a style and at a level that is appropriate to the audience;
- exclude industry-specific terminology or jargon;
- be complete, accurate, factual, and timely;
- have quotes to provide credibility and colour to the story;
- include background information and details; and
- provide contact information for media follow-up.

Preparing the media release
The first step in preparing a media release is to ensure that you have all of the necessary information. With this information in hand, you must then decide what is 'newsworthy' or, in other words, what an editor or reporter will perceive to have the biggest impact on readers or viewers. Think about which media would be interested in the story and what angles to promote.

On this basis, structure the order of information for the release, starting with the headline and first paragraph. Only then should you begin to write the copy. Once the copy has been written, edited, and formatted, print out the release and evaluate it as objectively as possible. If the news hook is unclear, rewrite the copy.

Bottoms Up!

Write your news story using an 'inverted triangle' approach—providing the most important information first, then filling in the background details. Because many people only scan the news, the essence of the story should be contained in the first paragraph. Keep in mind, too, that editors always cut a story from the bottom up.

How to Write a Media Release

COMPANY LOGO

FOR IMMEDIATE RELEASE	**FOR FURTHER INFORMATION:**
Date (release is sent) or	Contact:
Embargoed until (date):	Name, Title
	Company/Organization
	Telephone number(s), e-mail address

Headline

Make your headline an attention-grabber. It should summarize the 'news value' of the release and catch the interest of the reporter. The headline should also describe what is special about your story. Use upper-case type and keep the length to two lines or less. Reporters see a lot of media releases and you have to get their attention early. Always include a verb in your headline.

First paragraph
Place (slug line)

A well-written release will reflect a news style of writing. The five Ws (who, what, where, when, and why)—and H (how)—should all be contained in an interesting opening statement.

Second and remaining paragraphs

These paragraphs should include quotes from spokespeople and third party sources (from one to three quotes per release), background information on the organization and/or event, information on sponsors, event registration, statistics, survey results, etc.

Releases are usually not reprinted verbatim. A good release will provide the essential information for a future story and will encourage the reporter to seek out more information. Keep your writing tight and uncomplicated.

Always use the third person in your release—never use the word 'you' to talk to the reader. Similarly, avoid personal opinions, except for those expressed in direct quotes. Use simple language and don't use tech speak or jargon.

Finally, remember that a media release is not advertising copy—the media do not want to feel they are being 'sold' a story.

End of the page

If the media release is two pages, type '. . .more' at the end of the first page and number the second page. Always type '–30–' (the newspaper symbol for 'end of story') and centre it at the end of the one- or two-page release.

V. hot off the press

FOR IMMEDIATE RELEASE

Virgin Mobile Launches in Canada
Branson Delivers the Cure for the 'Catch'

(Toronto, ON – March 1, 2005) – Virgin Mobile came to the rescue of Canadians today with the launch of its mobile service across the country.   The company will bring competition back to the market and offer Canadian customers a mobile phone service with no catches: great rates, no hidden fees and no contracts to sign.

During an action-packed stunt in downtown Toronto, Virgin Group Chairman and Virgin Mobile Canada founder, Sir Richard Branson, zipped from the skies and crushed the competition in the Virgin Mobile "emergency services" monster truck. Richard Branson freed customers who were chained to long-term contracts, hidden fees and high rates.

 "More than 11 million Canadians are stuck with 'the Catch,' which means they're locked into long-term contracts that are riddled with hidden fees and extra charges," said Branson. "Customers are losing out and they're paying more than they need to for their mobile phone services. Virgin Mobile has taken out all the confusion and will right the wrongs of the industry."

"Our philosophy at Virgin is to break into markets where customers aren't getting what they deserve and deliver a better service. We've had a great deal of success with this approach in the mobile industry and now have more than 8.5 million customers worldwide. We plan to continue this success in Canada by bringing some much-needed simplicity to the market," added Branson.

Virgin Mobile's customer-oriented approach to mobile phone services has been successful in the UK, Australia and most recently in the United States.

"We know that Canadians are ready for Virgin Mobile and ready for a simpler, better deal," said Andrew Black, President and CEO of Virgin Mobile Canada. "With over 300 plans out there, buying a mobile phone is hard work. It's no wonder that over 50% of Canadians don't have one."

"We offer a simple service where customers buy a phone and pay only for the calls they make. With Virgin Mobile, Canadians will get a service with great rates all day, everyday; no hidden fees such as 911, System Access, voicemail or call waiting; no contracts to sign, and no catches," added Black.

The Facts:

Pricing
Virgin Mobile's rates start low and get even lower. Calls cost just 25 cents a minute for the first five minutes each day, then just 15 cents a minute. The credit customers purchase lasts for 120 days - the longest period before expiry in the market. Virgin Mobile customers can get even better value with a $25 monthly pass: only 20 cents a minute for the first five minutes of calls each day and then just 10 cents a minute.

.../2

Above: Media Release for the Launch of Virgin Mobile Canada

2/...

The Phones

Virgin Mobile phones are sold without contracts, so customers don't have to tie themselves into long-term commitments and high-priced plans. At launch, three sexy little phone models are available at affordable prices from leading manufacturers Nokia and Audiovox— the Nokia 6015i at $99; the Audiovox 8615 flip phone at $159 and the Audiovox 8910 camera phone at $219.

The Cool Stuff

Virgin Mobile has created its own customized menu and some fun and sexy extras such as: Musictones (download the real tune by the artist), Rescue Ring (program your phone to save you during a bad date), Skins (customize your menu to be a "playa", "it girl" or go "au naturel", Celebrity Dirt, Your Psychic, Date Generator and loads of games and ringtones. These can be found in the VXL section of Virgin Mobile's menu. Customers only pay 10 cents for unlimited access to VXL for the entire day, a one-time content fee for any extras they purchase, and no additional per Kb download fee.

"Customers have told us that they're sick of the techno-babble and simply want cool services. Our phones are about more than talking and listening. We give customers a whole new experience, from our easy-to-follow menu to our unique VXL service," said Black.

Where to get us

Virgin Mobile has made buying and using a Virgin Mobile phone easy for customers. Phones will be available at more than 1,500 stores nationwide, and customers can get turned on through customer service (1-888-999-2321), online (www.virgin.com/mobile) or at select retailers. Top up cards will be available at 10,000 stores across Canada, and customers can also top up online, through Virgin Mobile customer service or directly from their mobile phone.

What is Virgin Mobile Canada?

Virgin Mobile Canada is a partnership between Sir Richard Branson's Virgin Group and the Bell Mobility division of Bell Canada, bringing together one of the world's most respected brands with Canada's national leader in communications.

Virgin Mobile Canada will operate as a mobile virtual network operator or MVNO, which has proven to be a successful business approach for Virgin Mobile in other markets around the world. Virgin Mobile was first launched in the United Kingdom in November 1999, in Australia in 2000 and subsequently expanded to the U.S. in July 2002, and together the companies have attracted more than 8.5 million customers worldwide.

-30-

For more information, please contact:

Paula Lash; paula.lash@virginmobile.ca
416-655-5555
Nathan Rosenberg; Nathan.Rosenberg@virginmobile.ca
416-556-6000
Virgin Mobile Canada

Jen Koster/Selena Gardner
Hill & Knowlton
416-413-4615/416-413-4739
jen.koster@hillandknowlton.ca/selena.gardner@hillandknowlton.ca

Above: Media Release for the Launch of Virgin Mobile Canada (continued)

PUROLATOR AND THE [LOCAL CFL TEAM] WORK TOGETHER TO TACKLE HUNGER
Fans to donate food for a photo with the Grey Cup

[CITY]– Purolator, Canada's largest courier company, is proud to host a Purolator Tackle Hunger food drive in support of the [NAME] Food Bank at the [TEAMS] game on [DATE].

Purolator is asking football fans to participate in the food drive by bringing a non-perishable food item or cash donation to the Purolator Tackle Hunger trucks stationed at [STADIUM]. In return, fans can have their picture taken with the Grey Cup [*and names of members of the CFL Hall of Fame, depending on the city*] and enter a draw to win two tickets to the Grey Cup final in Winnipeg.

Last year, [CITY] football fans helped raise over XX lbs of food for the [NAME] food bank by participating in the Purolator Tackle Hunger food drive.

What: Purolator Tackle Hunger food drive in support of the [CITY] Food Bank

When: [DATE] – [TIME] until the end of the first quarter

Where: Food collection to take place at [GATE] at [STADIUM]. The Grey Cup will be located [GATE]

Who: [CITY] football fans, Purolator employees, [TEAM] coaches and players' wives/girlfriends, who will be on hand to accept donations.

In addition to the Purolator Tackle Hunger food drive, every time a CFL quarterback gets sacked throughout the regular season, Purolator donates the equivalent of the quarterback's weight in food to a CFL hometown region food bank. For the game on DATE, Purolator will donate approximately XX lbs. of food if [NAME of QB, if appropriate] is sacked.

Purolator Tackle Hunger food drives are part of Purolator's commitment to help alleviate hunger in Canada and will extend across Canada throughout the season at various CFL games. In 2005 alone, Purolator Tackle Hunger helped raise 223 truckloads of food, equaling over 275,000 lbs. for local food banks across Canada.

About hunger in [CITY]
The need for food bank donations in CITY over the summer is great. Many donors take vacation during the summer months and as a result donations drop even though food bank usage remains constant. *[this section will be tweaked according to the season]*

[CITY] Food Bank distributes food donations to more than XXX associate agencies. Last year, the food bank distributed nearly XX million kilograms of food, which included distributing food each month to over XX people.

For more information about the Purolator Tackle Hunger food drive, visit [website] or contact:

Above: Media Release for Purolator Tackle Hunger 2006

FOR IMMEDIATE RELEASE

Community Walk Raises Funds for Dog Guide Training Programs

More then 100 Canadian communities will host walks – including High Park, the Beaches and Scarborough on May 15, 2005

TORONTO, ON, May 5, 2005: Neighbourhood dogs, pet owners and animal lovers will gather at High Park, Ashbridges Bay and Thompson Memorial Park at 10:30 a.m. on May 15 for the annual Purina Walk for Dog Guides to raise money for Dog Guide training programs offered by Lions Foundation of Canada. Each year, thousands of people and their dogs participate from coast to coast.

"It's wonderful to see so many people from the community demonstrating their support for Dog Guides and the important service they provide to their human partners," said Joan Leeder, organizer of the High Park Purina Walk for Dog Guides. "Thanks to the events on May 15 and the support of corporate sponsors, Lions Foundation of Canada will be able to assist more disabled Canadians achieve an independent lifestyle."

Lions Foundation of Canada is the only facility in Canada to offer training programs for Dog Guides to serve the needs of people with visual, hearing, medical or physical disabilities. Clients receive a Dog Guide and all required training, including travel and accommodation, at no charge.

Fundraising activities, corporate sponsorships and private donations are primary sources of funding for Lions Foundation of Canada. The Foundation does not receive any municipal, provincial or federal government support. In addition to supporting the Purina Walk for Dog

Above: Media Release for the Purina Walk for Dog Guides

Guides as the event's title sponsor, Purina also provides food for all Dog Guides from the time they are puppies until they are finished their training.

"A typical Dog Guide provides eight years of service to its human partner, which makes proper health and nutrition very important," says Jennifer Clarke Maier, direct and interactive communications manager – Canada. "At Purina, we're proud to assist with the important work of Lions Foundation of Canada and ensure Dog Guides get proper nutrition to enhance their wellbeing and live a long, happy life."

Other corporate sponsors lending national support for the Purina Walk for Dog Guides include Urban Associates, Information Packaging Inc. and Super Pet. Local sponsors of community walks across Canada are also a key component of the event's success. Several local businesses in the High Park, Beaches and Scarborough communities have also generously pledged their support.

About Lions Foundation of Canada

Lions Foundation of Canada Dog Guides is a federally incorporated charitable foundation created by Lions clubs across Canada. Its mission is to provide service to physically challenged Canadians in the areas of mobility, safety and independence. Since 1983, Lions Foundation of Canada has provided specially trained Dog Guides to more than 1000 men, women and children aged eight to 84. The only Dog Guide training school of its kind in Canada, Lions Foundation of Canada's three programs are *Canine Vision Canada*, *Hearing Ear Dogs of Canada*, and *Special Skills Dogs of Canada*.

For more information or to locate your local Purina Walk for Dog Guides, visit www.purinawalkfordogguides.com, or call 905-842-2891 / 1-800-768-3030.

- 30 -

Media contact:
Kerry Collings
Argyle Rowland Communications
416-968-7311, ext. 227
kcollings@argylerowland.com

Michelle Gaulin, *Communications and Events Coordinator*
Lions Foundation of Canada Dog Guides
905-842-2891 / 1-800-768-3030 / mgaulin@dogguides.com

Above: Media Release for the Purina Walk for Dog Guides (continued)

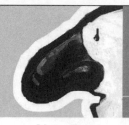

BLUE NOSE INTERNATIONAL MARATHON
1565 SOUTH PARK STREET
HALIFAX, NOVA SCOTIA B3J 2L2
T 902.496.1889   F 902.425.3180

information@bluenosemarathon.com   www.bluenosemarathon.com

News Release

The Second Annual Blue Nose International Marathon success despite weather storm

Harry Neynens wins his first Blue Nose Marathon

May 22, 2005, HALIFAX, NS– The second annual Blue Nose Marathon ran today. 5,000 runners participated in Marathon weekend - an increase of 1,500 from last year. Runners braved a spring storm that delayed the marathon start by one hour to 10:00 am. More than 3,000 runners, participating in the full, half and team relay events, ran a modified course that for marathoners included two laps through Halifax. Runners did not cross the Macdonald Bridge due to the weather.

Thousands of volunteers and spectators participated in the second annual event despite the extremely inclement conditions. The team relay – run in a modified format due to weather - raised over $45,000 for the YMCA Strong Kids program.

The marathon attracted runners from across Nova Scotia and every Canadian province and 11 US states. The "people's marathon" attracted runners of all ages and levels of experience, from ages 3-70, making the marathon an event that lives up to the name "the people's marathon."

"This weekend's event was a huge success," said Rod McCulloch, event co-chair. "Despite the wet, windy and cold weather, over 85 percent of the registered runners ran this morning. This truly shows the resiliency of runners and of Nova Scotians. We are more than thrilled with the unprecedented turn out and resolve of everyone involved in this race." McCulloch experienced the weather first-hand during his half-marathon run.

"An event like this is a huge undertaking. We know that this event wouldn't have been this successful if it wasn't without the help of our dedicated volunteers, our enthusiastic spectators and the support of the people of IIRM," said McCulloch. "We were really pleased to see so many runners, especially first time runners, weather the storm and embrace this event."

1,558 runners ran the Crystal Light Full Marathon and Volkswagen Half Marathon today, 623 ran The Chronicle Herald 10K, and 197 ran the Roger's Wireless 5K. Total registration numbers for the second annual Blue Nose Marathon were over 5,000 in all events.

Harry Neynens of Enfield, Nova Scotia and Holly Whitman of East Chezzetcook were the first male and first female across the finish line in the Crystal Light Full Marathon with times of 2:58:06.3 and 3:24:53.4.

The winners of the Volkswagen Half Marathon were Alex Coffin from Saint John, New Brunswick with a time of 1:21:11.0, and Denise Robson from Dartmouth, Nova Scotia at 1:26:18.3.

Sean Williams from Sydney, Australia was the top male in the Chronicle Herald 10K with a time of 37:08.3, and Kaitlyn Watters from Westville, Nova Scotia as lead female with a time of 45:54.9.

Above: Media Release for the Blue Nose International Marathon

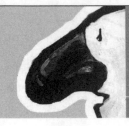

BLUE NOSE INTERNATIONAL MARATHON
1565 SOUTH PARK STREET
HALIFAX, NOVA SCOTIA B3J 2L2
T 902.496.1889   F 902.425.3180

information@bluenosemarathon.com   www.bluenosemarathon.com

Bruce Carr from Dartmouth, Nova Scotia and Mary Chan of Upper Sackville, Nova Scotia were the first male and female of the Rogers Wireless 5K Run-Walk to cross the finish line. Carr came in at 24:52.1 and Chan had a finish time of 24:37.1.

Over 80 teams registered for the YMCA Team Relay. The relay teams ran a modified course today, covering a distance of 5k starting at the Metro Centre. All proceeds from the Team Relay will go to the YMCA's Strong Kids Program.

""The money that has been raised through the Head Shoppe Team Relay is going to make a major difference in the lives of hundreds of children in our community this year. This year's success in raising these funds for YMCA Strong Kids will ensure that more kids than ever before can go to Y Camp this summer, take swimming lessons, or play basketball," said Bette Watson-Borg, President of the YMCA of Greater Halifax. The program allows for the development of programs emphasizing the core values of caring, honesty, respect and responsibility-tools to help build strong kids to grow up and thrive in our communities.

The winners in each race categories – from full and half marathon, 10K, 5K run/walk - will receive The Blue Nose Marathon Plate of Excellence, a handcrafted, custom designed by NovaScotian Crystal.

Prizes were also awarded in Junior (under 19), Masters (40-49) Senior Masters (50-59), Golden Masters (60-65) and Youth categories. Relay teams were awarded prizes for spirit, fundraising and for being the first across the finish line.

Over 1,700 Youth covered a distance of 4.2 km, 1/10th of a full marathon on Saturday, in the Doctors of Nova Scotia Youth Run. Participants have been training all year through fitness-training curriculum with the schools that saw students cover over 38 km, throughout the months leading up to the event.

The **Blue Nose International Marathon** is the people's marathon – with the diversity to encourage and challenge runners of all levels, first timers and seasoned marathoners. The ultimate goal of enhancing the quality of life and lifestyles of the people in our region, by creating an event that promotes not only active healthy living but also community involvement and participation. The Canadian Medical Association has recognized the Blue Nose Marathon organizing committee with its 2005 Award for Excellence in Health Promotion, for its efforts to create an event that promotes healthy activity in Nova Scotians of every age and activity level.

For information on the event and to get the results of the 5K, 10K, Relay and Half/Full Marathon visit ww.sportstats.ca.

-30-

For more information please contact:
Sarah Moses
Media Relations, Blue Nose International Marathon
(902) 425-1860 ext 258 or 489-2227 during event weekend
smoses@mctl.ca

Above: Media Release for the Blue Nose International Marathon (continued)

Hey, What Happened To My Media Release?

What happened	Why it happened
Discarded	• Incomplete information • Inappropriate for the audience, publication, or station • Addressed to the wrong person • Too long, rambling, and with no news value • Filled with misspellings and grammatical errors
Put in a file	• Publication or program has an upcoming article, segment, or supplement that could incorporate your information
Reported as a one-liner	• Publication or program felt it was worthwhile to mention your company or organization in a broader article or segment. This may be disappointing, but never underestimate the value of the mention. Readers or viewers will remember that they read or saw something about your organization or company—not the number of lines or minutes you received.
Reprinted as is	• Sometimes happens in trade magazines, newsletters, or community newspapers. Most media edit and add to the information in the release.
Contacted by the media	• Media representative books an interview with you.

The media advisory/photo op

The media advisory gives the media a quick overview of the five Ws (who, what, when, where and why)—and H (how)—and suggests photographic features of the event. Also known as a 'media alert', a media advisory/photo op (photo opportunity) is a type of release that is e-mailed or faxed to media one day before (or the morning of) your event to remind the assignment editors, reporters, producers, and photographers about the event. It uses short, bulleted points instead of the full paragraphs used in the media release.

MEDIA ADVISORY -- PHOTO OPPORTUNITY

Purolator and CFL TEAM Join Forces to Tackle Hunger
In Support of the CITY Food Bank

CITY – This DAY, CFL TEAM coaches, players [*specific names if team is able to confirm*], as well as their wives and girlfriends [*and families, if applicable*] will gather at NAME Stadium to show their support for the upcoming Purolator Tackle Hunger food drive which will benefit the CITY Food Bank. [*TEAM mascot will also be on site, if applicable*].

What:	Photo opportunity with Purolator employees, CITY Food Bank and CFL TEAM coaches, players, wives and girlfriends to support Purolator Tackle Hunger food drive.
Where:	NAME Stadium, Field Level.
When:	DATE, TIME

This is a great opportunity to remind football fans to participate in the upcoming Purolator Tackle Hunger food drive which will take place at the CFL TEAMS game this DATE. Fans can participate by bringing a non-perishable food item or cash donation to the Purolator Tackle Hunger trucks stationed at the stadium gates. In return, fans can get their picture taken with the Grey Cup. Wives and girlfriends of CFL TEAM coaches and players will be on site to accept donations.

All proceeds from the Purolator Tackle Hunger food drive support the CITY Food Bank.

Last year, Purolator helped raise the equivalent of 270,000 lbs. (223 truckloads) of food for local food banks across Canada.

For more information about the Purolator Tackle Hunger Food Drive please contact:

Contact

Above: Media Advisory/Photo Op for Purolator Tackle Hunger 2006

SAVE THE DATE / PHOTO OPP

High Park Purina Walk for Dog Guides

Neighbourhood dogs, pet owners, animal lovers walk to raise funds for Lions Foundation of Canada Dog Guide training programs

Join us at 11:00 a.m. on Sunday, May 15, 2005 for a walk in High Park with hundreds of community residents and their dogs to raise funds for Lions Foundation of Canada Dog Guides training programs.

Lions Foundation of Canada trains Dog Guides for Canadians with visual, hearing, medical and physical disabilities, and is the only Dog Guide school of its kind in Canada.

Did you know...
♦ Since 1983, Lions Foundation of Canada has provided specially trained Dog Guides to more than 1000 men, women and children ages eight to 84
♦ Funding for Dog Guide training is 100 per cent obtained from private donations, Lions Clubs, Service Clubs, foundations and corporations – with <u>no government support</u>
♦ Lions Foundation provides clients with Dog Guides <u>free of charge</u>
♦ The most successful breeds for Dog Guide training include Labrador Retrievers, Standard Poodles and Border Terriers

INTERVIEW:	**Joan Leeder**, organizer of the High Park Purina Walk for Dog Guides, about the important of this fundraising event.
	Lions Foundation clients and their Dog Guides companions.
	"Dog Guide in Training" puppies and their foster families.
WHEN:	Sunday, May 15, 2005 10:30 a.m. for interviews / 11:00 a.m. Purina Walk for Dog Guides starts

For more information:

Kerry Collings
Argyle Rowland Communications
416-968-7311, ext. 227
kcollings@argylerowland.com

Above: Media Advisory/Photo Op for the Purina Walk for Dog Guides

The Fact Sheet

A Fact Sheet is a one-page summary of basic information related to an organization, a product, or a program. It details the organization or company's areas of expertise and the names of spokespeople who can provide authoritative material in its field. A fact sheet is a resource document, which can be used to provide a quick overview of an organization, and it is often kept on file by the media.

A Fact Sheet for an organization or company should provide the following information:

- the full name of the organization or company;
- the street address, telephone and fax numbers;
- the website and e-mail addresses;
- the year the organization or company was founded;
- the focus of organization, through a mission statement and tag line;
- the unique characteristics and areas of expertise;
- the services, products, and events; and
- the names and titles of key contacts.

For special events, a Fact Sheet can be included with a news release or Media Kit in order to provide details about types of activities, schedule, speakers, participants, and photo opportunities.

BLUE NOSE INTERNATIONAL MARATHON
1565 SOUTH PARK STREET
HALIFAX, NOVA SCOTIA B3J 2L2
T 902.496.1889   F 902.425.3180

information@bluenosemarathon.com   www.bluenosemarathon.com

Myles Media Memo

Countdown: 2 days until race weekend!

With just 2 days to go excitement is building as over 6,000 runners prepare to race in the second annual Blue Nose International Marathon. Here's the latest up to date information on all the marathon news.

Areas of Interest:
For more information on any of these stories, please contact Sarah Moses at 425-1860 ext 258 or at smoses@mctl.ca.

Timing a Marathon Runner
With over 6,000 runners expected to cross the finish line it seems nearly impossible to have an accurate time for each runner right? Wrong. Thanks to modern day technology each runner will place a time chip to his or her shoelace. It's called the ChampionChip and allows each runner to know his or her total running time. The miniature transponder is activated when the runner crosses the start line. Antenna mats are placed throughout the race route that detect the chip and transmit the runner's data. Once the runner crosses a mat at the finish line his or her Chip ID and time are stored on to a computer system. This information is later processed so the runner knows just how fast they were going.

Name that Runner
Each runner who registered before May 13th will have his or her name printed on his or her runner's bib. This makes the runner easy to spot by family and friends. Plus, an added bonus to the name bib, it makes it easy for spectators to yell out your name and cheer as you head throughout the race route.

Great Big Pasta Party
Carbohydrates give us energy, so what better time to load up on them then the night before the big race. The MT&L Great Big Pasta Party will be held Saturday night at the Halifax Metro Centre. Chef Christophe from the WTCC will be helping to prepare the over 2,000 pounds of pasta that will be eaten at the event. Keynote speaker for the evening will be a former marathon champion, Dick Beardsley, who will also be running in Sunday's race. Entertainment will include Big Fish, the Mellotones and Jon Matheson. Eating begins at 6:00 p.m.

Spectator Party
What does it take to host a spectator party? Well how about a lawn and a BBQ for start. Families and friends across metro are gathering together to celebrate the runners as they make their way along the race route. Spectators are invited to hold up cheer cards, signs, use noisemakers, sing songs, cheer and holler to the runners as they travel through their neighbourhoods. Tonight, Geri Wallace, a longtime runner will be speaking at the marathon's volunteer orientation session about the importance of being an energetic spectator. The session takes place from 6:00-8:00 p.m. at the Halifax Metro Centre.

Wheelchair Athlete
This year the marathon is pleased to have wheelchair marathoner Anthony Purcell back on the race route. Andrew will be returning to participate in the 10 K event. The 26-year old Elmsdale native is looking forward to crossing the finish line again. Last year Purcell finished 150th out of 619 participants in a little more than 52 minutes. Can he make it in less time this year? Be at the finish line to see this determined young man's exciting finish.

Above: Fact Sheet for the Blue Nose International Marathon

BLUE NOSE INTERNATIONAL MARATHON
1565 SOUTH PARK STREET
HALIFAX, NOVA SCOTIA B3J 2L2
T 902.496.1889   F 902.425.3180

information@bluenosemarathon.com

www.bluenosemarathon.com

Media Centre (Race Weekend)
During race weekend, there will be a media centre set up in the World Trade and Convention Centre. All Blue
Nose International Marathon materials will be made available through the media centre as well as final runner
times. Any questions during race weekend should be directed to the media centre.

For more information or to view the race route, visit www.BlueNoseMarathon.com.

<u>**Schedule of Events**</u>

Doctor's Nova Scotia Youth Run Official Start	**Saturday, May 21, 10:00 am**
Pharmasave Health & Sport Expo	Saturday, May 21, 9:00 am to 6:00 pm
Youth Run Post Race Ceremonies	Saturday, May 21, 10:30am to 12:00pm
MT&L Great Big Pasta Party	Saturday, May 21, 6:00 pm to 9:00 pm
Official Start of the 10K race	**Sunday, May 22, 8:45 am**
Official Start of the Full/Half/Team Relay Events	**Sunday, May 22, 9:00 am**
Official Start of the 5k Event	**Sunday, May 22, 9:15 am**
Post Race Mixer and Awards Ceremony	Sunday, May 22, 10:30 am to 3:00 pm
Molson Post-Race Party Metro Centre	Sunday, May 22, 8:00 pm

On your marks. Get set. Giv'er!

Sarah Moses
Blue Nose Marathon PR Committee
425-1860 ext 258
smoses@mctl.ca

Above: Fact Sheet for the Blue Nose International Marathon (continued)

What is the Purolator Tackle Hunger Program?

- As part of Purolator's commitment to drive away hunger in Canada, Purolator Tackle Hunger is a food drive campaign that aims to increase food donations for local food banks in cities across Canada.

- As part of the program, Purolator organizes a fan food drive and fundraiser at select CFL games and encourages fans to drop off a non-perishable food item or a cash donation. In return, fans can have their picture taken with the Grey Cup and enter a draw for tickets to the Grey Cup final in Winnipeg.

- In addition to the food drives, every time a CFL quarterback gets sacked throughout the regular season, Purolator donates the equivalent of the quarterback's weight in food to a CFL hometown region food bank.

- Developed in partnership the Canadian Football League and the Canadian Association of Food Banks, the Purolator Tackle Hunger program is now in its fourth year and has helped collect more than 670,000 pounds of food (223 truck loads) for food banks across Canada.

When is the Purolator Tackle Hunger program coming to CITY?

- On **DATE** from **TIME** to the end of the first quarter, Purolator will host a Purolator Tackle Hunger food drive in support of the **CITY** Food Bank at the **NAME** Stadium where the CFL **TEAM** will take on the **OPPOSING TEAM.**

- Football fans heading out to the game are encouraged to drop off a non-perishable food item or a cash donation to the Purolator trucks stationed in the front of the stadium gates. In return, fans have the chance to get their picture taken with the Grey Cup (which will be located at **GATE #**) and enter a draw for two tickets to the Grey Cup final in [**CITY**]

- In the days leading up to the game, Purolator will also bring the Grey Cup directly to its customers at their places of business so customer employees can also get their picture taken with the Cup in exchange for a food donation.

What can fans donate?

- The need for food bank donations over the summer is great. Many donors go on vacation during the summer and as a result, donations drop even thought food bank usage remains consistent.

- Appropriate food donations include non-perishable items such as peanut butter as well as canned beans and fruit [*section to be updated by food bank*]. Cash donations are also welcome. CITY Food Bank distributes food donations to more than XX associate agencies. Last year, the food bank distributed nearly XX kilograms of food, which included distributing food each month to over XX people.

What has been raised so far by the Purolator Tackle Hunger program?

- Last year in **CITY**, the Purolator Tackle Hunger food drive was able to help collect **XX lbs** of food for the **CITY** Food Bank.

- During the 2005 season, the Purolator Tackle Hunger program helped raise over 270,000 lbs. (92 truckloads) for the Canadian Association of Food Banks.

For more information, contact:

Above: Fact Sheet for Purolator Tackle Hunger 2006

Lions Foundation of Canada Dog Guides
FACT SHEET

Lions Foundation of Canada Dog Guides is a federally incorporated charitable foundation created by Lions clubs across Canada. Its mission is to provide service to Canadians who are physically disabled in the areas of mobility, safety and independence.

Since 1983, Lions Foundation of Canada has operated Dog Guides Canada to provide specially trained Dog Guides to more than 1000 men, women and children ages eight to 84. The only Dog Guide school of its kind in Canada, Lions Foundation of Canada trains Dog Guides not only for Canadians who are blind or visually impaired, but also for people who are deaf or hard of hearing or who have medical and/or physical disabilities.

All Dog Guides and required training, including transportation and accommodation, are offered at no charge. Lions Foundation of Canada operates two facilities in Ontario, including the head office and training facility in Oakville, and the breeding and training facility in Breslau. Funding for Dog Guide training is 100 per cent obtained from private donations, Lions clubs, service clubs, foundations and corporations, with no government funding.

Dog Guide Training
- Training is completed over a period of six to eight months;
- Once a Dog Guide is fully trained, the dog is matched with a client who stays at the training school in Oakville for 10 to 26 days, depending on the program; and
- Trainers work one-on-one with clients and dogs to produce qualified Dog Guide teams.

Canine Vision Canada (CVC) Dog Guides
- CVC Dog Guides increase the mobility and self-confidence of people who are blind or visually impaired by enabling their handlers to travel safely through crowded areas, traffic and around obstacles.

Hearing Ear Dogs of Canada (HED) Dog Guides
- HED Dog Guides are trained to alert deaf or hard-of-hearing handlers to sounds they cannot detect, such as the telephone ringing, the doorbell, a child crying, the calling of their name and the sound of an activated fire alarm.

Special Skills (SSD) Dog Guides
- SSD Dog Guides are trained to turn off and on light switches, open and close doors and drawers, retrieve items dropped such as a pencil or keys and get help should assistance be required; and
- The constant companionship of a trusted canine partner brings independence to the lives of Canadians with disabilities.

Above: Fact Sheet for the Purina Walk for Dog Guides

LIONS FOUNDATION OF CANADA DOG GUIDES   *PAGE 2*

The Lions Foundation of Canada Breeding Facility, Breslau, ON
- Lions Foundation of Canada breeding facility provides quality puppies for the development of future Dog Guides. Generous breeders often donate puppies as well as breeding stock; and
- The most successful breeds for Dog Guide training include Labrador Retrievers, Standard and Miniature Poodles and Border Terriers.

The Foster Puppy Program
- The Foster Puppy Program is very important to the early development and training of Dog Guides;
- Qualified volunteers provide homes for puppies where, for the first year of their life, they learn proper house manners, and are socialized and exposed to many different situations; and
- The Foundation covers routine medical and veterinary expenses and Nestlé Purina PetCare provides the food.

Purina Walk for Dog Guides
- The Purina Walk for Dog Guides is the Lions Foundation of Canada's annual major fundraising initiative;
- Since the inaugural event in 1985, the Purina Walk for Dog Guides has grown to include more than 100 community walks across Canada during the months of May, June, September and October.

To locate your local Purina Walk for Dog Guides, visit www.purinawalkfordogguides.com or call 905-842-2891 or 1-800-768-3030

For more information about the Lions Foundation of Canada Dog Guides' programs, visit www.dogguides.com, or call 905-842-2891 or 1-800-768-3030.

- 30 -

Media contact:

Kerry Collings
Argyle Rowland Communications
416-968-7311, ext. 227
kcollings@argylerowland.com

Michelle Gaulin
Lions Foundation of Canada Dog Guides
Communications and Events Coordinator
905-842-2891, ext. 238 / 1-800-768-3030, ext. 238
mgaulin@dogguides.com

Above: Fact Sheet for the Purina Walk for Dog Guides (continued)

Backgrounder

A backgrounder is a document that is usually no more than one page in length. It provides biographical or historical information on a company or organization, its products or services, an event, a key executive, or a speaker.

Nestlé Purina PetCare
Nestlé Purina Soins des animaux familiers

Canada
2500 Royal Windsor Drive
Mississauga ON L5J 1K8

NESTLÉ PURINA PETCARE

THE COMPANY BEHIND THE ANIMAL HALL OF FAME

For over 100 years, Nestlé Purina PetCare Company has dedicated itself to creating innovative, nutritious products – all designed to enhance the well being of pets. Nestlé Purina PetCare is the world's largest producer of dry dog and dry and soft-moist cat foods as well as being a leading producer of cat box filler in Canada and the United States. In Canada, Nestlé Purina's leading brands include Dog Chow and Cat Chow, Pro Plan, Purina ONE, Fancy Feast,Friskies and Purina MAXX. Canadian operations are headquartered in Mississauga, Ontario.

Nestlé Purina PetCare has 400 employees and operates regional offices in Vancouver, British Columbia, Calgary, Alberta, and in Laval, Quebec. Purina operates 26 manufacturing facilities worldwide for the production of its pet products.

As you might expect from a company that is passionate about pets and created the Purina Animal Hall of Fame, Nestlé Purina is also committed to advancing animal health and nutrition. The company's Purina Pet Institute is staffed by nutritionists, food and flavour scientists, veterinarians, immunology specialists, and others. The Institute's wide focus ranges from animal health and behaviour, to genetics and molecular biology.

Purina's research-studies program includes a dedicated farm and pet-care centre, located just outside St. Louis, Missouri, staffed by veterinarians, nutrition analysts and pet-care specialists. The world-renowned pet-care centre is home to a wide variety of dogs and cats, and is the largest of its kind, drawing nearly 200,000 visitors a year.

Purina sponsors regional and national dog shows. It also works with and supports various pet-shelter programs and animal associations, such as the Assistance Dogs Training Programs run by the Lions' Foundation of Canada Dog Guides. Many Canadians rely on trained support animals, such as guide dogs for the blind, for people with muscular disabilities, and for children with autism who relate well to animals.

Above: Backgrounder for the Purina Walk for Dog Guides

The story so far...

Who are we?

Virgin Mobile Canada is a partnership between Sir Richard Branson's Virgin Group and the Bell Mobility division of Bell Canada, bringing together one of the world's most respected brands with Canada's national leader in communications. However, at Virgin Mobile, we've developed our *own* sophisticated technology that allows us to be incredibly innovative and respond to the desires of customers by offering them good value and great service.

We'll operate as a mobile virtual network operator or MVNO, which has proven to be a successful business approach for Virgin Mobile in other markets around the world. Virgin Mobile was first launched in the United Kingdom in November 1999, in Australia in 2000 and subsequently expanded to the U.S. in July 2002, and together the companies have attracted more than 8.5 million customers worldwide.

What we stand for...(and what we don't)

Richard Branson set up Virgin Mobile in Canada because mobile customers are not getting what they deserve today and are being forced to sign long term contracts, choose from hundreds of confusing plans, pay hidden fees and high daytime rates.

We're here to offer Canadians a simpler, better deal, with no catches.

Virgin Mobile Canada is:

> ➤ **Customer champion** – We'll offer our customers great rates all the time and they start low and get lower. We don't make our customers sign a contract. We have no hidden fees and are totally honest and upfront about ALL our charges.
> ➤ **Hassle-free and easy** – Buying a Virgin mobile phone and topping up when you want to is a breeze. And, we're available where customers shop – our phones are at 1500 stores and our top up cards can be bought at over 10,000 stores across Canada. There are no complicated plans to get your head around and you have 120 days to use your cash – the longest expiry in the industry.
> ➤ **Superior customer service** – We will WOW our customers by empowering our team to go the extra mile, and consistently exceed our customers' expectations.
> ➤ **Challenger to the competition** – Virgin Mobile will bring competition back to the Canadian mobile industry, shake up the market and appeal to people's passions in life.

.../2

Above: Backgrounder for the Launch of Virgin Mobile Canada

2/...

The Team...

There are over 100 people here and while we've only existed for a short time, our fun, energetic and "young at heart" Virgin Mobile Team has years of experience in the mobile industry and within the Virgin group of companies. We also have some people with experience in neither – which helps us think differently.

Located in Toronto, Virgin Mobile Canada is headed by 42-year old Andrew Black, the former President of Lego Systems, and General Manager of Brand Development of Nike Inc. Andrew brings over 20 years of global marketing experience to Virgin Mobile from Lego and Nike, and other leading international brands such as Cadbury Schwepps and Colgate Palmolive.

Richard Branson's globetrotting empire...

In the 1970s, Richard Branson was a 20-year old music lover who hated the idea of having to pay the big bucks for records charged by the big record companies of the era. So in 1970 he opened shop as a mail order record retailer, called it Virgin, and started offering great music at great prices. He was so successful that he decided to open up a music retail store and then a record label, all branded with the Virgin name. By the 1980s, Virgin was becoming a challenger brand – stepping into conglomerate-dominated industries like the airline industry with Virgin Atlantic, and shaking things up.

In the 1990s, the Virgin brand exploded and today represents over 200 companies, more than 30,000 employees and over $10 billion in revenue. It's now involved in planes, trains, credit cards, soft drinks, music, mobile phones, holidays, cars, wines, publishing... the lot! And what ties all these businesses together are the values of the brand and the attitude of the people.

-30-

For more information, please contact:

Paula Lash; paula.lash@virginmobile.ca
416-655-5555
Nathan Rosenberg; Nathan.Rosenberg@virginmobile.ca
416-556-6000
Virgin Mobile Canada

Jen Koster/Selena Gardner
Hill & Knowlton
416-413-4615/416-413-4739
jen.koster@hillandknowlton.ca/selena.gardner@hillandknowlton.ca

Above: Backgrounder for the Launch of Virgin Mobile Canada (continued)

V. bigwigs

The Virgin Mobile Canada Team

There are over 100 people here and while we've only existed for a short time, our fun, energetic and "young at heart" Virgin Mobile Team has years of experience in the mobile industry and within the Virgin group of companies. We also have some people with experience in neither – which helps us think differently.

Name	**Richard Branson (54 years old)**
Job	Chairman of the Virgin Group, founder of Virgin Mobile Canada
Responsibilities	Championing and growing the Virgin brand
Previous incarnation	What hasn't he done? For more on Richard, have a look at his autobiography "Losing My Virginity".
Likes	Saying "Screw it, let's do it!"
Dislikes	Defeatism and bitterness
Richard in one word	Entrepreneurial

Name	**Andrew Black (42 years old)**
Job	President & CEO
Responsibilities	Leading a dynamic team whose passion is to offer Canadians a simpler, better mobile phone service.
Previous incarnation	Though he's a newbie to the telecom industry, Andrew brings over 20 years of global marketing experience to Virgin Mobile. Previously the President of Lego Systems and General Manager of Brand Development for Nike Inc., Andrew's vision, enthusiasm and hands on approach are evident across each area of the business.
Likes	Making gravy around the holidays with his kids
Dislikes	Heights
Andrew in one word	Passionate

Name	**Nathan Rosenberg (33 years old)**
Job	Main Marketing Man
Responsibilities	The service. (And driving everyone on the team nuts.)
Previous incarnation	A Virgin veteran, Nathan joined Virgin Mobile in Australia in 2000 as brand manager. With seven years of telecom industry experience in his back pocket, "Rosy" has delivered on his promise of a clear brand message that's stayed true to the Virgin values.
Likes	Packing snow & Thai food
Dislikes	Spiders
Nathan in one word	Energetic

.../2

Above: Backgrounder for the Launch of Virgin Mobile Canada (continued)

2/...

Name	**Heather Gomes (43 years old)**
Job	Chief Financial Officer
Responsibilities	The cash.
Previous incarnation	Joined the Bell group of companies back in 1991 where she previously held a senior financial position with Bell Canada. She has a wall full of fancy degrees, a remarkable sum of financial know-how but what's most amazing about Heather is her dazzling wit. (And if you've ever worked with accountants, you'll know what we mean.)
Likes	Wine & spreadsheets (which she enjoys separately)
Dislikes	Being the grown up
Heather in one word	Adventurous

Name	**Christina Sanders (41 years old)**
Job	VP of Human Resources
Responsibilities	The people at 720 King St.
Previous incarnation	Previously held a senior HR leadership role at St. Joseph Corporation, Christina managed all of their human resource activities that resulted from six major acquisitions involving $75 million in direct investment. At Virgin Mobile, she's brought on she's ridiculously nice to everyone.
Likes	Shopping
Dislikes	Filling out expense forms
Christina in one word	Natural

Name	**Valdis Martinsons (42 years old)**
Job	Chief Technical Guy
Responsibilities	The IT department.
Previous Incarnation	We poached Valdis from Research in Motion where he held the title of Chief Information Officer. Practical, unassuming and very tall, Valdis brings a wealth of IT know-how and facilities infrastructure to the team. He also has an unblockable hook shot nicknamed "The Solution".
Likes	The great outdoors
Dislikes	GTA Traffic
Valdis in one word	Dependable

Name	**Nancy Tichbon (30 years old)**
Job	Director, Customer Service
Responsibilities	Answering the phones.
Previous Incarnation	Another Virgin veteran, Nancy joined Virgin Mobile as a Customer service manager at Virgin Mobile in Australia in 2002. A real sparkplug, Nancy is a bornb leader whose initiative and energy continually inspire her team to deliver the kind of customer satisfaction that's bound to make people feel good all over.
Likes	People of all kinds
Dislikes	Busy signals
Nancy in one word	Unflappable

...̸/3

Above: Backgrounder for the Launch of Virgin Mobile Canada (continued)

3/...

Name	Kevin Derbyshire (41 years old)
Job	VP, General Counsel
Responsibilities	Protecting our assets with his legal superpowers.
Previous incarnation	Held the acting counsel role at Bell ExpressVu since 2003, Kevin now provides legal support, litigation management as well as commercial and corporate protection for Virgin Mobile. We wanted to say something funny and irreverent about him here, but he strongly advised against that.
Likes	Closing the deal
Dislikes	Preparing his own bio
Kevin in one word	Intense

Name	**Lori Hansford**
Job	VP, Sales & Distribution
Responsibilities	The business.
Previous incarnation	Lori has worked for a range of packaged good companies and is an accomplished senior executive with an incredible sales and marketing background. We grabbed Lori from the Campbell Soup Co., where she was VP of Sales. In her spare time, Lori climbs mountains – and real ones, too, not just the metaphoric kind.
Likes	Her Blackberry
Dislikes	Anyone who says "no deal"
Lori in one word	Determined

Above: Media Release for the Launch of Virgin Mobile Canada (continued)

Testimonials

Testimonials are inserts included in your Media Kit that function as examples of customer feedback—via letters, e-mails, or praise given to a company or organization. Testimonials can be a powerful tool when the media are looking for people to interview or quote in an article or segment. Include three or four testimonials (two to three lines each) on one sheet in your kit.

Story ideas

Story ideas are the 'hooks' or 'angles' you provide to the media to encourage them to create a longer piece or segment. Each story idea should be about three sentences—just long enough to give the media a flavour for what makes your story different, interesting, and important to their readers or viewers. Story ideas can be based on profiles, a financial angle, a problem, a trend, or an issue in your industry.

Calendar listing

A calendar listing is a summary of an upcoming event, typically supplied to magazines and newspapers that feature 'What's Happening' sections on a regular basis. These listings include the name of the organization, date and name of event, location, admission fee, telephone numbers, and e-mail addresses for more information. This information is time-critical, so be sure to check on the submission deadlines.

Public service announcement (PSA)

PSAs are a great way to publicize an upcoming event and recruit volunteers. Radio and television stations (Community Bulletin Boards), newspapers, and magazines provide free time and space to charitable and civic organizations, in the same spots as paid advertising, according to space or time availability. Be sure to call in order to determine deadlines; each publication or station will have its own PSA deadlines and policies. Stations may ask you for copy (information on your event) and then have you designate someone to be taped for the PSA. Look for a local celebrity who would do this for you, particularly if they are part of a kick-off to launch your event.

PSAs are also used for events that partner a for-profit corporation or organization with a non-profit, such as fundraisers, or for events that are free (such as seminars). When preparing PSAs, be sure to include:

- a contact name and telephone number;
- the correct name and title of the media contact responsible for PSAs;
- the who, what, what, when, where, why, and how of the event;
- the release date;
- short and punchy (50 words or less) text for print PSAs; and
- loosely edited audio/video with natural sound and spokesperson clips, and an indication of the length, for broadcast PSAs.

Public Service Announcement:

**Traffic in HRM and Bridge Closure during the
Blue Nose International Marathon on Saturday May 21 and Sunday May 22**

Halifax is hosting the second annual Blue Nose International Marathon from May 21 to 22, 2005. Over 6,000 runners will be running the race routes on the streets of Halifax and Dartmouth.

Traffic on Saturday
The Youth Run on Saturday, May 21 begins at the Town Clock at 10 a.m. and continues up Brunswick Street and then on to Sackville Street. Runners will then circle the Halifax Commons and continue back to the Town Clock. Traffic may be impacted along Brunswick Street.

Traffic on Sunday
Traffic along the marathon race route will be affected on Race Day, Sunday, May 22. At 8:45 a.m. on Sunday, runners will begin in downtown Halifax at the Town Clock, circle the Halifax Peninsula including the Point Pleasant Park, cross the MacDonald Bridge, tour the Dartmouth lakes area, return across the bridge and conclude back downtown at the Town Clock.

Bridge Closure
The MacDonald Bridge will also be closed from 8 a.m. to 2 p.m. while runners cross the bridge.

To ensure the safety of all athletes and volunteers, there will be controlled vehicular access along the marathon course from 8 a.m. to 4 p.m. in Halifax and 10 a.m. and 2 p.m. in Dartmouth. (Attached is the race route schedule.)

Residents of HRM along the race route are reminded to:
* Please drive carefully and slowly, and follow the instructions of police authorities along the route.
* Please drive in the opposite direction of runners.
* Please refrain from parking on the street from Saturday night to Sunday afternoon.
* Please allow for the possibility of extra travel time along the race course.

Free Parking
The Waterfront Development Corporation has announced that they will provide free parking to Blue Nose participants along the waterfront on race weekend. There will be free parking provided for vehicles along the waterfront on Saturday, May 21 and Sunday, May 22 from 8:00 am to 2:00 pm. The parking lots include: Block M (Waterfront Warehouse Restaurant), Marine Park (south of Salter Street), and the Cunard Block (at the foot of Morris Street).

For more information or to view the race route, visit www.BlueNoseMarathon.com.

For more information please contact:

Sarah Moses
Media Relations, Blue Nose International Marathon
(902)-425-1860 ext 258
smoses@mctl.ca

Above: PSA for the Blue Nose International Marathon

Blue Nose International Marathon Race Route

Anticipated times runners will be passing through HRM is as follows:

Race Stage	Time
START – Town Clock	**8: 45 - 9:15 a.m.**
MacDonald Bridge (Note: Bridge closed to traffic between 8 a.m. and 2 p.m.)	8:50 a.m. – 2:50 p.m.
Russell Street	9:15am - 11:30am
Brunswick Street (Town Clock)	**9:15 a.m. - 12 noon**
Hollis Street	9:20 - 10:10 a.m.
Young Avenue	9:30 - 10:40 a.m.
Oxford Street	9:50 - 11:10 a.m.
Gottingen Street	10:10 - 11:45 a.m.
Woodland Avenue	10:35 a.m. – 12:45 p.m.
Shubie Park	10:45 a.m. - 1:45 p.m.
Waverley Road	11 a.m. – 1:40 p.m.
Maple Street	11:15 a.m. - 2:20 p.m.
MARATHON FINISH	**11:30am – 3:00pm**

Above: PSA for the Blue Nose International Marathon (continued)

Awards and recognition

Include a list detailing any special honours received by or given by your organization or company. The media are often looking for 'good news' stories and audiences enjoy reading and hearing about awards and successes.

Statistics

The Media Kit will also include an insert that provides a summary of statistics or recent surveys related to an industry, a trend, or an issue. Media appreciate having this information on hand when they are compiling an article or segment because it adds credibility to a subject.

Published works

If your organization or company publishes an external newsletter (for clients, potential clients, suppliers, etc.), send a copy to your key media; it will provide them with additional ideas for stories or interviews. If you have written an article that was published in a trade magazine or newspaper, be sure to include it in your Media Kit.

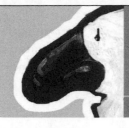

BLUE NOSE INTERNATIONAL MARATHON
1565 SOUTH PARK STREET
HALIFAX, NOVA SCOTIA B3J 2L2
T 902.496.1889   F 902.425.3180

information@bluenosemarathon.com   www.bluenosemarathon.com

Awards – Items & Categories

OPEN: FULL

Male

1st	Harry Neynens	2:58:06.3
2nd	Andrew Dacanay	3:05:49.1
3rd	Murray Lowery-Simpson	3:06:33.0

Female

1st	Holly Whitman	3:24:53.4
2nd	Tammy Hackett	3:37:02.4
3rd	Micheline Drisdelle	3:39:11.5

OPEN: HALF

Male

1st	Alex Coffin	1:21:11.0
2nd	Ray Moorehead	1:23:21.6
3rd	Terry Melloy	1:23:29.0

Female

1st	Denise Robson	1:26:18.3
2nd	Cindy King	1:28:25.1
3rd	Linda MacDonald	1:32:36.1

OPEN: 10 K

Male

1st	Sean Williams	0:37:08.3
2nd	Rami Bardeesy	0:37:27.0
3rd	Tyler Germani	0:39.22.2

Female

1st	Kaitlyn Watters	0:45:54.9
2nd	Virginia Bessette	0:45:55.5
3rd	Alexandra Bruce	0:47:44.9

OPEN: 5 K

Male

1st	Bruce Carr	0:24:52.1
2nd	Sandy Morrison	0:26:13.3
3rd	Louis-Etienne Marcoux	0:26:37.0

Female

1st	Mary Chan	0:24:37.1
2nd	Paula Stuart	0:30:28.5
3rd	Alicia Landry	0:31:43.4

Above: Awards and Recognition for the Blue Nose International Marathon

Matt story

A matt story is a completed article that is submitted directly to the media through a freelance writer or through a service. This type of story can highlight staff, a trend or issue, a promotion, or an event. The story idea is often pitched to community newspapers or trade magazines. Do not, however, pitch the same matt story idea to all editors, writers, or producers.

Product samples

Be sure to include a product sample with your media release or, when this is impossible, include an 8-inch x 10-inch photograph of the product.

Newsletter

Including a recent newsletter in a Media Kit often provides media with ideas that can be expanded into stories or features.

Other printed materials for your media campaign

Advertisements, postcards, Key Messages, publications, and web promos should also all be included in your Media Kit. Any type of documentation that will catch the media's interest, generate buzz, and provide information will increase the success of your campaign.

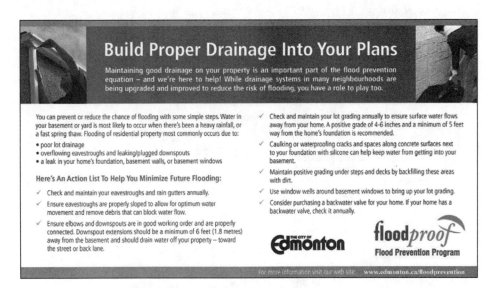

Above: Advertisement for the City of Edmonton Flood Prevention Strategy

Coming November 29th in the Province

Meet Fran Kary

Due to family circumstances, Fran Kary was in a residential care facility for 10 years. Now as a widow, the 84-year-old had the opportunity to move into an assisted living apartment a year and a half ago.

"I actually needed more independence," said Fran, "and I wanted a place of my own. Now, I can come into my own apartment, make myself a pot of tea, but I can join other seniors in the dining room for meals. I don't feel like anyone's telling me what to do. But if I can't manage, I just push the emergency button and help is there. It's the best of both worlds."

Watch for it!

Independently Healthy
A special publication on seniors' housing and care needs

Find out more about the benefits Fran enjoys through assisted living in the upcoming special seniors publication on Tuesday, November 29. There are more than half-a-million people in British Columbia over the age of 65 – that number will increase to about 1.4 million over the next 25 years. Today, more and more seniors and their families are discovering assisted living – housing that provides independence, but also some personal care services.

This special publication and resource guide explores creative partnerships such as the *Independent Living BC* program, and includes references and contacts you'll want to keep close by.

For more information, go to www.bchousing.org. To learn more about seniors' programs and services, call 1-800-465-4911.

Above: 1/4-page Advertisement for Independently Healthy—Changing Housing and Care Needs of Seniors

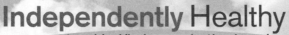

Independently Healthy
A special publication on seniors' housing and care needs

Coming November 30th in The Vancouver Sun

There are more than half-a-million people in British Columbia over the age of 65 – that number will increase to about 1.4 million over the next 25 years. Today, more and more seniors and their families are discovering assisted living – housing that provides independence, but also some personal care services.

This special supplement and resource guide explores creative partnerships such as the *Independent Living BC* program, and includes references and contacts you'll want to keep close by. **For more information, go to www.bchousing.org. To learn more about seniors' programs and services, call 1-800-465-4911.**

Above: Advertisement (Banner Ad) for Independently Healthy—Changing Housing and Care Needs of Seniors

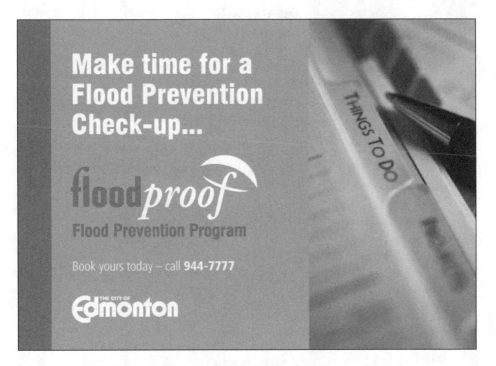

Above: Postcard for the City of Edmonton Flood Prevention Strategy

Independently Healthy

A special feature on B.C. seniors' changing housing and care needs

Seniors living longer, healthier

Seniors are living longer, healthier lives, according to a recent provincial report, A Profile of Seniors in British Columbia. Seniors in B.C. come from diverse backgrounds, many lead active lives, and 94 per cent live in the community in their own homes.

Population growing

Seniors age 65 and older make up 13.3 per cent of B.C.'s population, and will increase to 24 per cent, or about 1.4 million, by 2031. We also have the most rapidly aging seniors' population in Canada. Between 1991 and 2001, the number of seniors age 80 and over grew 54 per cent.

"This trend is expected to continue, with the most rapid growth among those 85 and older in the next five years," says David Baxter, Executive Director of the Urban Futures Institute.

continued on page 3

Inside: Check out our
*Seniors Resource to
Living Independently Healthy*

Above: Newspaper Supplement Cover for Independently Healthy—Changing Housing and Care Needs of Seniors

Independently Healthy

Now available on-line!

A special publication on seniors' housing and care needs

There are more than half-a-million people in British Columbia over the age of 65 – that number will increase to about 1.4 million over the next 25 years. Today, more and more seniors and their families are discovering assisted living – housing that provides independence, but also some personal care services. This special publication and resource guide explores creative partnerships such as the *Independent Living BC* program, and includes references and contacts you'll want to keep close by. **For more information, go to www.bchousing. org. To learn more about seniors' programs and services, call 1-800-465-4911.**

Above: Web Promotional Advertisement for Independently Healthy—BC Housing

ARGYLE ROWLAND
COMMUNICATIONS

PURINA WALK FOR DOG GUIDES KEY MESSAGES

1. The Purina Walk for Dog Guides is a major fundraiser for Lions Foundation of Canada Dog Guides

2. To locate a Walk near you or to donate, go to www.purinawalkfordogguides.com

3. Dog Guides assist people with visual, hearing, medical or physical disabilities

4. 100 per cent of the funds raised from the Purina Walk for Dog Guides goes to the training and placement of Dog Guides

5. Lions Foundation of Canada provides Dog Guides at no cost to people right across Canada

6. Each Dog Guide costs approximately $20,000 to raise and train, and has 6 - 9 months of one-on-one training

7. Thanks to Lions Clubs and volunteers, over 1,000 people between the ages of 8 and 84 have been provided a Dog Guide.

8. Since 1985 more than $20 million has been raised through the Purina Walk for Dog Guides for Dog Guide training programs

9. More than 110 communities across Canada hold a Purina Walk for Dog Guides

10. Optimal health and nutrition is very important for Dog Guides, just as it is with all pets. Thanks to Purina, all Lions Foundation Dog Guides are well fed as puppies and during training, meaning they can provide many years of assistance to their human partners.

Above: Key Message for the Purina Walk for Dog Guides

Virgin Mobile calling

A new kind of mobile service where the customer calls the shots.

★ **Why Virgin Mobile?**
'Cause we're different. No, really.

★ **Our great rates**
How do we stack up against the competition? Quite nicely, we think.

★ **Meet the sexy Virgin Mobile phone lineup**
Did someone say casting call?

★ **Accessories to go**
Safety first!

★ **The Virgin Mobile menu**
It's what's inside (the phone) that counts.

★ **Get in the zone at VXL**
All the fun stuff we stuff into our mobile phones.

★ **We're very available!**
Here's where customers can buy a Virgin Mobile phone.

Above: Key Messages for the Launch of Virgin Mobile Canada

Four Ways to Use a Media Kit

1. Use the Media Kit to pitch to media on a trend, issue, or problem they have been covering. Show how your company or organization ties in with their stories or segments.
2. Use the Media Kit to announce a major event, such as an opening, a product launch, an exhibition, or a convention.
3. Use the Media Kit to provide supplementary information for an interview that a reporter or writer has already requested. Always follow up three to four days after the Media Kit has been mailed. If possible, make sure all media and advertising contacts receive an updated Media Kit each quarter with new articles, media releases, and information.
4. Distribute the Media Kit to proclaim an official beginning (or successful completion) of any long-term public project, from a charity fund-raising campaign to a new recreation centre.

Getting On the Air

The most common formats in which to submit material to broadcast media are B-roll packages, video news releases, satellite media tours, radio news releases, and radio clips packages. In preparing for a B-roll or video news release, you must develop a news hook that will appeal to a wide viewing audience—give the story a human-interest angle. If possible, tie the story into a much bigger, related announcement by government or industry.

Video B-roll package

Video B-roll is a loosely edited package of visuals and interview clips sent via satellite to a targeted list of stations. It offers the most flexibility to the station, while providing a good story in broadcast quality. The television station can edit the footage into a news story using their own reporters in order to make the story fit their format and style. B-roll video must be in beta format and must consist of short clips of the most interesting footage. The entire video shouldn't be more than two minutes of short clips (clips of 30 seconds or less). There should be no emphasis on narration because most television producers use B-roll as a backdrop for their own story, rather than putting it in the forefront.

Video news release

A video news release is a 90-second broadcast-quality news report that provides visuals for a story. Like the B-roll, it's distributed via satellite to a targeted list of television stations as required. A satellite distribution can reach a local, regional, national or international market.

Radio news release

Used less often than audio clips, radio news releases remain a good vehicle for a story that requires the communication of a definite Key Message. In this case, the message must be heard, rather than read or seen. The sound for radio news releases must have broadcast quality. A broadcast news release script can be included in your Kit; a clear release helps the clarity of your message, so type and double-space your release.

Online Media Room

An Online Media Room is a specific area of your website that is filled with facts, reports, and newsworthy items that are important to your key media. Typically, you should provide an icon or link to this area of the website directly on the main page of the website. It is inexpensive to produce an Online Media Room and it provides the media with all of the related material in one easy-to-access location. The main disadvantage to an Online Media Room is that it must be up-to-date.

Essentials of an online media room

The following elements are essential if you wish to establish a successful, easy-to-use Online Media Room:

- accurate and current information;
- media releases—including current and archived releases—with a search tool that will provide easy access to a variety of topics;
- 24-hour contact information, including a specific contact person by name, title, phone numbers and e-mail address;
- corporate information, such as a company profile, backgrounder, executive biographies, and statistics;
- an FAQ page;
- a search page with a topic list to make it easy to access information on a certain topic;
- fact sheets;
- backgrounders on the organization or company;
- executive summaries;
- recent media coverage;
- information on upcoming events;
- testimonials and case studies;
- speeches;
- relevant financial information;

- links to other websites;
- downloadable, high-resolution photos; and
- forms for media to complete if they wish to obtain more information or to be part of future mailings.

To see what other companies and organizations have included in their Online Media Rooms, search the Internet for 'press rooms', 'online media rooms', or 'media rooms'.

Working with Outside Professionals

While media relations practitioners are often multi-talented individuals, they may not have the time or the skills to create a successful Media Kit on their own. In many instances, outside professionals are required for writing, design, and photography purposes.

How to choose a freelance writer

Contact writers' clubs and associations, such as the Professional Writers' Association of Canada, media clubs and local press clubs. Ask associates or editorial staff of publications in your field to recommend writers with whom they have worked. Look for someone flexible enough to do rewrites if you do not feel the copy reflects your company or organization. It's also important that you look at samples of a writer's work and client list to ensure that the freelance writer is well-suited to your media campaign. Contact past and current clients to get their perspective on the writer and his or her work. If you are adding a freelance writer to your campaign, you should spend as much money as you can in order to obtain the best professionals for the writing of your printed materials.

How to work with a graphic designer

Show the graphic designer all of your current material to give him or her a feeling for what you want. Specify your needs with a printed outline. The graphic designer will then either create from scratch or transform your originals into a design that you describe. You should find out what computer software/programs the designer will be using for your work because you may want to exchange files electronically; avoiding file conversion problems will eliminate many problems that could disrupt your campaign. If you cannot use the same program as your graphic designer, ask him or her to send you any text information electronically in a common word processing format (such as Word).

Setting a reasonable schedule will also be important. Designers require time to create your work. Do not expect a same-day or overnight turnaround. Furthermore, fees for a freelance graphic designer will range from entry-level to professional; most designers charge on a per-project basis.

How to choose a photographer

When choosing a photographer for your media campaign, it is crucial that you select a professional photographer who has experience with public relations photography. Ask clients and colleagues to recommend a photographer with whom they have worked before. Inquire about the services the photographer provides, such as commercial photography, annual reports, videos, publicity, special events, slide presentations, etc. Find out the photographer's rates, including hourly, half-day, daily, in-studio, and on location. Finally, check out the portfolio, training, and client references and testimonials of each photographer you interview.

How to work with the photographer at your events

Things will unfold with fewer obstacles if you write a script of what will happen over the course of your event. Include the agenda, times, and prominent people. You must decide on the objectives of photographs for your event. What image are you trying to convey of the event and organization? What do you want the photos to 'say'? It is your job to 'sell' the photo to the editor, and it is also your job to make sure the photographer knows what you need the photos to say. Discuss the kinds of photos you prefer and whether there will be room for horizontal or vertical cropping. The composition should include a clear, sharp image. Have people in action in photos, and include no more than three people at a time.

Analyze any special needs you will have for backdrops, lighting, or settings for photography at your event; it will be helpful to include your photographer in this analysis as they might see possibilities and problems that you would otherwise overlook.

After the event, order a contact sheet from your photographer. If a publication is interested, send the contact sheet to the editor. When media send their own photographer, arrange to meet in the on-site media room and ask the photographer if he or she has any special needs in terms of background, lighting, and types of shots. Arrange convenient times for photo sessions, which may include key speakers, interesting events, or other activities. Don't ask for copies of photos unless you know a newspaper has a policy that allows you to purchase them.

If You Don't Know Any Photographers. . .

Through joint ventures with Canada NewsWire (E-Pix) and Canadian Corporate News-ITG (E-See), CP Photo Assignment Services can transmit your commercial photos directly to photo editors at most Canadian daily newspapers. This service provides one-stop shopping for access to a network of more than 500 highly skilled news, studio, and specialty photographers across Canada and around the world, allowing you to have pictures shot—using traditional or digital cameras—processed, scanned, and transmitted or e-mailed to any location worldwide.

Understanding Publicity Photographs

The goals of publicity photography include:

- generating outside publicity for the organization;
- acknowledging those who have helped the organization;
- keeping people informed of on-going activities within the organization through its newsletter, annual reports, etc.;
- acknowledging the contributions of sponsors and supporters; and
- boosting morale and improving productivity of employees,

Publicity photography is often required by an organization or company to record, celebrate, and promote events. Typical events for which a photographer may be required include Annual General Meetings, awards presentations, sales and training seminars, and special parties and banquets.

Six Reasons to Include Publicity Photographs in Your Media Campaign

1. It can graphically describe and show what words cannot.
2. It cannot be edited, other than cropping for size.
3. The reader will rarely miss it, and your news story can be 'read' at a glance.
4. It can be used as a publicity plug for your event or organization, when the editor does not have room for the release but is short of eye-catching material for a page.
5. An eye-catching photo sent to an editor with a media release can convince an editor to set your story apart from others on the page, thus giving you more visibility.
6. A photo heightens the impact of a story and readers will remember your event longer.

Rules for Using Photography in Your Media Kit

When you are preparing photos for distribution to the media, it is important to remember a few simple rules.

- Research your target print media and examine how and when they use photographs. What are their needs for style and format, such as vertical versus horizontal format?

- Call publications and ask if they use photos received with media releases or submitted on their own.
- Get signed releases from participants in shots.
- Select a light background. It will reproduce better on newsprint. Check that the reproduction is as sharp as the original.
- The media will want black and white glossy photographs for publication, colour transparencies, or colour slides.
- Label and caption all photos. Label the back of photos for easy identification. Include full names and titles of everyone shown (spell out the names in full), clearly identifying from left to right in photo. Include the name of the organization, its address, your name and telephone number, all single-spaced. The caption, also called a 'cut line' is a sentence or a paragraph describing the action in the photograph. For example, 'ABC Inc. senior vice-president Joan Smith and president Paul Evans, in front of the new sculpture at the entrance to corporate headquarters. The carving by well-known artist Phillip Stark symbolizes the vigour and enthusiasm with which the company serves its customers.'
- When mailing photographs, protect them with cardboard. Do not attach anything to the photograph with paper clips or staples.

Above: Photograph from the Blue Nose
International Marathon

Above: Photograph from the Purina Walk for Dog Guides

Above: Photograph from the Purina Walk for Dog Guides

CNW Group's Breakfast with the Media

Media/Photography Panel (20 June 2006, Vancouver)
Whether you're holding a press conference, launching a product or making an announcement, photos are a great way to add visual and emotional impact to your story. CNW Group brings together editors and professional photographers to discuss what makes a photo worthy of pickup in the daily newspapers. Visit the following website to listen to the event: http://www.newswire.ca/en/extras/custom/bmail_037_vancouver/.

How to Make a Visual Impact in the News (15 June 2006, Calgary)
Find out what the media are truly looking for and learn what you can do to help your organization get the images you really need. Whether you're holding a press conference, launching a product or making a corporate announcement, visuals are a great way to add impact to your story and pique media interest. CNW Group brings together business reporters, photo editors, and professional photographers to discuss what makes photos and video footage worthy of pickup. Visit the following website to listen to the event: http://www.newswire.ca/en/extras/custom/bmail_036_Calgary/.

Exercises

1. Is the media release, as we know it, dead?
2. Describe the current image of your organization. How is it conveyed through your Media Kit and inserts? Describe your ideal image.
3. Develop a Media Kit for your organization or company. Describe its contents.
4. Based on your Media Kit, develop an Online Media Room for your company or organization. Describe the contents of your Online Media Room—both the permanent information and the changing information.
5. Select a special event (past, present, or future) and create a headline and first paragraph for a media release for the event.

Chapter 8

Contacting the Media

You've identified your audiences, developed your Key Messages, created your media list, and prepared a dynamic Media Kit. Now it's time to put your plan into action by contacting reporters, editors, producers, and other media representatives, and building personal relationships with them.

Chapter Summary

By the end of Chapter 8, you will be able to:

- call the media, pitch a story idea, and follow up efficiently and effectively;
- win the game of telephone tag;
- arrange an Information Session;
- meet with Editorial Boards;
- contact the media about special events;
- send media releases or media alerts;
- know when to contact the media;
- organize a media drop; and
- manage media call-backs, contact sheets, and after-event inquiries.

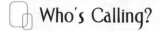

Who's Calling?

Designate one person to contact the media. This could be someone within your company or organization, a public relations consultant, or a public affairs specialist. The media prefer to deal with one person when they cover an event, need a quote, or want to arrange an interview.

Be prepared

Before contacting key media, get to know their products. Read their magazines and newspapers, watch their television shows, listen to their radio shows, and visit their websites and blogs. Study their columns, segments, and supplements. Look at the topics they have covered recently that relate to your industry, company, or organization. Your ultimate goal is to develop personal contacts with the trade, consumer, and Internet media who specialize in your industry or subject area. Once you have established this relationship, it will be easier to call and pitch story ideas or clarify information.

Making the First Contact

Before you telephone an editor or producer, think about how you can make your story or broadcast segment personally meaningful to the target audience. Tie your topic in with an issue, the news of the day, a current trend, or a new product.

When you make the initial phone call to a media outlet, the first question you should ask a reporter or producer is: 'Are you on deadline? Is this a convenient time to talk to you?' If your contact is too busy, find out when you can call back. Otherwise, proceed with the conversation, making it clear that you recognize the value of their time and that you will be brief.

In the first minute of your conversation, you should try to confirm that the person you are talking to is the decision-maker for editorial coverage. If so, let the person know that you would like to be a resource to them for quotes or for information. At this point, it is unnecessary (and unwise) to 'sell' your company. Keep your approach focused on 'how I can help you', rather than 'how you can help me'.

When you pitch a story idea

Briefly state your story idea, including what you can talk about in an interview or segment. You will have about 30 seconds to make an impression. Describe why you feel the idea is important to the audience, what makes it different, and any interesting visual aspects of the interview (for television) or reliable outside sources (for print).

Your job is to create interest on the first call. Make sure you get the name and title of the person you have spoken to and follow-up with an e-mail or fax within 24 hours of the first conversation. Expand on one or two 'hooks' that you believe would make an interesting article or segment for the target audience. Recommend that the editor or producer visit your website.

Always Follow Up

Follow up your first telephone call to the media by providing your contact with a tangible reminder of your conversation, such as an e-mail with your Media Kit and a suggested story idea. Even if the media do not respond right away, keep in touch on a regular basis to see if you can provide any assistance.

Getting through

Try to find out, during this first conversation, what kinds of stories or segments they have planned. If the producer or journalist is interested, he or she will usually respond by asking you to send printed materials.

Winning the Game of Telephone Tag

Leaving messages

In general, most media outlets are understaffed, overworked, and inundated with telephone messages from people looking for coverage. They often do not return a telephone call from someone they do not know or have not dealt with before. It is better to call back, at different times of the day, than to leave 10 messages. Try to call first thing in the morning or last thing in the day. Don't keep calling if you have already left several messages: the producer or editor has probably received them and is not interested in your idea or story.

Returning messages

If a reporter, editor, or producer leaves you a message, return the call promptly. Media are often under tight deadlines and will need to speak to you immediately. It could be that the writer or producer needs to verify information; to get additional details about you for a story or segment; to receive a product sample, quote, or photograph; or to set up an interview with the spokesperson, employees, or customers.

Arranging an information session

If possible, try to arrange an Information Session with key media. This is a short meeting (10- or 15-minutes) to introduce yourself, your organization or company, and your events. It is intended to provide information that may be useful to the media, and to learn more about how you can be of assistance. Community and trade media are often receptive to this type of meeting.

During the meeting, do not ask the editor, reporter, or producer to do anything that is clearly self-serving, such as writing a profile of your company or a story about one of its new products. Instead, use the meeting to gather information and, at the same time, demonstrate your interest in the media outlet's needs. Find out, for example, whether the media outlet:

- encourages unsolicited articles;
- wants photos submitted with a story (or do they take their own?); or
- prioritizes specialized editorial coverage, or themes, at certain times of the year. (If so, try to obtain an Editorial Calendar outlining future themes, dates, and deadlines.)

Meeting with editorial boards

Most daily newspapers have editorial meetings each morning to discuss the day's events and coverage. If you can, try to develop your relationship with the media so that you are invited to attend these meetings. Your chances of being invited will be much greater if you and your organization can bring some special insight to a current issue, or can provide specialized financial or technical information. Since editorial meetings generally include representatives from all of the newspaper's departments, they are a great way to both provide information and pitch a story to a number of different departments (such as business, lifestyle, financial, local news, etc.).

Calling the media about a special event

If you are calling the media to encourage them to cover an upcoming event on the evening news, be sure to contact them earlier in the day. For more important or elaborate events, contact TV planning and assignment editors two to three days in advance, with an explanation of the event and what is going to happen.

Touch base with key media with a telephone call the day of the event. E-mail or fax a media alert one or two days before the event as a reminder.

Sending a Media Release or Media Alert about a Special Event

There are many ways to send a media release to the media. The trick is to find out how your key media want to receive their information; each representative may prefer a different method.

E-mail

You can use e-mail to send an Alerts Bulletin with a headline that directs the media to the full media release posted on your website, you can e-mail the entire media release as an attachment, or you can email the media release as the text of your e-mail.

Although e-mail is easy and convenient, resist the temptation to rely on it as your only method for sending media releases. E-mailed information may get overlooked because of the sheer volume of e-mails received every day by the media. Many reporters and editors view e-mail as both a blessing and a curse—while it is very useful for background information and alerts, it also clogs inboxes with too much irrelevant information. Find out from each contact on your list whether they want to receive media releases by e-mail. In order to minimize the threat of computer viruses, some media outlets make it a policy not to open unsolicited e-mail attachments. Finally, keep in mind that e-mails are easily lost or destroyed—particularly if a mail server crashes. It's best to also plan another method for really critical releases.

Fax

You can fax a copy of your media release to the main newsroom or directly to an individual. While this method is generally reliable, remember that many newsrooms receive hundreds of faxes every day, and media releases can get lost or mixed up with the junk faxes that end up in the garbage. Also, when one central fax machine serves a number of different departments within a large media organization, it can sometimes take hours before a fax is distributed to the intended recipient.

Mail

While much slower than other distribution methods, conventional mail is still an acceptable way to get your media release to the print media, if it is not particularly time-sensitive.

Wire service

Many news staff prefer to receive media releases electronically on screen into the editorial newsroom via the newswire. When you send your media release by CNW Group, it is also posted on the Daybook Summary, which posts twice daily, at about 7 am and 7 pm EST. The 'daybook' is a daily log of events that will be covered in the news that day. It alerts media to news conferences, trade shows, awards presentations, photo opportunities, and other events planned by organizations. Assignment editors and producers often use the daybook to send a writer, photographer, or camera crew to cover events.

Sample Daybook Summary

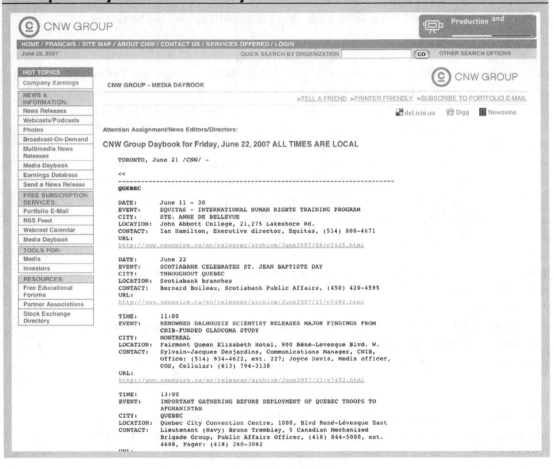

Following up on a Media Release or Media Alert

Call the contacts on your media list one week after the release is sent, just to confirm they have received it and, if the opportunity presents itself, to discuss possible coverage. If they did not receive the release (or if they lost it), e-mail or fax another one immediately and phone back.

Keep in mind, however, that some media representatives will not appreciate a follow up phone call. In their view, such calls are unnecessary. For best results, try to add a new piece of information to your telephone call, such as the name of the speaker or entertainer who has been confirmed for the event.

Talking Up a Big Event

When your media relations campaign focuses on a special event, you will typically contact the media a number of times well in advance of that event. A sample critical path for such a campaign is shown below.

A Sample Critical Path

Before the Event

5 months before	Initial meeting re: campaign
4 to 5 months before	Create proposal for campaign
4 months before	Conduct media audit
4 months before	Explore media sponsorship, PSAs and tie-ins
3 to 4 months before	Create Media Kit inserts
3 to 4 months before	First release and Media Kit to magazines
3 weeks before	First release to other media
	Media Kit to selected media
2 to 4 weeks before	PSAs to media
	Follow up with media
2 weeks before	Second release to media
1 week before	Media drop
1–2 days before	Media Alert

On the Event Day

Event day	Call Assignment Desks to remind media. Organize an on-site media room or media sign-in table

After the Event

1 or 2 days after	Fourth release to media
1 or 2 weeks after	Photo contact sheets and thank you notes to media
2 weeks after	Create media report
	Gather media coverage
1 month after	Final meeting and evaluation
	Submit final media report

Of course, the actual details of your critical path will differ according to the type of media coverage you are seeking. Just keep in mind that consumer magazines have three-month deadlines for editorial copy. If you miss the deadline, your event cannot be included.

If you have the time, staff, and expertise to send a series of media releases for your special event, here is one way to organize the series:

- *First release.* Provide an overview of the company or organization and the event. This includes the nature of the event, its purpose, features, who will be there, who can attend, the cost, the date, and the time. Always include a name, telephone number, and e-mail address of a contact person for the media.
- *Second release.* Focus on one interesting aspect of the event, such as seminars, entertainment, theme, etc.
- *Media Alert.* Provide final detailed information on the event, such as times and locations of activities. E-mail or fax to key media one or two days before the event.
- *Fourth release.* Summary of event's success, sent within days of event, which includes funds raised, speeches given, quote from attendee, and any news arising from the event.

Want an Academic Opinion? Look in the Blue Book

The Blue Book is an A to Z Guide of academic experts at the University of Toronto. The book, first shared with Canadian newsrooms in the 1980s, is a resource guide for journalists seeking expert opinion from faculty at U of T's three campuses. Its popularity with news organizations grew quickly and it is considered to be the standard bearer for media guides produced by Canadian universities. The guide, a staple in newsrooms across the country, went online in 1998 at www.bluebook.utoronto.ca allowing journalists to search via key word or name from their desktop or from any Internet connection while on assignment in other parts of the world. The last print version was published in 2004.

Telling the media about non-profit events
If you are promoting a charitable or non-profit event, e-mail or fax a public service announcement (PSA) to community newspapers, local and cable television stations, and local radio stations prior to your event. Call each media outlet to find out their deadlines for PSAs, as well as the name and title of the person who handles them.

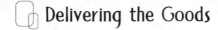 Delivering the Goods

In an environment where hundreds of people are competing for the media's attention, the media drop is an excellent way to stand out and cut through the clutter. Essentially, this term refers to the personal delivery (or courier delivery) of a Media Kit and products or samples to your key media 7–10 days before an event or product launch.

Phone the editor or producer two weeks before the event to let them know you will be doing the media drop and find out if you should ask for someone specific. Package the products and Kit in a colourful bag addressed to the right person, being sure to include his or her title. Make sure you follow up several days after the drop to ensure your contacts received the packages and to find out if they will be able to cover your event.

Sample Media Drop Route for Toronto Special Event

7:45 to 11:30 am

1. **CKFM**
   2 St. Clair West, 2nd floor
   Contact: Ace Maclean, Producer

2. **CFRB**
   2 St. Clair West, 2nd floor
   Contact: Ted Woloshyn

3. **CHUM AM** and **CHUM FM**
   1331 Yonge Street
   Contact: Roger, Rick and Marilyn Show

4. **CHFI-FM**
   777 Jarvis Street
   Contact: Erin Davis, Morning Host

5. **680 News**
   777 Jarvis Street
   Contact: Scott Metcalfe, News

6. **Eye Weekly**
   625 Church Street, 6th floor
   Contact: Christina, Advertising and Promotions Coordinator

continued

7. NOW Magazine
   189 Church Street
   Contact: Ellie Kirzner, Senior News Editor

8. **Toronto Sun**
   333 King Street East
   Contact: Assignment Desk

9. **24 Hours**
   333 King Street East
   Contact: Jennifer Bell, Senior Editor

10. **Toronto Star**
    1 Yonge Street
    Contact: Assignment Desk, Toronto Star

11. **Metro Morning,** CBC
    Front Street West
    Contact: Andy Barrie

12. **The Globe and Mail**
    444 Front Street West
    Contact: Assignment Desk

13. CITY-TV
    299 Queen Street West
    Contact: Peter Dworschak, Assignment, CablePulse 24

14. CTV
    9 Channel Nine Court, Scarborough
    Contact: Assignment Desk

If You Post It, They Will Come

In recent years, the print and broadcast media have become increasingly dependent on the Internet to search for and develop good stories. Consequently, a good company or organization website can be very useful in bringing the media to your door. And for reporters, editors, and producers, that means a website with useful, newsworthy content.

Take a critical look at your company's website from an editorial media point of view. The website may be visually attractive, with plenty of slick graphics, but does it include information that will be of interest to your target media?

Going the Distance

While national media are useful for reaching a cross-country audience, you can often get more effective coverage by contacting local media directly in markets across the nation. This type of approach is often used to launch a new product nationally, such as a book or a consumer product.

In general, it is better to connect with a local media relations' representative in each city you are contacting or visiting, since they often have established relationships with the local media.

Conducting a satellite media tour

The satellite media tour can be valuable when the objective is to gain coverage across the country. An organization or company spokesperson appears on camera from the studio to talk about a product, service, or idea, and is broadcast live via satellite to individual television reporters across the country for a series of exclusive, locally tailored, one-on-one interviews.

A satellite media tour allows users to travel to as many as six cities in one hour. It's cheaper than airfare, the spokesperson stays fresh—and so does the news. At the same time, the news reporter obtains a unique interview opportunity. It is convenient for the production of news coverage. The news director does not have to assign camera crews, a producer, or editing facilities.

Satellite news conferences are also an effective virtual PR tool. Here, a company announcement is broadcast live into television newsrooms as required. The option for receiving stations to participate in a question and answer period is possible.

Satellite technology can also be useful in sending time-critical audio clips to radio stations across the country. It is now common practice to take audio clips from a news conference and feed them to radio stations across the country. Within a very short time frame, companies such as CNW Group can record and edit audio clips, and feed them via satellite to all Canadian radio stations.

The return on investment of broadcast projects has proved invaluable for visual stories and campaigns. It's an element that can have the greatest impact on media coverage.

When the Media Call Back

Ultimately, all of your efforts to contact the media are intended to get the attention of editors and producers. You try to provide them with information that is sufficiently newsworthy, so that they will want to call you back. Being prepared for that call is clearly important. Be sure you brief the people who answer your telephone on the importance of calls from the media. They should be trained to find out precisely what the caller needs, make an accurate record of the call, and contact you immediately so that you can return the call. A sample 'media contact sheet' is illustrated below. Make sure that it is used to track every conversation with the media.

MEDIA CONTACT SHEET

Date/Time of call: _____

Name/Title of caller:_____

Media affiliation: _____

Address:_____

Telephone: _____   E-mail: _____

Information requested: _____

_____

Deadline: _____

Action required (specify): _____

_____

_____

Follow-up required (specify name of person responsible): _____

_____

_____

Recorded by: _____

Media Support for Special Events

CASE STUDY

Fashion Cares 2005, M.A.C. *VIVA GLAM* Bollywood Hollywood

A public relations team of 15 people from within Weber Shandwick and its members' network of public relations colleagues was onsite to manage the various areas and media requests throughout the evening. A team of this size was essential for an event held in an area the size of four football fields. Key responsibilities included:

- Media sign-in for the 200 accredited media—management of the media desk and organization and distribution of media passes and tickets at the event
- Coordination and management of a news conference and photo opportunity with event talent and host, Pamela Anderson
- Onsite media relations support—identifying story angles and opportunities, facilitating interviews with spokespeople, and granting backstage access where appropriate to help media put their story together and obtain visuals
- Identifying opportunities for media to profile event sponsors or sponsored elements—including providing 'social scene' media with a public relations committee runner to identify event sponsors to photograph and include in media coverage
- Management of photographers and videographers on the event risers and runway
- Facilitation of experiential packages with all eBay winners
- The team was managed from a central media desk, communicating via headset with team members.

 Executing The Plan

Fashion Cares 2005, M.A.C. *VIVA GLAM* Bollywood Hollywood
Launch Party & Pre-event Support:

- A Fashion Cares 'Launch Party', announcing the *Bollywood Cowboy* theme, unveiling the advertising creative and featuring entertainment and décor reflective of the theme, was held six weeks prior to the event. Invitations and a media kit including information on all aspects of the event were distributed to a comprehensive list of media. To complement the materials, the kit included Fashion Cares images for media use, which were also uploaded to an FTP site to provide media with easy access to high-resolution images.
- To sustain media interest in the weeks after the launch party, two updates were sent to media—one announcing a confirmed entertainment line-up, and another announcing the event host, Pamela Anderson.
- Media training was provided to all spokespeople to ensure effective delivery of program messages.
- Regular media coverage updates, with examples, were provided to share with key sponsors.

eBay.ca Partnership & Auctions:

- To sustain media interest and coverage, the public relations committee coordinated a partnership with eBay Canada. An 'About Me' page, featuring Fashion Cares 2005 M·A·C *VIVA GLAM Bollywood Cowboy* was created (www.ebay.ca/fashioncares)

including information and its beneficiary, ACT. It also used the event advertising creative to ensure consistent messaging and was linked to the main www.fashioncares.com site.

- Experiential packages, designed to generate pre-event buzz while communicating some of the key and unique event elements, were coordinated and auctioned on eBay.ca, including:
  - Front row tickets to the show
  - Early access to the Fashion Cares Boutique
  - An opportunity to go backstage and see the show preparation
  - A backstage first-person meeting with Pamela Anderson, autograph and commemorative photograph
- In partnership with event sponsor, M·A·C Cosmetics, celebrity-signed Levi's (another event sponsor) jean jackets from personalities including Tommy Lee, Cher, Lisa Marie Presley, Pamela Anderson, and rapper 50 Cent, among others, were sent to a host of Canadian designers, who created designs inspired by the celebrity and the cause.
- These auctions were staggered to ensure ongoing news hooks and supported with media relations.

Onsite Event Support:

- A public relations team of 15 people from within Weber Shandwick and its members' network of public relations colleagues was onsite to manage the various areas and media requests throughout the evening. A team of this size was essential for an event held in an area the size of four football fields. Key responsibilities included:
  - Media sign-in for the 200 accredited media—management of the media desk and organization and distribution of media passes and tickets at the event
  - Coordination and management of a news conference and photo opportunity with event talent and host, Pamela Anderson
  - Onsite media relations support—identifying story angles and opportunities, facilitating interviews with spokespeople, and granting backstage access where appropriate to help media put their story together and obtain visuals
  - Identifying opportunities for media to profile event sponsors or sponsored elements—including providing 'social scene' media with a public relations committee runner to identify event sponsors to photograph and include in media coverage
  - Management of photographers and videographers on the event risers and runway
  - Facilitation of experiential packages with all eBay winners
- The team was managed from a central media desk, communicating via headset with team members.

CASE STUDY

The Purina Walk for Dog Guides

Spokesperson Media Tour:

- A long-standing Dog Guide handler—a visually impaired woman accompanied by her Canine Vision Canada dog guide—was selected as the national media spokesperson.
- Several weeks in advance of the first Purina Walk for Dog Guides, Argyle contacted local and national media in the Greater Toronto Area to secure interviews with the spokesperson and promote the upcoming events in communities across Canada.
- We made use of the Lions Foundation's celebrity spokesperson, actress Sonja Smits, to help boost interest with national outlets.

Launch Event:

- Argyle designed, produced and staffed a portable event space, dubbed the 'Purina Neighbourhood', to help launch the Purina Walk for Dog Guides at High Park in Toronto. It was a fun, interactive space featuring a branded tent, product displays, and a series of four games and activities for people and their pets, all surrounded by branded white picket fencing.
- The Neighbourhood was set up adjacent to the registration area, so that participants would visit us before and after the walk.
- As an additional tool to encourage registrants to complete all four activities, participants who collected four stamps—one from each activity station—were eligible for a draw to win a year's supply of pet food.

Local Market Media Relations:

- Argyle managed a grassroots media outreach program for all 110 walks across Canada. Media materials, including a news release and fact sheet, were *customized* for each market and distributed in the weeks before the local event.
- We conducted one-on-one follow-up with each outlet in an effort to secure advance coverage for the events in calendar listings and feature articles, and to confirm media attendance at the event itself. We contacted more than 450 media outlets across the country, and conducted telephone briefings to help local organizers make the most of these interviews. This significantly increased the profile of the walk in smaller markets.

CASE STUDY

The Launch of Virgin Mobile Canada

The project was executed across Canada leveraging Hill & Knowlton's Toronto, Montreal and Vancouver offices. Pre-event and day-of PR activities included the implementation of the following tactics in Toronto and Montreal:

- Coordinating Sir Richard Branson's participation in outrageous, branded public 'stunts' to launch Virgin Mobile
- Managing media briefings in Toronto and Montreal, which a record number of journalists attended, and ensuring focus remained on Canadian offer via tag-team interview panel of Andrew Black, President and CEO of Virgin Mobile Canada, Nathan Rosenberg, Chief Marketing Officer of Virgin Mobile Canada, and Richard Branson
- Augmenting stunt coverage by arranging a series of high-profile one-on-one interviews for Richard Branson, with key print, broadcast and online media, which helped reach the target consumer with details on how Virgin Mobile differs from its competition
- Managing media at evening VIP launch parties to help build the Virgin Mobile brand character and reach social/party media
- Engaging in aggressive media follow-up to secure ongoing interview opportunities in the days following the launch with business, marketing, news, technology, lifestyle, youth, entertainment, and consumer media
- The Virgin Mobile Canada team also visited Vancouver, where media relations outreach was conducted
- Controlling release of launch event details to minimize competitor response
- Developing a comprehensive and creative media kit introducing Canadian media to Virgin Mobile's services, brand and the 'No Catch' messaging. A video news release with B-roll footage was also made available to television media

CASE STUDY

Purolator Tackle Hunger 2006

The 2006 Purolator Tackle Hunger campaign ran from June to November in each of the eight CFL cities. Most of the media relations activities took place during the days leading up to each game day food drive. During these days, Purolator brought the Grey Cup to its customers so they could also make donations to the local food bank in exchange for a picture with the Grey Cup. With multiple customer visits scheduled within tight timeframes, media appearances with the Grey Cup were carefully timed so they would not disrupt the customer visit schedule, identified as a key priority by Purolator.

Tactics:

- Engaged each regional food bank two weeks in advance to discuss each upcoming food drive, secure their participation, obtain local hunger statistics and key messages that could be used in media materials, and confirm the availability of a food bank spokesperson for joint media interviews.
- Contacted the sponsorship managers of each regional CFL team to discuss the upcoming food drive, confirm involvement of players' wives/significant others in the food collection, and propose joint photo opportunities.
- Signed deals with the QB's from each team to be the regional spokesperson for the Purolator Tackle Hunger program. The QB participated in all media events leading up to the food drive in each city.
- Wrote and distributed media advisories and fact sheets via email to alert local sports writers, city/community news editors, and broadcast media about the upcoming food drives and collection times in all CFL hometowns.
- Conducted aggressive phone follow up with reporters, television producers, and radio hosts to ensure media coverage.
- Pitched and arranged live TV and radio talk show appearances with Purolator regional managers and food bank executive directors. The Grey Cup was also brought to the stations in each region to provide a visual element of interest for both hosts and viewers.
- Organized joint media events with local food bank representatives, Purolator regional managers, and home football teams. Print and broadcast media were invited to interview relevant spokespeople about the food drive and photograph CFL coaches, players, and wives against the backdrop of the Purolator Tackle Hunger delivery truck with food props donated by the food bank.
- Organized Grey Cup photo opportunities with Purolator spokespeople and local food bank staff. Print media were invited to food bank headquarters to interview relevant spokespeople and photograph food bank staff and volunteers getting their pictures taken with the Grey Cup.
- Organized a photo opportunity with Purolator regional managers and a minor football team in BC (South Delta Rams). Community papers were invited to photograph young football players taking a break from practice by gathering around the Grey Cup against the backdrop of the Purolator Tackle Hunger delivery truck.
- Wrote and distributed letters to regional newspaper editors on behalf of Purolator regional managers to share the results of the local food drives and praise the communities for their efforts.
- Wrote and distributed via email news releases announcing the total 2006 collection figures for the program with references to results achieved in each region.

Exercises

1. Select a media representative you could contact to arrange an Information Session. Why would this person be interested in your company or organization and its programs and services? Make a list of questions you would ask during an Information Session.
2. Describe three media-friendly events or promotions you could organize or get involved in over the next year.
3. Develop a Critical Path for the editorial and advertising campaign for these events, including dates and media.

Chapter 9

Managing Media Interviews

We've all heard stories about people giving a media interview and then, as soon as it's printed or broadcast, complaining that their words have been taken out of context, given a sensational slant, or just simply reported inaccurately. Such situations can be avoided by taking a few simple steps to prepare for the interview.

Chapter Summary

By the end of Chapter 9, you will be able to:

• understand what the media want from an interview,
• choose a spokesperson,
• know what questions to ask before granting an interview,
• know when to decline an interview,
• know what information to supply to the media in advance of the interview,
• rehearse interview questions and answers,
• develop effective speech techniques,
• dress for the camera,
• handle a problem interview, and
• know what to do after the interview.

Answering the Media Request

An important part of managing successful interviews is to understand the process from the media's point of view. In most cases, the caller has no hidden agenda; he or she just wants the story, honestly presented, and in the shortest time possible. Being prepared, with a succinct story and with facts readily at hand, makes an interviewer's job easier. And that translates into a higher probability of positive media exposure for your company or organization. If you are not the right person for the interview, provide the media with information on another expert, if possible.

Choosing a Spokesperson

A spokesperson must be able to speak effectively to the news media during interviews and news conferences. An organization may hire a public relations practitioner as a spokesperson or may wish to train some of its own employees to deal with the media. A competent spokesperson makes all the difference in the media coverage an organization or company will receive. The media like having a reliable resource they can contact and count on.

What qualities does a successful spokesperson possess? Besides having the confidence of top management and a willingness to take on the demanding role, a good spokesperson is also:

- committed to their role as a long-term strategy (wants to do it);
- an expert in his or her field (understands the issues, problems, and trends);
- available for speaking engagements and media interviews;
- experienced or has a communications background (public speaking or broadcasting);
- well-spoken and well-written (conveys meaningful thoughts and idea to others);
- a story-teller (can draw analogies that an audience can understand);
- able to communicate complex thoughts and ideas simply and clearly;
- able to provide openness and transparency;
- respected by the Executive Team and is able to direct in a crisis;
- strongly in command of the language in which they are communicating;
- not afraid to talk favourably about the competition;
- looking for PR opportunities;

- on hand for good news stories and events;
- well-versed and able to understand the different types of media: print, electronic, and the Internet;
- able to develop relationships with specific media representatives that will enhance trust;
- aware of what is being said about him or her and the organization or company;
- certain about what they would *like* the media to say about their organization or company;
- able to create Key Messages geared to needs of media;
- able to listen carefully to questions;
- aware of the nuances of interviews; and
- more effective and polished as time goes on.

Questions to Ask Before Granting an Interview

To ensure that an interview results in a positive outcome for your organization or company, it is important to understand as much as possible about the time-frame, intent, and scope of the interview before agreeing to participate. Questions you should ask include:

- When is your deadline? (If not immediately, can I call you back in 20 minutes with information and other sources to interview?)
- What is the purpose/goal of the interview?
- Where will the interview take place? (On the telephone, in person, at the office, or in-studio?)
- Who else is being interviewed?

Confirm with the Reporter/Producer/Interviewer that you will be recording the interview (on tape or video). For broadcast interviews, be sure to ask the following:

- Will the program be a live, real-time show, or will it be taped?
- How much time has the producer, interviewer, and crew set aside for the interview?
- Will I be interviewed alone or on a panel?
- Will the host open up the show to telephone calls?

Record and file the necessary information following the format in the Sample Media Interview Form.

Sample Media Interview Form

Interviewer: _____

Representing: _____

Address: _____

Telephone: _____

E-mail: _____

Person interviewed: _____

Date of interview: _____

Time: _____

Location of interview: _____

Goal of the interview: _____

Length of interview: _____

Live or taped: _____

Airdate or print date: _____

When to Decline an Interview

There are certain instances when it may be appropriate to reject a media request for an interview. A number of potential situations are outlined below.

- The risk factors outweigh the potential gain. This involves your level of comfort with the medium, who the interviewer is, legal liability, the amount of time to prepare for the interview, and how much damage will be done if they do the story without you.
- The audience will not be responsive to your message.
- The audience is not a relevant market—demographically or geographically—for your company or organization.
- There is someone else outside the company, such as a scientific source or an association executive, who can deliver a more credible message.
- You do not have a trained spokesperson ready to do the interview.
- You know that the interviewer is well known for harassing, yelling at, or embarrassing guests.

The key is to decide how this interview will benefit you, your organization or company, your employees, and your clients and customers.

Supplying Advance Information to the Media

Once you have agreed to the interview, provide the interviewer with a Media Kit (see Chapter 8) containing background information on you, your organization and/or event, and a list of questions that you feel are important to your organization and the interviewer's audience. This list of questions is very helpful to interviewers who are pressed for time. Furthermore, it allows you to shape the content of the interview.

Preparing for the Interview

Check out the venue
- Become familiar with the interviewer, the format of the show, publication, or online media outlet, types of questions he or she asks, and what is expected of you.
- Look at the background and interests of the interviewer.
- Learn all you can about the audience of the program or publication, including the average age or age range of the audience, educational background, occupation, and buying habits.
- Ask for the station or publication's Sales or Media Kit to obtain this information.

Do your homework
- Know the three Key Messages you want to convey. Be prepared to repeat them several times during the interview.
- Make sure you can explain your organization and event in two sentences. Have the facts and figures on hand.
- For television interviews, prepare some effective visuals to present during the interview, including charts, pictures, posters, and products.

Key Messages

CASE STUDY

Fashion Cares 2005, M.A.C. *VIVA GLAM* Bollywood Cowboy
The key messages were modified for the pre-event period and the event, but overall the aim of the program was to communicate the following:

- The 19th annual Fashion Cares 2005 M·A·C *VIVA GLAM* Bollywood Cowboy is being held June 4, 2005 at the Metro Toronto Convention Centre. Tickets are available at Ticketmaster and through ACT.

- Fashion Cares 2005 M·A·C *VIVA GLAM* Bollywood Cowboy includes all that patrons have come to expect from Fashion Cares—an exciting and visual theme, hot entertainment, fabulous shopping, and a glitzy fashion show featuring a tribute to four legendary Canadian designers.
- Fashion Cares 2005 M·A·C *VIVA GLAM* Bollywood Cowboy is expected to raise close to $1 million dollars in support of the AIDS Committee of Toronto.

CASE STUDY

The Purina Walk for Dog Guides

The dog guide story is one that many people found extremely compelling, which risked Purina's health messages being overlooked. Argyle resolved that by ensuring messages about pet health were subtly woven into all the media materials, and that spokespeople were briefed on delivering these messages in the context of their interviews.

We prepared our spokespeople to deliver a unique 'pet health' message: 'Just as dog guides look after us, we have to look after them.' This opened the door to media coverage about Purina products as excellent sources of nutrition for dogs.

Practice, Practice, Practice

Whether you are participating in the interview or are coaching your organization's spokesperson, rehearsal is an essential part of being prepared.

- Brief the spokesperson on the type of story the reporter is working on (in-depth feature, survey piece, etc.) and what the reporter wants from the interview (quotes on corporate objectives, sales plans, organization's opinion on a trend or issue, etc.).
- Prepare a 'script' of anticipated questions and answers. Audio and videotape your questions and answers. Have someone with experience give you critical feedback about your answers and presentation style. Practice a clear, crisp delivery.
- Write out two or three Key Messages to convey during the interview, no matter what questions are asked.
- Role-play the situation. Prepare answers to the 'touchy' questions you anticipate and refine your answers.

Speech Therapy

Your voice is a tool that you can use to convey authority. Try the following exercises to practice voice control:

- vocalize: *aaaeeeiiiooouuu,*
  aaaeeeiiiooouuu,
  aaaeeeiiiooouuu;
- say '*unique New York, unique New York, unique New York*'; or
- repeat a personal mantra or affirmation.

Put energy in your voice through deep breathing. And to keep the vocal cords clear, be sure that you don't eat cheese or drink coffee, milk, or ice water just before you have to speak.

Presenting Yourself in the Interview

For any interview, but particularly for television appearances, how you present yourself is often as important as what you say. Here are some guidelines to keep in mind while preparing for the interview.

Body language is key. Find a comfortable position and lean forward toward the interviewer. Maintain an open demeanor—don't squint at the lights and keep your shoulders down, relaxed, and back. Sit still and don't fidget. Look at the interviewer, not the camera, and maintain eye contact with the interviewer.

Be relaxed and conversational. This is particularly important for television, because television magnifies your movements, expressions, and tone. Speak slowly, quietly, and remain cool. Avoid unsubstantiated comments and emotionalism. To calm your nerves before an interview, do neck and shoulder rolls and deep breathing.

Listen, listen, and listen again. Clarify your understanding of each question before you answer. Take some time to answer difficult questions. Don't fill the dead air—if you've finished your comments, stop talking. Be frank and open. Anticipate touchy questions and tell the truth. Remember that if you don't tell the truth, the reporters will find out and get the information somewhere else and that information could be incorrect. Make a statement and stick to it.

Show integrity and honesty. Know your facts and figures and be able to use them with authority. If you don't know the answer, say so and pass the question to someone who does or promise to get the information immediately and then *do it*.

Remember the three Cs:

- *concern* (for the issues and the people involved),
- *confidence* (knowledge of facts and hot issues), and
- *commitment* (to the issues, to the 'cause', and to a long-term plan).

Always speak in positive terms and avoid jargon or complicated terms. Speak in everyday language. Keep your answers simple; remember the KISS (Keep It Simple, Stupid) rule. Speak in sound bites of 13–15 seconds; your comments are less likely to be edited if they are short and complete. Always respond with a complete answer, not just 'yes' or 'no'.

Don't give away the store. Answer the question asked, and only the question that was asked. Reporters will have follow-up questions and interviews have a 'round-robin' quality.

Think, and speak, in threes. For example:

- time (past, present, and future);
- geography (Vancouver, British Columbia, and Canada);
- pendulum (some people feel this way, some people feel that way, I feel. . .).

Finally, if you are coaching a spokesperson, find out whether you can be present during the interview. This will enable you to:

- be on hand to introduce the interviewer to the spokesperson;
- promise follow-up materials, when necessary;
- clarify a point; and
- tape the interview.

Dress for Success

Through the eye of the camera, everything is magnified—your weight, your mannerisms and, particularly, the impact of the clothes you wear. Here are some sartorial tips for television interviews.

- Wear business attire.
- Avoid vivid colours, such as bright red, purple, and yellow, except as accents (tie, scarf, piping, etc.).
- White clothing is too glaring, but be aware that black clothing absorbs heat.
- Avoid outfits with stark, dramatic contrasts (light and dark).
- Fabrics with fine patterns (herringbones, checks, and plaids) should be avoided because they cause 'strobe' effects on the screen.

continued

- Double-knit clothing or sweaters will add visual pounds.
- Avoid horizontal stripes.
- In general, choose clothing in lighter tones (or in tones which complement your complexion) with slim lines.

Consider where and how the microphone is to be clipped or pinned to your shirt, blouse, sweater, or jacket. Men should unbutton their jackets before sitting down to avoid having the back collar ride up. And men who have fast-growing beards should shave closely just before the taping begins.

Tips for the Problem Interview

According to the University of Toronto's media guidelines, here are some guidelines they have prepared for their own staff which will help you to handle a problem interview:

- Prepare a Q&A—a list of potentially controversial questions a reporter may ask—and devise answers to those questions so you are prepared.
- Stay within your area of expertise and responsibility and don't be coaxed into making speculative statements that might backfire on you. Set up an additional interview for the reporter, if necessary.
- Remember to never speak off the record.
- Avoid saying 'no comment'. It sounds suspicious and unhelpful, leaving the impression that you are hiding something. Instead, give a reason why you can't answer the questions, such as the matter is before the courts or still being negotiated/reviewed, etc.
- In response to a negative question, answer with a positive. 'Why has your research failed to. . .' could be answered with 'My research has expanded understanding of. . .'.
- Always try to be patient and keep your emotions in check, even if the reporter is being aggressive and antagonistic—especially if you are being interviewed on camera.
- Don't feel you have to accept unfamiliar facts or figures or that you must answer a hypothetical question. Clearly state your main points and offer your own example.
- Remember that for an issue-oriented story, other sources will also be contacted for their version of events. Avoiding a tough interview won't kill the story but it will kill your chance to get your message out.

continued

After the interview, they suggest the following:

- Ask the reporter when the story may run and monitor the coverage.
- Don't ask to see the story before it goes to print or air. If you have concerns about accuracy, offer to check specific facts.
- If you feel something you said might be misinterpreted, don't hesitate to call the reporter back to clarify the issue.
- If you have offered to provide additional information, make sure that you do. It is the best way of ensuring the story will be accurate and well-rounded.
- If you feel you have been misquoted, read the story very carefully before making a complaint. A five-paragraph statement condensed to two sentences can look like a misquote when it is really only a close paraphrase of your statement.
- If your comments or research have been so distorted that you feel your professional credibility has been harmed, the best means of recourse is contacting the reporter's editor or the media's ombudsperson.

Reprinted with permission from the Public Affairs Department, University of Toronto.

Exercises

1. Henry Kissinger said in a press conference, 'I hope you have the questions for the answers I am going to give.' Discuss this statement.
2. Create three Key Messages you would include in a media interview for your company or organization: pro-actively and in a crisis. Would the Key Messages differ depending on the situation?
3. Describe five questions you wish the media would not ask (and that they probably will ask). Provide your answers.

Chapter 10

Staging Media Events

It is often difficult to capture the media's attention with a simple media release. A Media Kit, no matter how well prepared, can sometimes be forgotten in a file drawer. But an invitation to an interesting or unusual media-focused event is almost certain to excite a greater level of curiosity. In this chapter, we'll examine the function of different types of media events and how to make them successful.

Chapter Summary

By the end of Chapter 10, you will be able to:

- define and organize a media-focused event;
- contact the media about your event, and follow-up after the event;
- prepare Media Kits for the event;
- organize all elements of a media event, including setting up, booking speakers, and distributing materials;
- ensure media sign-in at your events;
- arrange other types of media events, such as media receptions, media previews, and publicity stunts;
- coordinate an online conference;
- organize the media at your event;
- follow up with the media after the event; and
- understanding the media value of celebrities.

Making the News

One of the most effective ways to attract the interest of the media is to stage an event that is, in itself, newsworthy. Events like these are more compelling than simple media releases. But, they are also more complicated and expensive to set up.

A **media event**, in short, is an event targeted to attract and persuade target media to attend and to provide media coverage. In general, a media event can be anything that is arranged to inform the media, involves their participation, or provide them with an opportunity for coverage. Specific types of media events include news conferences, media receptions or tours, media-driven publicity stunts, media previews of a special event, and the launch (or completion) of a fundraising campaign.

Organize a 'media-focused event' to bring media attention to your company or organization and to provide speakers, visuals, and interview opportunities.

Contact and Follow Up for Media Events

The goal of staging a media event is to ensure that the media attend. Decide who will be there and circulate a proposed invitation list to key people early. Where appropriate, invite government officials (local, provincial, or national) and other key stakeholders. Limit the number of officials to be introduced and who will be speaking.

Where possible, obtain advance commitments from the media to attend the event. The invitation and media release should be sent to the media 10–14 days before the event. You should then follow up with a telephone call. Finally, fax or e-mail a media alert one or two days before the event. When you send your invitation and media release, be sure to note clearly that Media Kits will be available at the event.

E-mail or mail invitations (include date, time, location, focus, agenda, and speakers), mark an RSVP, and make arrangements for media who cannot attend so that they will still receive a Media Kit.

How To Invite Media

- You can invite media by phone, fax, or mail. A telephone call first will ensure that you will find the right writer or producer.
- Find out which media outlets or freelancers report on issues relating to your event or issue.
- Keep an up-to-date mailing list or database of journalists.
- Focus on getting the most influential media to attend.
- Consider inviting international and foreign media if the topic warrants.
- Get your event information to media 10–14 days before the event.
- Always make a follow up call after the invitation has gone out to ensure that the right media representatives have received the information.
- Provide general background briefings to important journalists prior to the event, without disclosing your main news story to them.
- Don't forget Daybooks (newswire service listings of upcoming conferences, CNW Group, etc.).
- Organize telephone interviews for no-shows.

Media kits for media events

Prior to a news event you can use an embargo to prevent journalists from publishing anything before the event takes place. To do this, write 'Embargoed until *(date and time of release)*' at the top left side of all media releases you distribute prior to the news event. In general, media will respect the Embargo. In the Media Kit, include an agenda, a media release with the full story provided at the event, the position papers, backgrounders, photos, fact sheet, speaker biographies, copies of speeches, list of news conference participants (who was on the panel and their titles), and any other audio/visual materials.

Types of Media-focused Events

The news conference

A **news conference** is a business affair in which a spokesperson, and two or three other speakers, make a major significant announcement of importance to the attending media. New conferences provide a formal opportunity for a company or organization to address the media with an important announcement and to answer media questions.

As a media relations specialist, you might organize a news conference to:

- release new information relating to a big story being followed by the media;
- make a statement on a controversial issue;
- benefit from the participation of high-profile speakers or celebrities;
- release important new findings or research data;
- launch a major new initiative;
- announce something of local importance;
- make political announcements;
- mediate labour disputes;
- begin or end a major fundraising campaign or groundbreaking;
- unveil major product developments;
- announce the results of an important survey or report;
- add important visual elements to your story, such as a video or demonstration; or
- disseminate information during crises, emergencies, or catastrophes.

Is Your News Conference Newsworthy?

Before going to the time, trouble, and expense of organizing a news conference, you should ask yourself the following questions:

- Would a simple media release be enough, or is this item especially important and newsworthy?
- Does the announcement have a high level of urgency?
- Can you afford to do an event?
- Can you prepare everything in time or will your message be outdated by the time the media event is arranged?
- Will your message be enhanced through direct meeting with the media, either through understanding, explanation, or appreciation?
- Is it easy for the media to get to you? Have you selected a convenient location and time?
- Is there an eventual return on your investment? Will the media use your story?

Staging a news conference

Typically, a news conference has a moderator and begins with a formal presentation to the media representatives, followed by an opportunity for attendees to ask public questions and receive public answers (formal Q and A). Then, the conference often includes an opportunity for individual question-and-answer sessions or interviews.

Reporters are served refreshments following the event and are supplied with a Media Kit relating to the topic(s) discussed at the conference. News conferences should be limited to 45 minutes to one hour in length.

Getting ready

Preparing for a news conference involves many details. Just keep in mind that the overall objectives and theme of the event must support your organization or company's goals and overall media relations plan.

Select the speakers

A news conference should have no more than three speakers, plus the moderator. These could include one speaker from your company or organization, one from a government agency or an outside expert, and one from a sponsor/charitable agency.

- Select strong speakers who are articulate, authoritative, engaging, and clear.
- Brief speakers carefully on the Key Messages of the event; try to hold a meeting to brief all speakers before the event.
- Prepare speakers in advance on how to answer difficult questions.
- Offer to provide speakers with Question and Answer material.
- Ideally, each speaker should present for only three or four minutes.
- Make sure that each speaker makes *only* one or two important points.
- Keep speeches short, simple, and aimed at a general audience. Avoid technical jargon.
- Select a moderator who will manage questions from the floor after the formal presentations.
- Encourage the media to ask questions.

Keep answers to questions short

If necessary, provide media training for key executives who will be speakers at the news conference. Then, make a list of difficult questions and rehearse and videotape the answers. Prepare a package for your key executives containing a detailed agenda, Key Messages, Q&As, and a schedule of potential concerns to be addressed.

Tips for success

1. If possible, stage the event on Tuesday, Wednesday, or Thursday, between 10 am and 2 pm.
2. Choose a central location that is close to your key media, with easy access and easy parking, and that is appropriate to the event.
3. Avoid a room that is too large because it could give the appearance that few people attended.

4. Make sure the noise level of the room is low. Reserve an additional quiet room for interviews following the news conference.

5. Have a 'sign-in' table, with a book in which media print their names, media outlets they are representing, and telephone number. This is often the only record you have of who attended for following-up and for a final report.

6. Distribute Media Kits at the sign-in table.

7. Ensure that the light and sound systems at the venue are in working order.

8. If possible, have a phone available.

9. Make sure there is a podium for the speakers and a table long enough for all speakers to sit behind.

10. Consider displaying large visuals, such as graphs, logos, or charts.

11. If you are including a tour of a new facility, time it beforehand with a group so that you know how much time to allow.

12. Arrange for media resources at the event.

13. Book a photographer to take photos of the event.

14. Arrange for distribution of Media Kits to those who did not attend.

15. Invite people other than media to event.

16. Check that you are not competing with other important news events on the same day.

17. Begin and end on time.

Ready for Prime Time:
Tips for Preparing a Televised News Conference

- Television reporters need time to process and edit film, usually to meet a 6 pm news deadline, so schedule your conference earlier in the day.
- Make sure television crews do not have to walk too far with heavy equipment.
- Make sure the walls and decor are neutral; otherwise they will create a distracting backdrop for television coverage.
- Ensure there are sufficient power outlets to enable television crews to plug in extra lighting equipment.
- If your speakers are to be seated around a table, avoid using a white tablecloth, which tends to glare on camera. Provide a table on which media can prop their own microphones.

continued

- Make sure you have supporting photographs, graphics, or posters to depict the theme or goal of your company or organization. Set these behind the spokesperson or in a separate area where post-conference interviews will be conducted.
- Certain media representatives may want to arrange a brief one-on-one interview with key participants following the main conference. It is normal to allow television the first opportunity to conduct on-camera interviews, followed by radio and print.
- Reserve space at the back of the room for television cameras, possibly on a raised platform.
- Designate space for print media.

Following up

Within a few hours of the news conference's conclusion, you should fax, e-mail, or otherwise deliver information to important media who were unable to attend. Make sure the receptionist from your organization is advised on where to direct follow up calls from media. Be sure to gather press clippings of the coverage that results from the news conference and, immediately following the event, you should monitor the coverage your news conference receives in the newspapers, on television, and online.

A month after the event, when all of the press clippings have been gathered, put together a summary that includes information on objectives and a brief analysis of how they were met. Put together a formal scrapbook and video program on the event. This should be part of a complete file that includes everything connected to the occasion, from the official speech to Media Kits.

Hosting a media party

A less formal alternative to the traditional news conference—and one that is popular with media people—is the media reception or party. Combining business and pleasure, these events can involve cocktails or a meal, or both. Typically they are used to attract media attention to news of less immediacy and importance than that presented at a news conference. For example, a media reception might be held to preview a new product before it is launched. Media receptions are often accompanied by a buffet-style meal. The formal question-and-answer period is often briefer than at news conferences, since media can mingle and ask questions one-on-one.

Media Previews

Often scheduled in connection with some event to which the general public is invited, media previews are usually held an hour before an event begins. Media preview events can include the opening of a new building, an important convention, or special occasions such as trade shows, consumer shows, fairs, and community events. By inviting the media to attend early, they can experience the event without the crowds. Have two speakers on hand who are prepared to talk to the media, and a selection of light food. Be sure to provide sufficient time for the media to walk around and time for their questions to be asked and answered. Distribute Media Kits and invite them to stay for the remainder of the event.

Launch Party and Pre-event Support

CASE STUDY

Fashion Cares 2005, M.A.C. VIVA GLAM Bollywood Hollywood

- A Fashion Cares 'Launch Party', announcing the Bollywood Cowboy theme, unveiling the advertising creative and featuring entertainment and décor reflective of the theme, was held six weeks prior to the event. Invitations and a media kit including information on all aspects of the event were distributed to a comprehensive list of media.
- To complement the materials, the kit included Fashion Cares images for media use, which were also uploaded to an FTP site to provide media with easy access to high resolution images.
- To sustain media interest in the weeks after the launch party, two updates were sent to media—one announcing a confirmed entertainment line-up, and another announcing the event host, Pamela Anderson.
- Media training was provided to all spokespeople to ensure effective delivery of program messages.
- Regular media coverage updates, with examples, were provided to share with key sponsors.

Product launches

A product launch is a commercial event designed to allow the media the opportunity to see, test, and take a new product. Editorial media will often not attend product launch events because they consider them to be too commercial; instead they might tell you to take out an advertisement.

Media events as publicity stunts

In many cases, the media will gladly participate in events that benefit the community. Examples include fundraisers or other activities undertaken strictly for fun or to build visibility for the media outlet. The most important requirement is that the event be newsworthy, unique, high-profile, relevant to their audience, and provide interesting photo opportunities.

Events done strictly for media attention often backfire, however, due to a lack of planning for the event or a lack of excitement or educational value around the event.

Conferencing Online

As online speeds have grown faster through cable and broadband connections, the Internet has become an increasingly effective way to distribute audio and video information. The generally accepted use of the term webcast is the 'transmission of linear audio or video content over the Internet'.

A webcast uses streaming media technology to take a single content source and distribute it to many simultaneous listeners/viewers. The largest 'webcasters' include existing radio and television stations who 'simulcast' their output, as well as a multitude of Internet-only 'stations'. The term webcasting is usually reserved for referring to non-interactive linear streams or live events. Webcasting is also used extensively in the commercial sector for investor relations presentations (such as Annual General Meetings), in e-learning (to transmit seminars), and for related communications activities.

Web conferencing is designed to accommodate a many-to-many interaction. It is a service offered by a number of companies that can help you to organize a press conference at your website, and enables media around the world to hear and see your spokesperson explain a position, product, or issue. Then, they are able to ask questions live and directly.

To announce a web conference, write a media release and distribute it via e-mail to your media list. For example: 'ABC Company is pleased to announce (*subject*). A news conference will be held live on our website (*URL*) on Monday, 21 March 2008 at 9:30 am. Spokesperson (*name*) will be available to answer questions, which can be e-mailed during the news conference.' One of the advantages to web conferencing is that all statements, questions, and answers are public. This allows you to avoid any misinterpretation of the information. Additionally, the audio and video record of the news conference can be archived on your website and made available for download after the event.

Media At Your Events

Media pre-registration

For larger events, it is a good idea to send out media application forms, and then issue media passes that can be presented at the door. This is a good way to find out which media are planning to attend, as well alleviate the congestion at the event's registration desk and, subsequently, in the on-site media room.

Setting up an on-site media room

It is an excellent idea to set aside a room dedicated to media at your event so that they can have easy access to information. A newsroom that is too small, poorly located, or understaffed can result in poor coverage. Follow these rules for success:

- Make sure all information is easily available, including background material and media releases, copies of speeches, and the people to be interviewed.
- Select staff members for the media room who are experienced, helpful, and friendly. The number of people needed depends on the size of the event and the anticipated coverage. Make sure staff are able to handle emergencies, opportunities, and delicate media or personality problems.
- Separate the media room from the traffic of your event.
- Include a telephone in your media room for incoming calls from media who want to book interviews throughout the day.
- Find out what electrical outlets and other essentials are needed for television crews.
- Provide food to both keep the media from wandering away and to ensure they stay as long as necessary. Sandwiches, muffins, tea, coffee, and water are all standard menu items.
- Make sure there are hook-ups for media who want to file stories while they are still at the event.

Media Support for Special Events

CASE STUDY

Fashion Cares 2005, M.A.C. *VIVA GLAM* Bollywood Hollywood

- A public relations team of 15 people from within Weber Shandwick and its members' network of public relations colleagues was onsite to manage the various areas and media requests throughout the evening. A team of this size was essential for an event held in an area the size of four football fields. Key responsibilities included:

- ○ Media sign-in for the 200 accredited media, management of the media desk, and organization and distribution of media passes and tickets at the event
- ○ Coordination and management of a news conference and photo opportunity with the event talent and host, Pamela Anderson
- ○ Onsite media relations support to identify story angles and opportunities, facilitate interviews with spokespeople, and grant backstage access where appropriate to help media put their story together and obtain visuals
- ○ Identifying opportunities for media to profile event sponsors or sponsored elements—including providing 'social scene' media with a public relations committee runner to identify event sponsors to photograph and include in media coverage
- ○ Management of photographers and videographers on the event risers and runway
- ○ Facilitation of experiential packages with all eBay winners
- • The team was managed from a central media desk, communicating via headset with team members.

Managing Media After Your Event

A successful media campaign depends on how you manage the media after an event, which is just as important as the event itself. Distribute copies of any speeches and a follow up media release to everyone on the media list. Also include information detailing the success of event, attendance, amount raised (for charity), several quotes from speakers and/or attendees, and any additional news. Send Media Kits to any key media who did not attend. Offer additional information or extra photographs to reporters. Be sure to send this material soon enough to arrive in time to make their deadlines. Send a handwritten thank-you note to media who provided coverage.

Keep in mind that if the media haven't shown an interest in your event it could be because they are the wrong media, the event is not newsworthy, or you have missed their deadlines.

The Media Value of Celebrities

The presence of celebrities, or Very Important People (VIPs), at a media event can contribute significantly to the success of an event. A celebrity association generates both higher attendance at the event and a positive image for your company or organization, and its products and services. More importantly, the presence (or, better yet, the participation) of a VIP or celebrity is almost certain to attract media attention.

Who qualifies as a celebrity? While a popular musician or film star may be ideal, such a person is generally difficult to get. In some cases, however, the celebrity may have a personal interest in the event or the cause behind it. For example, singer Anne Murray was willing to help raise the profile and generate funds for Sheena's Place in Toronto, a day program for girls and women with eating disorders, because her own daughter had an eating disorder.

Still, depending on the market and the nature of the event, any number of people can add some measure of celebrity status to your event. These can include high profile corporate executives or a local disc jockey. The point to including a celebrity presence is to provide your event with a name recognition that it otherwise would not have had.

When planning to include VIPs at your event, be sure to consider the following:

- *Financial arrangements*. While VIPs are typically not motivated to attend events for financial gain, there may be a nominal fee or honorarium. In addition, there may be expenses—such as travel, lodging, and meals—that will need to be covered.
- *Managing the VIP's appearances*. Assign someone to meet and greet any VIPs, and to ensure that he or she appears for scheduled publicity opportunities and media coverage for the event. This can include a pre- or post-event news conference, photo opportunities, and interviews.
- *Communication*. Provide the VIP with a complete agenda of the event, as well as background on the event and organization.

Exercises

1. Select the best type of media event for your company or organization: a News Conference, a Media Preview, a Media Drop, or an On-site Media Room. Describe why this is the best tool.
2. Describe the reasons why you would or would not organize a News Conference for your company or organization. If you had selected this type of media event in the previous question, answer the following questions.
   a. Why is this the best vehicle for your news?
   b. Where and when will it be held?
   c. Who will be featured at the event and why?
   d. What are your Key Messages?

Chapter 11

Monitoring the Media, and Measuring and Evaluating Success

Once a media campaign has progressed through the first three phases of RACE—Research, Analyze, and Communicate—you need to monitor, measure, and evaluate its success. Media relations practitioners work in a field of many intangibles: opinions, messages, and impressions—all of which are notoriously difficult to measure. But in today's business environment, success must be proven with hard numbers. This is a challenge, although a useful one, since it forces us to be rigorous in evaluating the outcome of every media relations campaign and to learn from our experiences.

The evaluation process is also essential to understanding the effectiveness of the strategies used in a media relations program, and to improving those strategies in the future. Once you understand what you have accomplished, the Evaluation step logically leads back to the Research phase.

Chapter Summary

By the end of Chapter 11, you will be able to:

- recognize the importance of tracking the media,
- monitor the media on your own,
- use a media tracking form and various media monitoring services,
- understand the importance of evaluating success,
- conduct a communications audit,
- evaluate media relations strategies,
- conduct a media image survey and analyze media coverage,
- calculate the dollar value of media coverage,
- develop a media content analysis,
- document your program, and
- wrap up your campaign.

Keeping Track

The success of a media relations program is measured by the quantity—and quality—of the exposure obtained for your company or organization. Evaluating that success (or lack of it) therefore requires you to monitor the media, both during and after the program.

Apart from any specific media relations campaign, however, it also makes sense to monitor the media on an on-going basis. This allows you to:

- keep up-to-date on what is being broadcast or printed about your company, its products, its competitors, or the industry as a whole;
- learn about emerging trends and issues; and
- be knowledgeable about relevant news stories across the country or around the world.

There are two ways you can monitor the media: on your own, or through a media monitoring service.

Monitoring on your own

Since it doesn't require the assistance of an outside service, monitoring the media on your own is less costly—but only where the media to be monitored are clearly defined and relatively limited in number. For example, if your media list is restricted to specific newspapers and/or local television stations or networks, you can keep track of any coverage quite easily. Radio, which broadcasts news throughout the day, is the most difficult to monitor on your own, even if it is local.

MEDIA TRACKING FORM

PRINT

Publication/Location	Date/Length	Circulation	Ad Value
_____	_____	_____	_____
_____	_____	_____	_____
_____	_____	_____	_____
_____	_____	_____	_____

BROADCAST

Station/Location	Date/Length	Audience	Ad Value
_____	_____	_____	_____
_____	_____	_____	_____
_____	_____	_____	_____
_____	_____	_____	_____

Media monitoring services

With thousands of different print and broadcast media across North America, it is virtually impossible for you to monitor them all on your own. Where widespread coverage is required, you will need a media monitoring service. What follows is an overview of the largest of these services.

MediaVantage

MediaVantage is offered exclusively by the CNW Group as a web-based media monitoring, management, and measurement service, powered by dna13. It scans online, print, and broadcast sources for content related to its client's keyword entries with real-time results. Online news and information is collected from an expansive list of sources, including premium international and regional publications, corporate and government press pages, industry trade journals, and focused niche publications.

CNW Group's suite of communications management and online TV, print, Internet monitoring tools deliver results within four minutes of the media coverage being printed, aired, posted, or blogged—and you can search it all from your desktop.

In 2007, CNW Group expanded the existing reach of MediaVantage to cover more than three million blogs and 19,000 Canadian and international online news sources that offer 200,000 daily news headlines. Other highlights of the upgraded offering include breaking news items, available within two minutes of publication, and ongoing updates of over 150,000 headline links.

Cision Media Monitoring (formerly Bowdens Media Monitoring Limited)

With over 50 years serving the PR industry in Canada, Cision is best known for providing comprehensive media monitoring services. Cision offers comprehensive broadcast media monitoring coverage extending over 100 local and national Canadian markets and more than 160 top US markets. In Canada, the company monitors more than 2,300 news and public affairs programs on over 350 radio and 150 television stations. The US broadcast monitoring coverage includes over 50,000 hours of news and public affairs programming on over 1,000 broadcast stations.

Cision's service, MediaSource, provides clients with consolidated delivery of both print and broadcast coverage, increased scope of monitoring, customized reporting options, and the added convenience of access to media coverage via a secure online portal from anywhere. Cision also delivers international media monitoring through the same MediaSource Monitoring portal.

CP Television News Monitoring

CP's television monitoring service delivers relevant full-text TV newscast transcripts to you within minutes of the program's sign-off. Clients can find out what's being reported in TV newscasts about their company, products, clients, and competitors. With immediate broadcast monitoring access to the latest transcripts of TV news programs from across Canada, they can maximize positive coverage and monitor emerging issues, trends, and opinions, as well as identify competitor innovations or business opportunities (business development).

The Canadian Press tracks TV media coverage in more than 90 news and public affairs programs in 14 Canadian markets. CP Command News, the service for PR professionals, lets you know about developing stories as they happen and before they hit the headlines because it monitors stories on the CP wire in real time. Your company or organization can proactively call media to respond before a crisis develops, or identify and correct misinformation before it is widely published or broadcast to the public.

Burrelle's Media Monitoring

Burrelle's Press Clipping service monitors over 18,000 US and international publications. The company's NewsExpress™ service compiles keyword-matched news stories from early morning newspapers and newscasts, and delivers them via e-mail or fax by 9:00 am each business day. The company also offers a proprietary software product, Burrelle's Information Office™ (BIO), which enables clients to download their clips each day; maintain a customized archive locally; and search, retrieve, and redistribute whatever clips are required.

Burrelle's NewsClip Analysis Service provides both quantitative (for example, the number of stories, extent of coverage, advertising value, etc.) and qualitative analysis, which evaluates the tone and general favourability of coverage received. The company's Web-monitoring services—NewsAlert, CyberTalk, and Web Clips—provide varying levels of keyword-based search capability. For a full suite of monitoring tools, Burrelle's offers its 'Insight Farm' service, which covers all print, broadcast, and media outlets, and features a range of proprietary indices such as Reputation Yardstick™ and Impact Quotient™.

eWatch™

Traditional media monitoring services all feature Internet-searching capability, but eWatch™, which focuses exclusively on cybermedia, claims a leadership position in this market. Its services include Web Pubs (keyword-based monitoring of over 4,700 online newspapers, e-zines, broadcast sites and portals), Newsgroups (over 66,000 Usenet groups and electronic mailing lists), Online Service Forums (includes CompuServe and America Online message boards), and Investor Message Boards (searches for company mentions on investor message boards on Yahoo! Finance, Motley Fool, Raging Bull, and Silicon Investor), as well as WebWatch™ (an automated daily monitoring of changes in customer-specified websites, excluding Web publications, search engines, and e-zines).

E is for Evaluate

How do you evaluate the success of a media relations program?

Was the editonal coverage beneficial? Can a dollar value be assigned to it? These are the sorts of questions that, traditionally at least, have been difficult to answer. Part of the reason is that the cost–benefit relationship in media relations is not as clearly defined as, say, marketing, where the value of a campaign can be measured directly by increased sales. As a result, 'old school' practitioners often evaluated their campaigns according to informal or anecdotal findings. Today, however, media relations campaigns are expected to show tangible business results that can be measured against specific objectives.

Why Evaluate?

The evaluation process is useful to both practitioners and their clients. Specifically, it

- demonstrates to top management the importance and value of the media relations program and budget;
- provides comprehensive, objective, and accurate data, in order to understand a company, organization, or industry's image in the public arena;
- gains strategic and tactical information to be used in building relationships with key media and in developing future strategies;
- monitors and improves PR processes;
- measures the success of the communications efforts (What message is getting to the public? How is it being perceived?) to show accountability;
- identifies where the communications effort is not reaching its potential;
- tracks issues so as to understand progress on a range of topics, demonstrates which media are pursuing which angles, and tracks the organization or company's image;
- allows you to understand trends and to identify opportunities to improve communications on important issues;
- helps to maintain a competitive edge; and
- secures more resources for future campaigns.

# Conducting a Communications Audit

Earlier in the book we learned about the importance of conducting a communications audit before initiating a media relations campaign. A similar process is equally useful in evaluating the campaign once it is completed.

Evaluate your media relations strategies

Your goal is to assess the media relations strategies developed in this book—including the media list, Media Kit inserts, media events, and crisis management plan—to judge their strengths and weaknesses. For example, ask yourself, did the media:

- respond to your materials?
- use the information in your Media Kit?
- contact you for information or interviews?
- attend your media events?
- attend your special events and visit your on-site media room (and/or your Online Media Room)?

Analyze data collected during the campaign

Your goal is to look at the data—the measurable responses to the media relations program—that was collected over the course of your media campaign. Data examined can include the following:

- number of people who attended your event;
- sales and orders for products and services;
- telephone and hotline calls;
- funds raised through event;
- number of new sponsors and partners;
- feedback and complaints from clients and attendees;
- comments from focus groups used to evaluate the perceptions of key markets after a program;
- in-depth interviews; and
- recruitment of celebrities (at no cost).

Develop post-campaign research

Your goal is to conduct research that provides additional qualitative data that you can use to evaluate the campaign's effectiveness. This can involve surveying your key markets to get feedback and to measure the effectiveness with which your campaign conveyed its messages, as well as analyzing awareness levels, assessing behavourial changes, and analyzing whether the program produced favourable reactions. Research methods can include telephone surveys, personal interviews, mailed questionnaires, and focus groups.

Conduct a post-campaign survey of media representatives

The purpose of a survey is to determine the media's perception of your organization or company's image following a media relations campaign. The goal is to obtain feedback from those media—including reporters, assignment editors, editors, news directors, and local bureau chiefs—who have first-hand experience working with you or your representatives.

Specific measures in the survey include:

- professionalism,
- credibility,
- accessibility,
- promptness in returning calls,
- responsiveness to the media's needs,
- sensitivity to media deadlines,
- timeliness of media releases, and
- newsworthiness of media releases

Analyze your media coverage

Your communications audit should include an analysis of the following aspects of media coverage:

- Total number of placements and total audience reach. Did it surpass the projected goal? Based on your budget for fees and expenses, what did the audience reach cost per person?
- Types of media coverage: national versus local, community, or daily newspapers, ethnic media, magazines, radio, television, or Internet section or program
- Quantity of coverage: number of articles or broadcast segments
- Placement of coverage: size of articles (number of column inches), length of television or radio appearances or segments (number of minutes), location, and headlines
- Photos captured and photo placement
- Matt story publish rate
- Success in generating coverage in key markets, as defined by the client
- Sources: who was quoted (for example, third-party experts)
- Competitors' coverage
- Attendance at media events

SAMPLE SURVEY

1. What is your current position?
   - ☐ Reporter
   - ☐ News Director
   - ☐ Program Director
   - ☐ Editor
   - ☐ Senior Editor
   - ☐ Assignment Editor
   - ☐ Producer
   - ☐ Other (specify)

2. How long have you been in that position?

3. Indicate type of media:
   ? Radio ? Television ? Newspaper ? Magazine

4. When was the last time you dealt with the company's media relations representatives?
   - ☐ Within the last month?
   - ☐ Within the last 6 months?
   - ☐ Within the last year?
   - ☐ More than a year ago?

5. For a given issue, would you prefer to speak with:
   - ☐ A media relations specialist?
   - ☐ An expert from the specialist's company?

6. Do you feel that the company's media relations department (or firm)
   - ☐ Helps you to obtain information?
   - ☐ Is more of a barrier to getting information?

7. What could our media relations department or consultants change or improve upon to make your job easier?

   _____

   _____

8. Describe your current knowledge or understanding of our company.

   _____

   _____

9. Would you prefer to have your responses
   - ☐ Identified to our client?
   - ☐ Be given only as part of a group?

- Advertising value: How much is it worth? 'Ad Value' is the amount it would have cost to purchase the same amount of space (for print media) or time (for broadcast) allocated to the coverage you received had you purchased it for advertising. For example, if a newspaper article about your company is 200 agate lines in length (about 15 column inches), and the advertising rate is $2.50/line, the ad value would be $500.

Develop a media content analysis

Your goal is to analyze the content and tone of media coverage. This includes factors such as the

- types of media impressions: positive, negative, or neutral;
- issues talked about, such as financial, environmental, or industry issues;
- penetration of Key Messages;
- use of message clips and quotes from spokespeople; and
- third-party quotes, such as those from students, doctors, etc.

Media Ratings Points (MRP™)

MRP™ is the Canadian standard for evaluating and reporting editorial media coverage. Members of the Canadian Public Relations Society Measurement Committee (CPRSMC) developed MRP after consulting with the Public Relations Industry for $3^1/_2$ years. The Canadian Public Relations Society, International Association of Business Communicators of Canada, Canadian Council of Public Relations Firms, and News Canada endorse MRP. MRP measures planned and unplanned media coverage by awarding points for quantitative and qualitative criteria. By pre-selecting tailored criteria that meet the objectives of individual campaigns, MRP creates a customized report that is both client specific and standard across Canada.

CPRS selected News Canada through a Request-for-Proposal (RFP) process to provide standardized audience reach data (in addition to running and supporting the web site). News Canada is the only vendor endorsed by both CPRS and IABC Canada to provide audience reach data for the MRP system.

continued

News Canada has created a website that enables subscribers to complete an MRP report in an easy, efficient manner. Subscribers can use the template; establish the criteria to evaluate their media coverage (photo/image, call to action, spokesperson quote, Tier 1 media, etc.); evaluate the media coverage (clips, airings, etc.) for tone and criteria; enter an audience reach number; and calculate their MRP score, Return-on-Investment (ROI), or Cost-Per-Contact (CPC). Subscribers can also export their MRP report to MS Excel.

The MRP standard does not use advertising equivalency values (AEVs), nor does it use multipliers. Instead it uses the same data that the marketing and advertising industry uses to determine audience reach.

Develop a media report

A media report is a summary document designed to provide an analysis of the communications' goals and how they were met, not met, or exceeded. In addition to summarizing the results of your communications audit, it provides the chance to discuss the following: surprises (if any); reasons for lack of media interest, along with any suggestions as to how to generate greater interest in the future; and media requests that could not be met, and why. In particular, be sure to review any weaknesses of the campaign, such as:

- your key contacts with media (spokesperson, receptionist, or volunteers); and
- inconsistent messaging (different people talking to the media and delivering different messages).

Organize a wrap-up meeting

About a month after the completion of the program, arrange a debriefing with everyone involved in the media campaign to discuss all aspects of the campaign. Specific elements for review should include

- the media report and the media tracking forms;
- a re-examination of your pubiicity goals and objectives;
- an analysis of projected budget and final costs of media campaign; and
- an assessment of the range of the campaign and whether to expand into new markets.

Questions to ask

Is your company or organization in a better position—in terms of its finances, sales, awareness, and support—than when you started your media campaign? What have you learned? What is your next step?

Document your program

Create a final document for the media relations program, and be sure to include the following elements:

- program overview
- current media list
- program tactics
- samples of media strategies:
- pitch letter
- media invitation
- media releases (from advance to follow-up)
- print PSAs and scripts for radio and television PSAs
- fact sheets
- backgrounders
- profiles
- feature articles
- media alert
- testimonials
- agenda for special events
- news conference(s)
- media call form
- Key Messages
- Q & A sheets
- all correspondence with the media
- photos, negatives, and slides
- media monitoring report that summarizes media coverage by date, outlet, circulation, and ad value
- press clippings book

Pyramid on previous publicity

Media interest in your company or organization often occurs when the media read or hear about you through other media. Make it a point to let key media know when you have been featured in an article or a television or radio interview, when your coverage has moved from local to national media, or when it has crossed from one type of medium to another (for example, from print to television or radio).

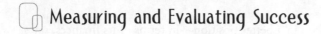

Measuring and Evaluating Success

CASE STUDY

Fashion Cares 2005, M.A.C. *VIVA GLAM* Bollywood Cowboy

Overall the event was a huge success, with extensive coverage of the launch party, featured designers, talent and host announcements and eBay auctions. The media coverage for the event was overwhelmingly positive, profiling the unique aspects of the event, and highlighting various sponsors.

Quantitative coverage
- 228 total hits—a 100% increase in number of hits over the previous year and
- Of the total hits, 113 (49.5%) occurred in the pre-event timeframe—surpassing the previous year by 40%
- 143,157,610 impressions—more than an 80% increase over the previous year
- More than 80% of the pre-event coverage highlighted the key event information, Bollywood Cowboy theme, event entertainment or shopping
- The eBay auctions generated close to 20 extra hits for the event, profiling event title sponsor M.A.C Cosmetics, supporting sponsor, Levi's, while also raising more than $10,000 for ACT
- 'Free' media passes were limited to 200
- Although attributed to all of the elements of the event and its marketing activities working together, including media relations outreach, ticket sales surpassed previous years' sales

Qualitative coverage
- Pre-event coverage included announcement of the event theme and key details, but also included profiles of expected entertainers, the eBay auction items (experiential event packages and celebrity-signed jackets)
- The tone of the event coverage clearly communicated the entertainment elements and 'outrageous' brand image of Fashion Cares
- The majority of the media provided passes, were 'working' the event and either provided significant pre-event coverage, or delivered satisfactory coverage for the actual event
- Key event night coverage from the *National Post*, *Toronto Star*, *Toronto Sun*, *Metro*, *24 Hours*, CITY TV and Global TV mentioned one or more event sponsor in addition to title sponsor, M.A.C Cosmetics
- Coverage for the event appeared in daily newspapers across the country, providing sponsors with national profile

The Purina Walk for Dog Guides

Measured against its goals and objectives, the Purina Walk for Dog Guides program was a resounding success.

Awareness of walk, link to Purina brand

- 170 total media stories generated an audience reach of more than 9.7 million Canadians.
- 70 per cent of coverage identified the event by its complete name and highlighted the involvement of Purina.
- 40 per cent included quotes/interviews from local or national spokespersons.
- 30 per cent included photos with appropriate branding for Purina and the walk.

Participation

- Participation and attendance numbers increased by 14 per cent, with the largest growth shown in midsize to large population cities.
- On-site exposure to Purina brand:
- 100 per cent of walkers at the largest site visited the Purina Neighbourhood for samples and information about pet nutrition.

Financial support

- Online donations via the Web site increased by 428 per cent over 2004, and total funds raised grew 8 per cent to $515,000.

The Launch of Virgin Mobile Canada

Media impressions and quality of coverage were used to measure the project's success. The launch of Virgin Mobile Canada generated 155 million media impressions—considerable in a country with a population of 36 million.

Furthermore, the domino factor stemming from the Toronto, Montreal, and Vancouver launches sent a wave of coverage across Canada. Ultimately, media relations activities helped to bridge the gap between the launch of Virgin Mobile Canada and the advertising campaign.

Highlights included:

- More than 5.5 hours of television coverage
- Visuals of the stunt in 75% of the overall coverage

- 117 print articles in 56 unique outlets across Canada
- 'No Catch'—an important Virgin Mobile key message—was included in more than half of media hits
- 45% of coverage included quotes and sound bytes by Richard Branson
- One to one interviews delivered coverage to target consumer (102.1 The Edge, Breakfast Television, Flow 93.5, Canada AM, Canadian Press, *Toronto Star*, Much Music, Musique Plus, JR Dufort, SRC, etc.)
- PR effectively shut out the competition—competitors' role in Virgin Mobile coverage was insignificant with quotes in only 7% of print hits
- 185 members of the media attended Virgin Mobile Canada launch events over the three-day launch period in Toronto, Montreal and Vancouver
- Andrew Black, president of Virgin Mobile Canada, was effectively represented with quotes in 15% of print coverage
- Just two weeks after launch, before the mass advertising kicked in, an independent poll reported unaided awareness of Virgin Mobile reached 24% of respondents in Toronto, and 18% in Montreal
- Fuelled mainly by media relations, the company was more than 20% ahead of its sales projections before other marketing initiatives kicked in.

CASE STUDY

Purolator Tackle Hunger 2006

- Extensive national visibility for the program including 125 media hits (48 TV, 37 print, 17 radio, 23 online and one wire service)—almost double the amount of media coverage received in 2005. In total, the 2006 program generated over 15 million impressions, a 140% increase over 2005.
- 16 media interviews with Purolator spokespeople; six live appearances on top shows in Calgary, Winnipeg, Toronto, Edmonton, and Hamilton.
- Almost 47 per cent of the media coverage noted the importance of helping alleviate hunger and the need for donations all year round.
- Over 60 per cent of the media coverage included the call to action to make a donation to each local game day food drive.
- Purolator was positioned as the driving force behind the food drives in 80% of the media coverage.
- Enhanced relationships with local food banks through numerous joint TV/radio interviews.
- 2006 proved to be a banner year for Purolator Tackle Hunger, raising the equivalent of 348,000 lbs of food—a 24% increase compared to 2005.
- 2006 was also a milestone year for the Purolator Tackle Hunger program as it reached the 1 million pound mark for the amount of food raised since the inception of the program.

Exercises

1. Are mainstream media outlets seeing a return in their online investments?
2. Since editorial coverage is perceived as having greater credibility than advertising, many media relations practitioners' multiply the ad value of media coverage by a factor of three to seven, depending on the medium and the placement. There has been a great deal of controversy related to this form of measurement. Discuss the pros and cons of advertising equivalency value.

Part 4

Issues Management and Crisis Communications

Chapter 12

Defining Your Issues and Creating a Plan

Every company or organization faces a variety of issues that can impact its level of client trust, reputation, assets, and interests, as well as its ability to operate. By identifying emerging issues that could escalate into a crisis, your company or organization can create a strategy to influence and alter the direction of the issues. In this way, you can 'manage', rather than 'react' to issues.

Chapter Summary

By the end of Chapter 12, you will be able to:

- clearly define an issue, an issue statement, and issue management;
- understand the four factors that influence an issue;
- recognize types of issues;
- delineate key markets and media for issues;
- develop goals and strategies to identify and manage issues;
- create an eight-step issues management plan; and
- handle the situation with confidence when an issue turns into a crisis.

An **issue** is a trend, concern, or event with the potential to substantially impact your company or organization and key audiences. It is crucial that you are aware of any issues that could affect your media relations campaign either well in advance of the start of the campaign or as soon as possible after they emerge. This enables you to have time to deal with each issue in a satisfactory manner. When issues arise during the campaign, you will need to release an **issues statement**, which clearly outlines your company or organization's position on a specific issue. It is important that you have an **issues management** strategy—a process for anticipating, identifying, and tracking events, trends, and concerns—in place. This will enable the organization to develop strategies designed to communicate the best position, deflect concern, and minimize consequences.

There are four factors that influence an issue:

1. your past history, management style of leadership, and operational philosophy;
2. local sensitivities;
3. the time, place, and intensity of the potential fallout; and
4. the depth and strength of opposing views.

Types of Issues

Issues as problems
This category includes the following:

- Industry-related issues, such as chemicals, technology, or airlines;
- Discrimination suits;
- Shareholder action;
- System failures;
- Customer service problems;
- Environmental impact and allegations of violations;
- Proposed legislation;
- Competitor initiatives;
- Plant closures;
- Mergers/acquisitions;
- Work force reductions;
- Strikes;
- Health pandemics;
- Regulatory violations;
- Bankruptcy;
- Impact on a politically-sensitive geographical area; and
- Ethnic concerns.

Issues as opportunities

Positive issues (or positive elements in issues) offer the chance to increase understanding and support for your company or organization. They provide opportunities for you to differentiate and educate your key audiences and media. This category includes the following:

- Plant approvals and expansions,
- Presentations of an award,
- Successful contract negotiations,
- Initial public offering,
- Regulatory approvals, and
- Facility openings.

Key Markets and Media for Issues

As you conduct your media relations campaign, and as you deal with the issues that may arise, you must know which market (and which media) is appropriate for each issue. Consider the following key markets:

- Employees and their families;
- Political leaders;
- Regulatory agencies;
- Government officials;
- Community leaders and advocacy organizations;
- Local, national, and international communities;
- Web-based markets;
- Stakeholders; and
- Media/Editorial Boards (print, broadcast, Internet, Internet-based, blogs, newsletters, etc.).

Ways to Develop Goals and Strategies to Identify and Manage Issues

It is important to have a clear understanding of what you are trying to achieve, in order to set, and evaluate against, your goals. These could include:

- gaining an understanding of internal and external factors that could evolve into issues;
- increasing your understanding, awareness, and support from key markets;

- controlling factors before they emerge or escalate into critical problems;
- communicating corporate policy to key markets;
- generating support from key markets;
- correcting misinformation about your company or organization; and
- projecting a positive message.

Create an Eight-step Issues Management Plan

Step #1: Gather information and conduct market research
- Conduct research—through questionnaires, one-on-one interviews, focus groups, and email and telephone surveys—with key markets to understand their concerns and issues.
- Analyze your company's history, operations, culture, and philosophy as they relate to emerging issues.
- Conduct a risk assessment audit to identify and prioritize areas of vulnerability. Organize meetings with representatives from different departments or divisions within your company.
- Study public perception, emerging trends, and business practices that could affect your organization or company.
- Monitor websites, blogs, and chat rooms to identify and understand issues and information related to your company or organization.
- Track media to see what issues they currently cover and review Editorial Calendars to see what issues they plan to cover.

Step #2: Classify, prioritize, and monitor issues
- Identify emerging issues and track their escalation.
- Decide which issues could cause significant damage. Focus on these issues.
- Continue to monitor these issues on a daily and monthly basis to understand changes in the intensity of an issue or its likelihood of occurrence.
- Analyze mainstream and alternative media, blogs, online chat rooms, and newsletters from activist groups.

Step #3: Organize an issues management response team
- Include your CEO or Executive Director, Senior Management, communications experts, legal and technical experts, and political strategists.

Step #4: Select key media for coverage
- Analyze potential media outlets that could reach and influence your target markets on key issues.

- Contact them and build relationships with them on an on-going basis, not only when an issue erupts into a crisis.

Step #5: Develop an issues strategy and action plan

- Include the following elements:
  - ways to anticipate likely issues,
  - ways to optimize management actions,
  - Key Messages,
  - printed materials,
  - third-party alliances, and
  - media training and simulations.

Step #6: Implement the plan when an issue escalates

- Develop a written issues statement to explain your point of view, as well as FAQ's and Key Messages.

Step #7: Monitor and evaluate your handling of the issue

- Analyze news and information, opinion research, media monitoring (during and after the issue), websites, and online discussions.
- Ask yourself these questions:
  - Are we responding effectively?
  - What are we doing right?
  - What does the public still need to know or what is confusing?
  - Was the news coverage positive or negative?
  - Has the issue lessened in severity?
  - Is it still a concern moving forward? (Stigmas take a long time to recover from, so work with the media to turn the negative into a positive.)
  - How can we restore confidence in our reputation?
  - Did we achieve our goals?

Step #8: Start to rebuild

- Make issues management an integral part of your communications' strategy and plan.

When an Issue Turns into a Crisis

Don't ignore the warning signs. Often, companies and organizations hope that a problem will not escalate into a full-blown crisis and ignore the symptoms as long as possible. You don't want to wait until an issue has major consequences before you address it.

CASE STUDY

Fashion Cares 2005, M.A.C *VIVA GLAM* Bollywood Cowboy

Although ACT had enlisted feedback from the South Asian community prior to approving the Bollywood Cowboy event theme and materials, there was backlash from a small group of community members who found the theme and collateral materials disrespectful to their culture and religion. The public relations committee provided the following short-term strategic counsel and support:

- Counselled the Steering Committee and ACT that to protect the event 'brand' and event sponsors, ACT spokespeople should speak to the issue rather than Fashion Cares representatives
- Advised ACT to issue a written statement explaining its point-of-view, expressing regret for any insensitivities on its part, outlining its process for ensuring it doesn't happen again and reinforcing the good that Fashion Cares does for AIDS-service organizations in all communities. The final statement issued by ACT reflects most of this counsel.
- When ACT was repeatedly pursued by media to engage in debate on the issue, the committee counseled that it stick to the strategy of delivering its key message via written statement
- Drafted and distributed a FAQ document to key event sponsors to provide them with information, and arm them to answer questions from their employees and/or partners. The FAQ's were also provided to members of the Steering Committee and its sub-committees to ensure that everyone was onside with messaging
- Advised ACT to invite three of the more vocal opponents to sit at one of ACT's tables at the Gala dinner to see first-hand how the theme was being portrayed.
- Counseled ACT on the need to develop a longer-term strategy to reconcile its relationship with the South Asian community

Although the issue initially generated some negative publicity for the event and for ACT, the strategy for managing the controversy worked to its advantage in the longer-term, with media continuing to use ACT's written statement in coverage and ultimately leaving the story, while sponsors continued to support the event and its theme. It also succeeded in distancing the Fashion Cares brand, and its sponsors, from the controversy.

CASE STUDY

Independently Healthy: A BC Housing Campaign

Title: Independently Healthy—Changing Housing and Care Needs of Seniors
Author: Susan Thom, ABC
Organization: BC Housing
Timeframe: November 2005

Need/Opportunity

BC Housing is a provincial government crown corporation responsible for the development and administration of subsidized or social housing in the province of British Columbia. With the aging demographics, BC Housing's mandate has shifted from the provision of subsidized housing mainly for low-income families to the development of a subsidized assisted living option for frail seniors. A key mandate is the development of 3,500 assisted living units under the Independent Living BC (ILBC) program—a housing and health partnership with provincial health authorities, the federal government, and the private and non-profit sectors. This type of housing provides some form of personal assistance/health services for seniors who do not want or need to be in a 24-hour residential care facility or nursing home.

The care for seniors will continue to put increased financial pressure on the health care system as the population ages. In BC, health care already accounts for over 40 per cent of the provincial budget. As seniors grow frail, they face more challenges to live independently. It used to be that the only other option to living at home, especially for low-income seniors, was to go to a government-subsidized nursing home. As a middle option between living at home and institutional care, assisted living has been available in the past for those who could afford it. With the ILBC program, assisted living is now available to low-income seniors. It's a more cost-effective option for government than providing around-the-clock care in nursing homes or hospitals. More importantly, it gives frail seniors more autonomy and independence, delaying or preventing the need to go to institutional care facilities.

Currently, there are over 500,000 seniors over the age of 65 in BC and this number will almost triple to 1.4 million in the next 25 years. A telephone survey conducted in the fall of 2004 by the two main newspapers in Vancouver (*Sun/Province*) indicated over 90 per cent of the respondents (500 newspaper subscribers) were concerned about the future of seniors housing and care. There was evidence of a need to increase public awareness and understanding of:

1. the social and economic implications of an aging population and to broaden overall public understanding of assisted living;
2. the continual need for the provincial government to focus its resources in providing appropriate housing and care for frail seniors; and
3. the myth that seniors' housing is institutional nursing homes.

Intended Audiences

The newspaper supplement is targeted to a broad community audience to garner public and media awareness/support of the role BC Housing and its partners play in the development of assisted living. More specifically, the goal is to increase awareness among seniors and their family caregivers of the availability of a subsidized assisted living option under the ILBC program.

Seniors: We wanted to increase awareness amongst seniors that research indicates they are living longer, healthier lives, and of the housing and care implications. Two informal focus groups with seniors were conducted last September to determine what they wanted to know about the future of housing and care in the supplement. One of the key suggestions was for larger font size in the publication. Another suggestion resulted in a comprehensive seniors' resource guide in the front part of the supplement. As well, articles in the supplement provided information on trends, programs and services, including 'frequently asked questions'.

Seniors' family caregivers: Another key target audience includes family members and caregivers, many of whom are aging baby boomers themselves who may need assisted living in the future. The supplement was designed as a pull-out resource guide for seniors and their family care givers to keep as a future reference, or to pass on to someone who may need subsidized seniors' housing.

General public and media: With the aging demographics, it's important to garner public understanding and support of government's role in the future of seniors' housing and care options in the province. Especially with limited housing resources, some housing advocacy groups have been critical of government's role in diverting subsidy dollars from family housing to seniors' assisted living.

Non-profit and private seniors' housing groups: These groups were targeted to participate in the supplement by purchasing ads to support the publication and to cross-promote the supplement by posting it on their websites or distributing it to their tenants or clients. Partnerships with these groups were also highlighted in the articles.

Goal/Objectives

The goal is to measurably increase public awareness, understanding, and support of government's role in the future need of seniors' housing and care in the province by:

1. Providing a cost-effective and useful resource guide (based on feedback from seniors' focus groups) that seniors and their family care givers can pull out, save and refer to in future for information about housing and care for seniors in BC;
2. Developing an informative newspaper supplement as a vehicle to increase public awareness of the future of seniors' housing and care in partnership with the media and targeted seniors' housing groups—before, during, and after the publication of the newspaper supplement;
3. Increasing public understanding and support about the trends and implications of the aging population and why government is focusing its housing dollars along with other public, private, and non-profit partners in the provision of seniors' housing and care; and
4. Involving various government, health authorities, media, private, and non-profit partners in financially supporting this newspaper supplement through editorial content, advertisements, and cross-promotion of the published supplement through distribution to its members and posting on their organizations' websites for up to five months.

Solution Overview

Given that our key objectives were to increase public awareness, understanding, and support about the future needs of seniors' housing and care, how it has evolved, and the role of the Province in collaboration with its partners under the ILBC program, I chose to produce another multi-dimensional 16-page newspaper supplement as a pull-out seniors' resource guide. As in any marketing endeavour, frequency is key to hitting home a message. The first newspaper supplement focused on partnerships; the second one in the fall of 2004 focused on seniors and their caregivers. The theme of the 2005 seniors' newspaper supplement was 'Independently Healthy'—a play on the words independently wealthy. It was inserted in *The Vancouver Sun* and *The Province*, the two major daily newspapers in Vancouver, both owned by the Canwest/Global company. Given the audience, *The Vancouver Sun* offered an older/educated readership and *The Province* offered a younger but province-wide distribution. To allow the supplement to stand out, it was integrated in the newspapers during mid-week when the volume of information is not as high. I negotiated with the newspapers for a publication that is not a typical newspaper supplement, but one that would be cost-effective, multi-dimensional, and marketed before and after its publication date to maximize its visibility and usefulness.

- *Promotional ads to raise public awareness of the Independently Healthy supplement prior to its publication*: two quarter-page teaser ads (in Section A of each of the two newspapers); six promotional banner ads (three in each paper); and 62 thirty-second primetime ads on Global TV leading up to the publication of the supplement.
- *Staggered publication dates for the supplement in the two newspapers*:   We decided to publish the supplement in *The Province* (29 November 2005) and in *The Vancouver Sun* (30 November 2005).
- *Posting of the PDF of the full supplement (with bookmarks) identified by a seniors' graphic icon on the splash page of both* The Province*'s and* Vancouver Sun*'s websites*: I had arranged this posting for at least four months (free of charge) as part of the agreement with the newspapers. As well, both newspapers ran a total of four turn-to ads (two each) promoting the supplement on the papers' websites.
- *Post-supplement survey commissioned by Pacific News Group (advertising arm of the* Vancouver Sun/Province*)*: A prominent polling firm was hired by the newspaper group to do a telephone poll of 500 of *Province* and *Sun* subscribers to ascertain increase in awareness, readership, and understanding of the assisted living topic over previous supplements. We also took the opportunity to survey the public about their level of support for government partnership funding of assisted living under the ILBC program.
- *Over-run copies of the supplement*: Over 3,000 copies of the supplement were provided to BC Housing from the newspapers (free of charge), allowing us to send copies to key seniors' organizations and partners for their members and clients. Copies will also be used at seniors' conferences and tradeshows.

- *Cross-promotion of Independently Healthy supplement by various partners*: The supplement is visibly posted on BC Housing's website, as well as other partners' websites including the BC Non-Profit Housing Association; the Canadian Home Builders Association of BC; the national Care Guide; the Canadian Housing Renewal Association; and Vancouver Coastal Health and Fraser Health authorities.

Implementation and Challenges

Given the multi-dimensional aspects of this partnership initiative, there were many challenges:

- My first approach was to anchor the newspapers as media sponsors for the supplement. Once that partnership arrangement was secure, it was easier to get other partners and advertisers on side. The newspapers, in turn, helped bring on Global TV as promotional partner.
- We had a new Minister following the June 2004 provincial election. Through a comprehensive proposal and a cost-effective arrangement with both the newspapers and Global TV, the Minister's Office gave the green light to proceed. Overall, BC Housing's share was $32,500 for a total package worth $180,000 of which $115,000 was free space both in terms of advertorials and promotional ads from the media. I also demonstrated that this multi-dimensional supplement was not just a 'one-shot deal', but that it would have some lasting value after its publication.
- This work on this supplement was on top of our regular workload. My Manager of Communications, Sam Rainboth, took the lead to coordinate the timeline, editorial plan, and worked with our ad agency in the design of the supplement. One of the incentives for the newspapers was my offer to provide them a list of key potential advertisers, such as health authorities, private and non-profit housing sectors, construction firms, architects, developers, and other levels of government.
- I stood firm that the design of the supplement had to be warm, appealing, and the articles useful and interesting to seniors and their family care givers as a resource. It was crucial that this not look like government 'propaganda'. As such, there were various 'real-life' human-interest stories. A professional photographer was hired to capture some strong close-ups of seniors to make the supplement visually appealing. Given our joint partnership with the Government of Canada, the only 'government' presence in terms of logos was in the centre spread pages profiling the Independent Living BC program.

Overall Budget

As part of a joint federal/provincial communications initiative, BC Housing, and Canada Mortgage and Housing Corporation each paid $32,500 for our share of the upfront cost charged by the newspapers and Global TV for the supplement and the promotions. We assisted the newspapers to sell advertising to support the supplement. BC Housing spent another $10,000 in the photography, layout, and design of the supplement, and supported the Pacific News Group with $7,000 for their post-supplement subscribers' survey. BC Housing's budget for this initiative was about $49,500.

Measuring/Evaluation of Outcomes

1. Provided a cost-effective and useful resource for seniors and their family care givers:
    a. As part of this unique partnership with *The Vancouver Sun/Province* and Global TV, BC Housing was able to leverage over $115,000 of free advertorial in the supplement, promotional ad space in the newspapers and 62 thirty-second primetime ads on Global TV. This also included a total of two quarter-page teaser ads (in each of the two newspapers) and six promotional banner ads (three in each paper) leading up to the publication of the supplement. In addition, we received two turn-to ads on the day of the publication (one in each of the newspapers) and a total of four turn-to ads (two each) promoting the supplement on the newspapers' websites.
    b. Key partnership this year with Global TV promotions—62 primetime ads in a 10-day period—helped to generate awareness among its viewers of the newspaper supplement contributing to the significant awareness increase of 62 per cent of newspaper readers.
    c. To ensure lasting value and public awareness of this resource guide supplement, arrangements were made to have a special bookmarked PDF of the supplement posted on the splash pages of both the *Vancouver Sun/Province* websites with a graphic seniors' icon, as well as other partners' websites. Other cross-promotional efforts included hard-copies of the supplement being sent with a covering letter to all advertisers, key seniors' groups and stakeholders to distribute to their clients/members.
2. Increased public awareness, understanding and support of seniors' housing and care:
    a. The results demonstrated considerable gains from the last supplement with increase in awareness and readership, layout improvements, and support of government.
    b. A survey of 500 of the newspapers' subscribers in Greater Vancouver commissioned by *The Vancouver Sun/Province* immediately following the publication of the supplement indicated a significant increase in awareness of 62 per cent of those polled as compared to 41 per cent in the December 2004 supplement. This survey had a margin of error of plus or minus 4.5 per cent at 95 per cent level of confidence. When this percentage is projected against the total number of the newspapers' subscribers, it equates to 483,102 *adults* in Greater Vancouver where *total* population is about two million. This is compared to about 263,384 readers in the fall of 2004. Furthermore, a total of 15 per cent recalled seeing the Global TV ads.
3. Developed a useful and informative resource guide for seniors:
    a. Based on feedback from two seniors' focus groups, three pages in the front section of the supplement were devoted to resource information, including programs, contacts, eligibility and frequently asked questions. Other pages included informative articles profiling trends and housing and care options in the province. The

survey indicated that about 36 per cent (280,512 readers) spent about 15 minutes on average reading the supplement. This is a significant increase as compared to 21 per cent (143,904 readers) in the fall of 2004. Two-thirds of the readers said they were better informed.

b. Also based on seniors' feedback for this year's supplement, 96 per cent of respondents felt the font size was big enough and easy to read. (This was a key objective for improvement.)

c. About one-third of the respondents kept a copy of the supplement for future reference, or to pass along to someone else. (This was another key objective.)

4. Garnered public support of the provincial government's role and funding of seniors' housing and care:

a. Levels of concern in seniors' housing and care options continue to be high at 92 per cent, consistent with last fall's subscribers' survey.

b. About 92 per cent supported the federal and provincial governments' efforts to fund developments under Independent Living BC.

c. A total of 86 per cent of respondents believe the Independent Living BC program will be very or somewhat beneficial.

5. Involved various governments, health authorities, private and non-profit partners:

a. Generated strong support in the public/private housing and health sectors to advertise in this resource supplement. Based on the list of potential contacts BC Housing provided to the newspapers, they were able to sell all eight pages of advertising space in record time before the closing deadline.

b. There was a good selection of both advertising and editorial content by the partners resulting in a useful publication to seniors and their family care givers. This was the result of detailed editorial planning.

c. Further support from the housing and care sector was measured by the agreement of a number of partners to post a bookmarked version of the supplement PDF on their websites. Partners involved included BC Non-Profit Housing Association, Canadian Home Builders Association of BC, the National Care Guide, Vancouver Coastal Health Authority, Fraser Health Authority, the Canadian Housing Renewal Association, The O'Keefe, Ministry of Health, and Ministry Responsible for Seniors.

Exercises

1. Develop a Risk and Threat analysis for your company or organization.
2. Select a company or organization. Discuss what issues could arise because of their industry or scale. Choose an issue related to this company or organization. Track it online, and monitor chat groups to see how it moves around.
3. Describe an issue that could become an opportunity.

Chapter 13

Avoiding/Preparing for a Crisis and Creating a Plan

One of the major benefits of building and maintaining strong relationships with your key media is that when a crisis strikes these media are much more likely to treat you with fairness and understanding. Still, even the best of relationships will not guarantee that your company or organization receives positive coverage or that the media will minimize the negative coverage. It is crucial to develop a plan to detect, prevent, reduce, and deal with a potential crisis. Management plays a major role in the process of crisis planning, management, response, and recovery.

Chapter Summary

By the end of Chapter 13, you will be able to:

- define a crisis, crisis preparation, and crisis communication;
- know the types and causes of crises;
- understand the key audiences for crises, including internal and external audiences, partners, and media; and
- develop an eight-step crisis preparation strategy.

A crisis management plan should be an essential part of every company or organization's annual business plan; yet most companies do not develop a plan until a crisis has occurred. Even when they create a plan, many organizations forget the most important component—describing the ways they will communicate during a crisis.

According to the *Canadian Oxford Dictionary*, a crisis is 'a turning point. . .a decisive moment'. In terms of media relations, a **crisis** is a major event or occurrence that severely affects a company or organization's ability to operate. A crisis—which can happen suddenly or which can build up over time—can threaten balance, compromise trust, ruin credibility, and destroy reputations. In terms of **crisis preparation**, your goal as a media relations specialist is to recognize and prevent potential threats and risks, and to avoid mistakes and problems associated with crises, whenever possible. In addition, it is important to distinguish between a crisis, a problem, and bad publicity. Many companies and organizations turn a negative or embarrassing story into a crisis simply by overreacting. **Crisis communication**—the visual, written, and verbal interaction between a company or organization and its key markets before, during, and after a crisis—is of key importance throughout a media relations campaign.

Types and Causes of Crises

Some crises provide lead-time, like a hurricane, while others happen without warning (a tornado). There are several different types of crises to consider, such as event-driven crises, issues-driven crises, and litigation-driven crises. **Event-driven crises** include fires, hurricanes, earthquakes, accidents, contamination, workplace accidents, epidemics, droughts, bombs, explosions, leaks, death, product tampering, acts of terrorism, health epidemics, bankruptcy, employee layoffs, strikes, and boycotts. **Issues-driven crises** can include ethical issues, damaging rumours, sexual or racial discrimination, harassment claims, and downsizing/restructuring. In contrast, **litigation-driven crises** are often concerned with corporate lawsuits, product defects and recalls, government probes, trademark disputes, patent infringement, and challenges from activist groups and non-governmental organizations.

Key Audiences Affected by Crises

When developing your crisis management strategy, it is crucial that you consider the key audiences that could be affected by the crisis in question.

- **Internal audiences**
  - Employees and their families
  - Shareholders

- **External audiences**
  - Victims
  - Past and current customers

- ◦ Suppliers
- ◦ Competitors
- ◦ Financial community
- ◦ Government representatives and agencies
- ◦ Sponsors and donors
- ◦ Volunteers
- ◦ Special interest groups
- ◦ Web audience
- ◦ Local, national, and international community
- **Partners**
  - ◦ Organizations
  - ◦ Associations
  - ◦ Government agencies
  - ◦ Corporations
- **Media**
  - ◦ Print
  - ◦ Broadcast
  - ◦ Internet
  - ◦ Newsletters (politicians, associations, corporations, and community)

Create an Eight-step Strategy and Plan for Crisis Preparation

Step #1: Review and critique past crises
- Review past crises in your company or organization, and your industry, to understand where your company is vulnerable.

Step #2: Develop a risk and threat analysis
- Design worst-case scenarios that reflect your risks.
- Categorize these risks by event-driven or issues-driven; preventable/not preventable; internal; external.
- Create an inventory of crisis scenarios.

Step #3: Conduct research with key audiences
- Talk to clients; listen and ask a lot of questions. Identify crisis 'hot spots'.
- Use a variety of research tools, including questionnaires, focus groups, phone calls, e-mail, and online surveys.
- Find out audiences' level of knowledge, understanding, and attitudes towards scenarios that might affect your company or organization.
- Understand how audiences might respond to certain issues or events.
- Define misconceptions and unrealistic expectations.
- Remember to conduct research with employees, since they can be your best ambassadors or worst enemies during a crisis.

Step #4: Create a crisis response team

- Involve key personnel within your company or organization in the process of creating and updating your Crisis Communication Plan. Assign responsibilities for internal and external communication during a crisis.
- The Chief Executive Officer or Executive Director usually heads the team, which includes management personnel, legal counsel, communications experts, and technical experts.
- Keep a list of Crisis Response Team members—with telephone numbers, fax numbers, e-mail addresses, and pagers—easily accessible and up-to-date.
- Remember to double your usual resources for the crisis team.

Step #5: Develop or update your written crisis management/communications plan

- Create a comprehensive plan for crisis management and response planning, training, and simulations.
- Address the *Who, What, When, Where, Why,* and *How Much* of crises.
- Spell out resolutions to vulnerabilities (risks and potential crises).
- Designate one person to be in charge of the plan.
- Include the following components in your Plan:
  - A letter from the CEO or Executive Director, outlining the organization's philosophy on crisis management
  - A list of types of issues or situations that could cause a crisis, with information and background that would be necessary to respond to, and resolve, these potential crises
  - A list of primary and secondary spokespeople, with a directive prohibiting anyone else from talking to media during a crisis
  - A list of key media to be contacted during a crisis, with telephone numbers, e-mail addresses, and fax numbers
  - The most recent Media Kit inserts, including Key Messages
  - A list of emergency contacts, such as nearest hospital, fire department, and police departments
  - A list of public officials who should be informed and kept up-to-date, with office and home telephone numbers
  - A list of key industry and market analysts
  - A preliminary plan explaining how information will be released to the media, from the first steps to follow up
  - An Internet plan that describes how you will use the company's Internet site, Online Media Room, and blogs
  - An Intranet plan for employee communication and e-mail in order to move information to your key markets. You should also include a plan for updating the Intranet to ensure staff are aware of the key spokespeople and how to direct inquiries from external audiences to them

- ◦ A plan for advertising and advertorials
- ◦ A designated budget for crisis management activities
- ◦ A plan for document transfer protocols for your company. Practice transferring articles and documents to HTML and then downloading them to a secure area on the company website.
- ◦ A plan for your web management team, which allocates responsibility for posting information on the site as needed, for monitoring issues and coverage on the Internet related to the crisis, for 'manning' your site's inquiry pages, and for responding to requests for information during the crisis
- • After you have created or updated your plan, practice 'mock' executions of the plan to achieve the results you need during a crisis. Arrange weekly, monthly, and annual practice sessions with employees, including meetings with key executives and spokespeople.

Step #6: Identify and train media spokespeople

- • Designate primary and secondary spokespeople to speak on behalf of your company or organization during a crisis. Include spokespeople with technical and financial expertise, as well as third party sources.
- • Why wait for a crisis to occur before you do media interviews? The earlier you start to train and practice 'what could be asked in a crisis' (as well as the answers), the more prepared your spokespeople will be when under pressure during an actual crisis.
- • The goals of media training are to give spokespeople the tools and techniques to:
  - ◦ be conversational, energetic, natural, and unrehearsed;
  - ◦ take control of interviews;
  - ◦ arrive prepared with Key Messages and facts;
  - ◦ speak clearly and simply; and
  - ◦ explain complicated information in simple language

Step #7: Develop the communications tools you will activate during a crisis
The crisis media kit

- • Fact Sheet, with contact information (including names and titles of spokespeople and security and night telephone numbers)
- • Backgrounder on your organization or company
- • Backgrounders/biographical information on the principals
- • Information on activities of the company or organization, such as services, products, equipment, and research
- • Descriptions of facilities, with layout, square footage, and number of people
- • Statistics and charts
- • Visuals, including photos
- • Statement from the spokesperson about the crisis

The Internet

Turn the Crisis Media Kit into a crisis-ready website that can be activated when needed. This often becomes the hub of the crisis communication team. Your website can become a virtual newsroom or a public focal point for details on crisis events or issues. E-mail can serve as a relatively secure way to exchange and track documents quickly.

The dark site

A 'dark site' is a website that is prepared and ready to 'go live' when a crisis occurs, but that cannot be viewed by the public until then. The site includes all the background information, media release templates, fact sheets, crisis communication plans, images, maps, and links that you will need in a crisis.

PIER Ready Sites operate on the PIER (Public Information Emergency Response) platform; that is, they are designed specifically to enable the crisis communications teams to make full and efficient use of the Internet during a crisis. PIER ReadySites are only available through authorized PIER partners.

Step #8: Test, simulate, and evaluate your crisis communication strategy throughout the year

- Once your strategy is developed, be sure to review it often.
- Gather your crisis communication team together on a regular basis and ensure that the information is up-to-date and relevant.

CASE STUDY

City of Edmonton Flood Prevention Strategy

Who: Godfrey Huybregts, ABC, Marcomm Works; Elaine Trudeau, Public Information Officer–Drainage Services, and Romana Kabalin, Infrastructure Policy Advisor, City of Edmonton

When: September 2004–December 2005

Winner: 2006 IABC International Gold Quill (Customer Relations) and 2006 CPRS Award of Excellence (Communications Management)

Division and Category: 1.3 Communications Management, Customer Relations

Brief description: This project was a communications and consultative process that moved homeowners in 15 residential neighbourhoods from a position of anger and frustration to one of satisfaction and support.

Need/Opportunity

In the first week of July 2004 torrential rainstorms resulted in the flooding of a record 4,000+ homes in Edmonton, a city of 700,000 in Alberta, Canada. Flooded streets, sidewalks, parks and yards were commonplace in 15 neighbourhoods hardest hit by the storms. The 15,000 homeowners and 60,000 people living in these neighbourhoods were negatively affected by the flooding, some incurring tens of thousands of dollars in damage.

Insurance and a provincial disaster relief program compensated most people for damages but residents believed much of the flooding could have been prevented by an adequate municipal drainage system. The City was accused of poor planning and maintenance and placing citizens unnecessarily at risk. More than 600 people expressed their anger and frustration at three information meetings held in September 2004. Hundreds of others expressed similar emotions through letters and phone calls to the City and media. Residents and City Councillors from the affected wards demanded a quick resolution from the Drainage Services Branch, which is responsible for the City's 32,000 kilometres of storm and sanitary sewers.

Surveys completed by flooded homeowners, visual inspections by Drainage Services staff and engineering reviews completed by December 2004 showed the majority of the flooding was caused by poor lot grading, disconnected drainpipes and faulty or non-existent sewer line valves on residential properties. The studies also showed some municipal sewer lines lacked sufficient capacity to carry floodwaters away. Research made it evident that the 15 hardest hit neighbourhoods are at risk of severe flooding in the future but that reducing the risk would require a joint effort by homeowners and the City.

Godfrey Huybregts, ABC, Partner and Senior Consultant with Marcomm Works was contracted by Romana Kabalin, Communications Business Partner with Asset Management and Public Works in late 2004 to work with her, City Public Information Officer Elaine Trudeau and Drainage Services staff to develop and implement a communications plan. A plan was needed to support Drainage Services desire to work with neighbourhoods and other stakeholders to implement viable solutions to improve flood prevention.

Target audiences
External

- The 16,500 homeowners who live in the affected neighbourhoods. Most of the neighbourhoods are 30 years of age or older. Most homeowners have lived in their homes for more than 10 years.
- The other 16,000 adults living with a homeowner in a single family home and condominium in the affected neighbourhoods. There is an even gender mix with an age range of 30–80 years. There is no language or cultural barrier to communications. However, this target group knows little or nothing about the municipal drainage system and has only minimal knowledge about the drainage system on his or her property.
- Community League presidents and their Boards in affected neighbourhoods.
- Edmonton Public School Board and Edmonton Catholic School Board, as well as principals of schools in the flooded areas.
- City of Edmonton media, especially City Hall reporters.
- Business and community leaders in the flooded areas.

Internal
- Drainage Services staff.
- General Manager, Asset Management and Public Works.
- The Mayor and 12 members of City Council, in particular the six councillors from the three most heavily impacted wards.
- City of Edmonton Community Services staff responsible for community league liaison, outdoor sports facilities and parks in the flooded neighbourhoods.
- City Manager and other members of the City's Senior Management Team.

Goals and Objectives
Goal
- Engage concerned citizens and other stakeholders in affected neighbourhoods in a manner that results in their support and involvement in viable flood prevention solutions.

Objectives
1. Gain the support of 80% or more of residents in affected neighbourhoods for a Drainage Services' system improvement plan prior to Drainage Services seeking financial approval from City Council.
2. Achieve 90% satisfaction levels for educational programs.
3. Convince the majority of homeowners with flooding issues to take action on their own properties to reduce the risk of flooding.
4. Gain approval from City Council for Drainage Services' implementation plan.

Solution Overview
Interface with target audiences through questionnaires, meetings, focus groups, phone calls and emails in the fall of 2004 showed there was a general lack of understanding and knowledge about how the drainage system works, the connection between surface flooding and sewer backup, and the important contribution private property flood proofing makes to overall drainage efficiency. This resulted in misconceptions or unrealistic expectations of what the City can and cannot do to prevent flooding.

Residents wanted to be informed and involved in resolving flooding problems. They also harboured some mistrust that the City would act quickly and decisively. It was determined that an integrated communications approach with public education and public consultation components was needed to raise the level of education, shift public opinion, mobilize homeowners to take action on their property, and secure public support for flood prevention solutions.

Key messages included:

- Flood prevention is a top priority for Drainage Services.
- Drainage Services is committed to working collaboratively to develop and implement viable solutions that work for all stakeholders.
- Reducing the flood risk requires a joint effort between homeowners and the City.

The first challenge was to facilitate additional input and build communications bridges for information, consultation and educational needs. A stakeholder database composed of individuals who wrote letters, signed petitions, attended open houses, sent emails or made telephone contact was developed and used to make direct mail contact with concerned citizens. An information bulletin was produced and distributed to people on this database and other key stakeholders.

A part of the City's website (www.edmonton.ca/floodprevention) was dedicated to the flood prevention program to allow for a 'one stop' source of information for interested individuals. Community League presidents in affected communities were surveyed and asked for their advice and interest in being information conduits to local residents. An advertising feature was placed in Community League newspapers that covered affected areas. The same information was reformatted and provided for attachment to Community League newsletters in affected areas.

These communication vehicles were used to develop communication links, begin the educational process and advertise consultative sessions with residents in the spring of 2005. Nine meetings were held in March and April of 2005 for residents in the 15 affected neighbourhoods (neighbourhoods were grouped into one meeting where studies showed commonality of problems). These meetings shared engineering findings, laid out various options and got residents' input, comments and options with the 480 people who attended. This input, additional study and feedback from Community Leagues, School Boards and others was absorbed and incorporated into a proposed implementation plan. This implementation plan was presented to residents at subsequent consultation sessions in November 2005.

In April 2005, the flood prevention program was branded with the word mark *Floodproof!* This was incorporated into all public awareness materials, the bulk of which were launched as part of a summer long promotional campaign in May 2005. Components included television and newspaper advertising, postal drop postcards and flyers, a media kit and tip sheets. Edmonton television station Global TV was the major media partner.

To deal with core information and education gaps among homeowners, the communications plan recommended two new programs be created. The first was the *Home Flood Prevention Check-up Program*. This was a new, free service for any residential homeowner in Edmonton who wanted a drainage specialist to come to their home for a one-on-one drainage evaluation and assessment. This program was launched in May 2005. A 32-page self-help booklet called *"Homeowner's Guide to Flood Prevention"* was produced in support of this program.

The second was a series of educational workshops hosted by a college plumbing instructor on a specific home drainage element. The first topic chosen (based on homeowner demand) was on backwater valves.

Implementation and Challenges

The project budget was $250,000. Approximately $100,000 of this went to operate the *Home Flood Prevention Check-up Program*. The remainder was spent on advertising, graphic design, printing, distribution and contract fees. Substantial savings were realized from the media partnership with Global TV, advertorial discounts in newspapers, and inserts in community newsletters. The approach to Community Leagues at the beginning of the communications process garnered considerable cooperation in communicating information to neighbourhood residents.

The communications plan was completed in November 2004 with the first wave of communications to resident occurring before Christmas. Information bulletins, special features in newspapers and newsletters, web updates, and contact with Community League presidents have continued on a regular basis since then. The first consultation sessions were held in March and April of 2005, with a second wave in November 2005. A promotional campaign was launched in May 2005 in advance of Edmonton's flood season. To maximize dollars, a three-week spike of ad placement was done instead of spreading it out through the summer. This was supplemented during the summer with editorial placement and media contacts. The *Home Flood Prevention Check-up Program* operated from May to October of 2005.

A take-over bid for Drainage Services by a major private utility company in the summer of 2005 caused considerable disruption to Drainage Services' flood prevention work plans. This caused a two-month delay in getting back to residents on implementation recommendations (this did not occur until November 2005). Strategic scheduling of the education workshops in July and September of 2005, an October 2005 newsletter, and a September 2005 promotion of an enhanced City subsidy for backwater valve installation ensured stakeholders did not feel a communications vacuum during this delay period.

Evaluation

All of the objectives were achieved. Surveys show that:

- 53% of residents in the affected neighbourhoods recalled seeing or hearing information about flood prevention. Forty-two per cent of these individuals said this prompted them to make changes to their home to reduce their risk of flooding.
- 93% agreed or strongly agreed information provided by Drainage Services would help them resolve their property's drainage problems and encourage them to take action to improve and maintain good drainage.
- 97% agree or strongly agree that offering information and educational programs and services such as *Floodproof!* to help homeowners is appropriate for the City of Edmonton.
- 96% of backwater valve educational workshop attendees said it met their expectations.
- 98% of *Home Flood Prevention Check-up* program participants believe it is a valuable public service.
- 90% agree or strongly agree that the City should make improvements in drainage systems where flooding has been a problem.

Focus groups showed:
- Reaction to *Floodproof!* communications materials was positive.
- Homeowners understand and accept that flood prevention in their homes is their responsibility. They accept that there is a shared responsibility among homeowners and the City to prevent flooding and work together for an efficient system.
- Most homeowners see value in the City of Edmonton continuing the *Floodproof!* program. It is viewed as a public service by some and as a duty of the City by others.

In addition:
- Approximately 400 people attended the six educational workshops offered in July and September of 2005.
- The *Home Flood Prevention Check-up Program* was oversubscribed in a month. Extra staff had to be added to handle the demand, which exceeded estimates by 25%.
- Many homeowners have asked to be informed when the presentation to City Council on funding for flood prevention work will take place so they can be in attendance to show their support.
- Community Leagues, School Boards and others impacted by recommended plans have provided their approval in principle.
- The vast majority of consultation participants at the November 2005 sessions have indicated their support of Drainage Services improvement plans for their neighbourhoods. More than 2,500 people are on the *Floodproof!* distribution list.

The $110 million implementation plan will be presented to City Council for approval in April 2006. It is expected funding for the plan will be approved, as six City Councillors from the three most heavily impacted wards have expressed satisfaction to date with the process and have been informed of residents' wishes and expectations.

Exercises

1. Provide examples of problems, negative publicity, and crises. Discuss the differences.
2. Describe the Crisis Communications' team you would create before a crisis. Who would it include and why?
3. Develop a written Crisis Communications' Plan and include the steps you would take to deal with the crisis in your company or organization.
4. Create five questions you wish the media would not ask during your crisis (and that they probably will ask). Develop answers for the questions.
5. Discuss how you could turn a crisis into an opportunity.

Chapter 14

Crisis Communication and Management

With contributions from Kim Taylor Galway,
Perfect 10 Communications*

The true test of how well you have prepared for a crisis can be seen in how success-fully you communicate, manage, and recover from a crisis. This chapter provides information on how to stay focused from beginning to end. A well-handled crisis will actually enhance the reputation and credibility of your company or organization.

Chapter Summary

By the end of Chapter 14, you will be able to:

- define crisis management;
- know what your goals should be when a crisis occurs;
- understand the concerns, interests, and needs of the media; and
- understand the five stages of crisis communication and know how to manage each stage.

*Kim Taylor Galway, Perfect 10 Communications
Website: www.kimtaylor.ca
E-mail: kimtaylorgalway@rogers.com

All companies and organizations are vulnerable to crises. When a crisis does occur, you've got to get your story out—especially when your efforts may be carefully scrutinized and your company may be mistrusted. The first few minutes—and the first 24 hours—are crucial in deciding the public and media perception of your company or organization. This is your 'window of opportunity'. This is when a Crisis Management Plan (described in Chapter 13) is invaluable. **Crisis management** is a series of activities that are designed to minimize the damage related to a crisis, and it is easier to implement an established, well-designed plan when a crisis occurs than to create one on the spot.

In addition, a number of elements add a sense of urgency to crisis communications today. Blogs, picture and video sharing, and the ease of online publishing mean that information about your company or organization can be spread with an unprecedented speed. The advent of 24-hour cable news, the Internet, increased competition for media attention, media competition to break news, and the media's attraction to drama and conflict all contribute to an intense setting for crises.

The speed with which you recognize, respond, and emerge from a crisis can make a critical difference to the long-term success of your company or organization. Once a crisis occurs, it is important to take a systematic, open approach to dealing with the media. Always keep your short-term and long-term goals in sight.

Your Goals When a Crisis Occurs

- To position sensitive situations
- To manage difficult news
- To divert the negative impact
- To deliver your Key Messages as accurately and as often as possible
- To minimize financial and reputation damage
- To show caring, concern, and empathy
- To convey your values and beliefs
- To gain control
- To preserve your reputation
- To restore the status quo
- To build goodwill
- To regain lost sales and prevent market erosion

The Concerns, Interests, and Needs of the Media

Since their job is to educate and inform the public, media seek answers to their questions when a crisis occurs. If you are not open and available, they will obtain the

IABC Survey: Only 67 Per cent of Companies Prepared for the Next Crisis, Crisis communication plans found to be critical to businesses in 2005, but not yet widespread

San Francisco, CA – 23 February 2006   Despite a year of natural disasters and organizational crises, only two in three companies are prepared to manage and respond to the next crisis that affects them, according to a recent survey conducted by the International Association of Business Communicators (IABC). The survey also reports strong support for crisis communication plans: An overwhelming 99 per cent of respondents who had crisis plans found them to be effective in dealing with crises in 2005. Additionally, if a crisis occurred tomorrow, 80 per cent of respondents said implementing a crisis communication plan would help limit the overall negative impact on business.

According to the IABC survey of over 600 communicators, one in three companies did not have a formal crisis communication plan in 2005. After experiencing a crisis with no plans in place, 46 per cent of respondents said their organizations were beginning to develop crisis communication plans, while 42 per cent said their organizations were still taking no action. Of the communicators who work in organizations without crisis communication plans, 54 per cent said they didn't have plans because of lack of senior management support.

The crisis communication survey was conducted by Robert Holland, ABC, owner of Holland Communication Solutions LLC, and Katrina Gill, president and founder of Gill Research LLC, in collaboration with the IABC Research Foundation.

According to Holland, 'Communicators who seek a more strategic role in their organizations often find it difficult to link their work with critical business functions. Organizational crises—not just natural disasters, but also events such as leadership transitions and sudden market changes—provide opportunities for communicators to demonstrate their value with skills in planning as well as tactical execution.'

The survey reported that 69 per cent of the organizations that had crisis communication plans, implemented these plans in response to crisis events in 2005. Almost all respondents who had crisis communication plans found them to be effective (66 per cent cited plans as 'very effective' and 33 per cent as 'somewhat effective') in responding to crisis situations.

'These results add further evidence of two trends: Communicators today are approaching their work with more business discipline, and internal communication is increasingly viewed as an important business function,' said Gill.

For more information, contact Katrina Gill, Gill Research, LLC, Office: 773-857-7797, Mobile: 312-860-1314, katrina@gillresearch.com, www.gillresearch.com

information they need from other sources, and that information is often incomplete or incorrect. Therefore, it is important to prepare your answers to media questions as truthfully and completely as possible, throughout the course of the crisis.

Five Stages of Crisis Communication

Stage #1: The warning signs and how to prepare
- Track trends and issues, both on and off the Internet.
- Monitor the blogosphere; many crises are born and nurtured there. Blogs and bloggers are also key ways to deliver information during a crisis.
- Conduct primary research to understand what key audiences think about a crisis situation and how they think a company or organization should respond. Find out what they care about.
- Use this information to prepare Key Messages that address their wants and needs.

Stage #2: What to do when a crisis occurs
18 action tools
1. Understand the type of crisis and its severity.
2. Move forward in good faith to resolve the crisis.
3. Bring your Crisis Communications Team onsite.
4. Create a Media Communication Centre, at or near the scene in a safe, appropriate location. Include laptops, a printer, fact sheets, backgrounders, bios, Annual Reports, brochures, statistics, media releases, quotes from principals, visuals, daily summaries, and news briefs.
5. Establish a telephone number for media inquiries and ensure staff and partners know the number.
6. Set up a media message area and establish a file of incoming media requests, deadlines, and Key Messages relevant to their stories.
7. Coordinate media pool activities and photography session.
8. Prepare your spokesperson.
9. Evaluate the information you have, confirm the facts, and decide what you can do to improve the situation.
10. Activate your Crisis Management Plan.
11. Communicate internally first, through e-mail, Intranet, emergency phone trees, toll-free crisis lines, instant messaging, or face-to-face announcements. Get to your employees before the media do.
12. Ensure your employees understand exactly what has happened. They can be your biggest allies or your greatest detractors.
13. Be the first to deliver the news—good and bad. Then concentrate on the solution.

14. Respond to key media within two hours, if possible.

15. Carefully craft a statement to read or send to media that includes four things: acknowledgement of the crisis, concern and empathy for the people who have been affected, details of what you can confirm and what you don't know so far, and your plans for moving forward.

16. Supply media with experts who can speak on your behalf as quickly as possible, including financial, technical, and environmental experts. Outside resources provide credibility.

17. Use the Internet as a fast, potent, cost-effective communication tool for key markets.

18. Create a video clip and sound clip for your CEO or company spokesperson to make a statement. Broadcasters can download and use the sound clip. For the general public, the broadcast clip provides an opportunity to see and hear directly from your organization. These clips can also be linked to updated text and downloadable photos, charts, and background material.

What to Talk About Initially

- Thank partners, employees, and other key markets.
- Choose succinct and descriptive words wisely and ahead of time. Strong Key Messages are rarely 'born on the fly'.
- Talk about the process.
- Leave technical jargon out of the interviews
- Avoid broad-brush stroke statements that you can't back up with statistics or factual descriptions.
- Don't say 'no comment'. It is important to get your story to the media and the public in order to avoid rumours and mistrust.

When media contact you—and you aren't ready

- Thank them for calling.
- Document their needs.
- Request their format preference.
- Find out their deadlines.
- Ask what information they are looking for specifically.
- Find out who they have spoken to already.
- Tell them you need time to get answers (and tell them when you will get back to them).
- Set up a time and place for an interview.
- Ask if there is anything else they need.
- Update their contact information.

When you don't respond to media requests, you instantly lose credibility with the media and the general public. You want to address the bad news right away, so that you can concentrate on the solution.

Stage #3: As the crisis unfolds
20 things to remember
1. Decide what is to be said and how to say it.
2. Apologize, when appropriate.
3. List your process, procedure, and policies.
4. Draw upon your record and statistics.
5. Use active language: done, doing, will do.
6. Avoid personal opinion, speculation, unconfirmed information, blame, and topics outside your areas of expertise.
7. Take and maintain control of an interview.
8. Project empathy and openness.
9. Use word pictures, narrative, and description in your interviews.
10. Listen to the question and don't answer what you thought you heard. If you are not sure about a question, ask to have it clarified.
11. Tell the truth, even if it hurts.
12. Take positive action and remain upbeat in your attitude.
13. Find out the media's deadlines, promise to get back to them, and follow up.
14. Don't exaggerate with overly optimistic claims, denials, and half-truths.
15. Unqualified denial creates the impression of guilt.
16. Don't repeat negative words and phrases.
17. If you cannot respond or it is inappropriate to do so, provide a reason.
18. Nothing is 'off the record'. Think of everything you say as appearing in four-inch-high headlines.
19. Refer all inquiries related to an investigation to the external authorities involved.
20. Correct inaccurate information immediately.

Stage #4: Throughout the crisis
Select the best tools to communicate with the media, including:

- press briefings and media conferences;
- your website and partners' websites;
- blogs;
- written statements;
- telephone interviews and updates;
- media releases, video news releases, and media advisories;
- conference calls;

- answering machine messages;
- desk side chats; and
- faxes.

Track and document everything

- Monitor news coverage and/or hire a media monitoring/Internet media monitoring service.
- Document all calls and conversations with the media, including names and titles, media outlet, telephone number, and nature of the call.
- Keep a daily log of all events, printed materials distributed, and action taken.

Organize news conferences during a crisis

- Arrange and monitor all aspects of formal and informal news conferences, including supplies, props, and technical support. Audiotape and videotape the news conferences and send information to media who could not attend.

Stage #5: Crisis recovery and evaluation

- Implement recovery initiatives for your company or organization.
- Collect all media releases, articles, electronic coverage, and Internet coverage.
- Archive print, electronic, and Internet media reports.
- Analyze media content, Key Messages, and media coverage.
- Organize a debriefing and summarize the crisis in the company newsletter.
- Prepare post-emergency communications to deliver to the media.
- Prepare a full report on the handling of the crisis and make recommendations for your Crisis Management Plan. Review the report with key management.
- Answer the following questions:
  - How did you behave?
  - How effective was your Crisis Management Plan?
  - Did you emerge as a company or organization that acted fairly and openly during the crisis?
  - Did you build goodwill?
  - Continue to review and modify your strategies, guidelines, and policies throughout the year, based on what you have learned.

CASE STUDY

Blue Nose International Marathon 2005

Entrant's Name: Sarah Young/Blue Nose Marathon Public Relations Committee
Organization's Name: Blue Nose International Marathon and MT&L Public Relations
Division/Category: External Communications—Issues/Crisis Management
Title: Outrunning a Storm: Blue Nose International Marathon Triumphs Over Weather 'Bomb'
Time Period of Project: January–May 2005

Need/Opportunity

Launched in the spring of 2004, the Blue Nose International Marathon was an instant success, attracting runners and walkers of all activity levels from across Canada and the United States. Although triumphant, organizers of this non-profit, volunteer-run marathon realized that a second successful year was essential to ensuring the event a place on the runner's calendar.

Building on the framework of the first year's event, exhaustive preparations by the marathon's 2005 public relations committee included in-depth research and analysis of potential crisis scenarios, culminating in a comprehensive crisis contingency plan.

Participant profiles for the 2005 Blue Nose International Marathon included existing runners and first-time runners with the goals of undertaking a new physical endeavor. Marathons in Canada are generally run in the spring and fall to avoid extreme weather conditions that come with winter and summer. Regardless of poor weather conditions, there is always a risk of injury. Some recent high-profile marathons have experienced runner deaths or injury, including Toronto, Boston, and Big Sur in California. Medical concerns surrounding long-distance running include hydration, dehydration, heat illnesses, and finish line injuries. Running on streets open to vehicular traffic and lined with spectators was identified as another potential source of injury and issue.

Just 24 hours before race day, with over 5,000 participants and countless officials set to attend, a weather 'bomb' of unexpected proportions took Halifax by surprise, whipping the area with wind gusts of 56 km/h accompanied by 70 millimetres of rain. At 4:30 am on race day, an emergency meeting was called. SportsStat officials (the timekeepers for the event who travel to marathons around the world) advised that cancellation or postponement of the event would put the future of the marathon in jeopardy. At 6:30 am, in consultation with police and bridge officials, a decision was made to continue with the event, underscored by the need for immediate and seamless crisis intervention.

Target Audiences

- Registered runners of the Blue Nose International Marathon
- City and safety officials in Halifax Regional Municipality (HRM), including Police and Fire, EMS Ambulance and Hospital, Halifax/Dartmouth Bridge Commission, and HRM officials

- Blue Nose volunteers, including logistic and race operations chairs and committees, and marathon co-chairs
- Media, including print and broadcast media in Halifax and Nova Scotia
- Runners' families and friends, and spectators

Goals and Objectives

Goals

- To continue to build the reputation of the Blue Nose International Marathon as the 'people's marathon'
- To deliver a safe and successful event for 2005 and to positively position the event for future years

Objectives

- To prepare communications in the event of an issue or crisis during race weekend
- To integrate communications with operations and logistics responses in the event of an issue
- To assist appropriate agencies with any potential communications surrounding incidents or crises
- To ensure the event and its sponsors are shielded from negative publicity and to minimize any impact of issues on the event, participants, volunteers, and spectators
- To communicate effectively with media in advance of the event and, in the event of an issue or crisis, to give context of the issue with respect to the overall event

Solution Overview

In the lead-up to the event, concerns were identified and addressed proactively to avoid potential crisis situations arising on event weekend. The PR committee focused on ensuring that all groups were contacted prior to event weekend to ensure that the lines of communication were open. Although a key role of the PR committee was runner recruitment, the committee also attempted to identify and mitigate potential issues. Concerns were identified surrounding the route, specifically with the event route going through Point Pleasant Park, an issue that was resolved by responding to the needs of the city, parks department, and the community group 'Friends of Point Pleasant Park'.

Businesses, churches, and residents along the route were also contacted and notified of potential impacts. The community at large was notified of potential traffic implications. Runners received regular updates via e-mail, notifying them of the importance of training, hydration, and preparation for the event and identifying prime spectating locations for their friends and families. Volunteers attended training sessions, and the media was briefed via a series of media memos, identifying locations, event routes, and potential story ideas. Bridge, fire, and police officials as well as regional councilors were kept informed with update memos and information about the event and its impacts. Regular e-mail contact, the media, and the Blue Nose Marathon website were established as primary sources of information about the event.

During the first year's event, the PR committee worked to ensure that organizing committee members understood the importance of the role of communications in the race infrastructure. During the lead-up to the event, the public relations committee carefully monitored every aspect of the race's operations in an effort to ensure that potential issues were resolved before they became problems. Committee members were made aware of the importance of proactively notifying and consulting communications of any issue or potential issue as it occurred.

In preparation for the event weekend itself, a comprehensive crisis contingency plan was developed. The plan included weekend contact information for bridge, fire, police and municipal officials, a comprehensive media list, holding statements, and identified spokespersons and potential scenarios for the event weekend. In the week prior to the event, HRM officials and health officials were contacted to confirm emergency contact information and protocol. On Friday, May 20, an onsite media centre was established whereupon media centre volunteers were briefed, assigned roles, and informed about the importance of identifying any potential issue and notifying the media spokespersons. The media centre was equipped with laptops, a printer, and was located near a wireless 'hotspot' to enable releases to be issued to media 'on the spot' after each event. Extensive media outreach had also taken place leading up to the event to distribute information and stories and key contact and operational information in advance of the weekend, and so the PR team had identified which media would be covering the event.

Key Messages

Key messages were developed as part of the crisis plan and customized on race day to fit the specifics of the crisis.

Crisis messages from crisis plan

- The Blue Nose International Marathon, as the people's marathon, is set up to encourage participation and involvement from as many people as possible, regardless of running ability.
- The organizing committee has taken every precaution to ensure the safety of all runners, volunteers and spectators on course to make the enjoyment and excitement of the event as inclusive as possible.
- We will certainly review all aspects of this year's event, especially where safety is concerned to look for ways to improve the event in the future.

Messages in response to actual crisis

- Despite the weather, the Blue Nose Marathon will take place today.
- Blue Nose Marathon officials are working closely together with HRM officials to ensure a safe experience for all participants.
- Officials and volunteers and HRM officials overcame significant obstacles to deliver a safe and first-class experience for runners of the Blue Nose Marathon.
- Runners, volunteers, and spectators showed true Maritime tenacity by conquering unusual and severe weather conditions.

Implementation and Challenges

Once the decision was made to go ahead with the marathon (an hour later and on a modified route), the principal strategy was to remain focused on the event and not the weather. The second strategy was to move the start/finish area from its original location on Brunswick Street to inside the city's stadium, the Metro Centre, allowing runners to stay warm and dry until the actual start of the race. The onsite media centre was also relocated to the Metro Centre. The challenge then became communicating these changes to stakeholders within a three-hour timeframe.

With an additional hour before race time, the logistics committee was able to re-mark the route, pump the flooded streets, and distribute supplies to volunteer stations along the route. Runners and spectators needed to be redirected to new locations and the general public needed to be informed of the change in traffic implications. Broadcast and print media with a 'live body' on early morning Sunday were identified in order to report the changes on air and continue with updates of the most current information. The PR team began rolling out revised messaging, positioning the event as 'continuing despite the weather and overcoming the obstacles'.

The webmaster was immediately provided with updated information for the front page of the Blue Nose Marathon site and the PR chair was stationed at the Metro Centre to oversee operations. Meanwhile, a marathon chair took centre stage to provide assembled runners with updates, including the message to 'contact friends to tell them the event was delayed'. Signs were posted on each door of the Metro Centre (which covers four city blocks) and all associated answering machines were updated with the appropriate information.

Other tactics to communicate the changes within the timeframe included:

- *Role and responsibility implementation*: Following the full organizing committee meeting, the logistics, operations, and PR chairs confirmed roles and next steps for outreach to stakeholders. Logistics would work with volunteers to get routes established, operations would maintain contact with police and bridge officials, and PR would communicate changes to runners and media.
- *Media outreach*: Media volunteers began contacting local broadcast newsrooms to distribute the messages that the event would prevail and logistics changes. A media advisory was faxed to local newsrooms.
- *Spokespeople*: As outlined in the plan, the PR chair recommended one of the co-chairs remain at the Metro Centre to oversee operations and be available to media (both co-chairs were scheduled to participate).
- *Onsite announcements*: The marathon chairs, who had been official media spokespeople during the lead-up to the event, took to the stage of the centre and provided the assembling runners with updates, including the message to 'contact friends to tell them the event is delayed'.
- *Telephone tree*: The chair of the team relay committee, who had established contacts with each team relay captain, called each team to notify them of the delay, and

of the re-formulation of the team relay route Announcements were also made in the Metro Centre to encourage anyone that knew other runners planning on participating to call them and let them know of the changes.

During the event, designated media vehicles staffed with pre-trained media volunteers took reporters and photographers onto the route, and staff used a list of pre-developed ideas to ensure that the human-interest stories surrounding the marathon were the main focus.

Media relation's activities focused on the message that 'despite the weather, the event goes on.' A significant effort was made by the media relations team to ensure that the runners, the event, and the significant effort and accomplishment required by organizers and volunteers to respond to the conditions, and not the damage caused by the weather, became the focal point of the stories. As one journalist from an international running magazine who travels to marathons throughout the world stated, 'I've only seen conditions worse than this once—and that was in Antarctica', so the focus on allowing the weather to triumph over the event was significant. Calls were made to broadcast media with regular updates live from the event.

The PR team recognized it was a long day for media to remain in the Metro Centre (winners of the marathon would finish several hours later). Media centre volunteers were redeployed in the Metro Centre to provide assistance to media seeking story ideas or to interview participants. The chair of race operations was briefed as a spokesperson and made available to media to outline the complex undertaking of re-routing the event with its safety and logistics considerations. The chair of PR, logistics and operations regularly conferred to review updates and any required follow up to mitigate any issues. Further liaison with the Chief Medical Officer addressed any occurring concerns.

Evaluation

Despite the extremely inclement weather conditions, over 85% of registered runners participated in the event. (Typically there is a 5%–10% 'no show' of attendees on race day.) At the outset of the day, although SportsStats had recommended proceeding with the event, they had predicted that participation would be less than 30% given the conditions.

On May 23, over 95% of articles appearing in print and broadcast media carried the message that 'despite the weather, the marathon was a success' and a tribute to Maritime tenacity. In the province's largest major daily paper, *The Chronicle Herald*, an entire page of the editorial section was filled with positive feedback from runners, family members and visitors.

The organizing committee received over 100 e-mails and letters from runners heralding the success of the event despite the weather conditions. In addition to accolades from participants, The Running Room's president and founder recognized the organization saying: 'Your team rallied under some incredible conditions, adapting to the challenges and presenting all runners and walkers with a very classy event. Wind, rain, sinkholes, road closures, and the many challenges did not deter your dynamic team. The positive atmosphere exuded by your leadership group and the change to the indoor venue was sheer brilliance. Having attended several hundred marathons I have seen the good, the bad, and the ugly. Your team was without a doubt the very best! ...Truly a classy event staged by a first class group of individuals.'

Media feedback was extremely appreciative of the effort made by the PR team. For example, an e-mail from the sports editor of the *Chronicle Herald*: 'Just wanted to drop you a note to say what a great job I thought you did on Sunday (and before) under wacky conditions. You kept your head and allowed us to get the job done. Hope you'll be back next year with better weather.'

In total, more than 5,000 runners participated over the course of the weekend. Thousands of volunteers—both inside the Metro Centre and outside in the rain—and runners from across Nova Scotia, every Canadian province, and 11 US states came together to participate in the event. Registration for the 2006 event exceeded previous years.

SARS in Canada and the Media

A few months after the 2003 severe acute respiratory syndrome (SARS) outbreak, a sample of Canadian undergraduate university students completed a questionnaire that showed that, despite believing media coverage of the outbreak was excessive, they had little anxiety about acquiring SARS. Additionally, 69% of participants failed a SARS-specific knowledge section of the questionnaire.

The 2003 outbreak of severe acute respiratory syndrome (SARS) underlined the importance of fast and accurate risk communication to the public. Several studies have attempted to evaluate the media's performance during the outbreak and the general consensus is that the media coverage was excessive, sometimes inaccurate, and sensationalist. Whether this excessive coverage had a beneficial or detrimental effect on the public remains unknown. A logical assumption would be that, in response, the public would not only have high anxiety of acquiring SARS, but also would be more informed about the cause, symptoms, and other aspects associated with the syndrome. The purpose of this study was to determine, in an undergraduate university student population, preferences and use of various types of mass communication media, anxiety levels of acquiring the infection, and general knowledge of SARS. . . .

Conclusions

Mass communication media are valuable resources for efficiently communicating risk information to the public. However, extensive collaboration among public health departments and media outlets is essential to deliver health information to all sectors of society. During the SARS outbreak, a deficient communi-

continued

cation strategy among national and international public health agencies led to conflicting messages that created confusion and uncertainty in both the media and the general public. In reporting the events as they unfolded, the media communicated this confusion to the public. This study was undertaken only 5 to 8 months after the last known viral transmission and sampled a particular sector of the population, young students attending a university in southern Ontario, 105 km from Toronto, the epicentre of the outbreak in Canada.

Most participants reported access to and use of several forms of media; the Internet as the most used, followed by television and radio. Newspaper and magazines were the least popular, which suggests that these forms of media are less appealing to young populations.

Overall knowledge about the cause, transmission, symptoms, and treatment associated with SARS was very low for this population. As expected, knowledge was higher among health majors but was not associated with any other variable. However, Internet use seemed to increase baseline SARS knowledge. A possible explanation for this observation is that, in contrast with television and radio, in which passive communication occurs, the Internet requires more participation, attention, and information processing as the user must search and choose to read the information. For a young population that prefers the Internet, this medium could be a great tool for delivering health messages.

When anxiety levels of acquiring SARS were assessed, the results did not support the assumption that the media created anxiety in this young population. The only predictors of high anxiety levels were sex (women) and area of residence in the greater Toronto area. Although anxiety levels for older age groups have not been studied, this finding may suggest that younger persons have different perceptions of health risks and that health messages should be designed with these differences in mind.

In summary, this study showed that predetermined assumptions did not hold true for a young population. Despite believing that media coverage had been overdone, they reported low anxiety of acquiring SARS and showed poor knowledge of this emerging infectious disease. . . . The discrepancy between the amount and type of information dispersed by the media and what was actually absorbed by the young population suggests that mere exposure to copious information is not enough to strengthen knowledge or elicit feelings that would induce persons to modify behaviour.

Excerpted from S.L. Bergeron and A.L. Sanchez, 'Media effects on students during SARS outbreak', *Emerging Infectious Diseases* 11, 5 (2005): 732–4. Available at http://www.cdc.gov/ncidod/EID/vol11no05/04-0512.htm.

Exercises

1. Imagine your worst case, but very possible, scenario for the position you hold now.
   a. What issue would draw the media to you like flies? Give this issue/crisis a title:
      Crisis Title:
      Your Name:
      Your Title During Crisis:
   b. What are the three greatest challenges to your role in the earliest stages of this crisis?
   c. What kind of information is likely to be missing and is going to make this issue tough for you to deal with early on? List what would be missing in the beginning.
   d. What would the public want/need to know most in the first 24 hours?
   e. What kind of reporter questions would you hope not get asked in the first 24 hours?
   f. List some things you could tell the media in the first 24 hours. *(This exercise was designed by Kim Taylor Galway, Perfect 10 Communications.)*
2. Create and describe a situation where a company cannot communicate as freely as it would like to during a crisis.

Appendix
Media Relations Past and Present

Creating media exposure for a company, product, or event is not a new idea, although the techniques for doing so have become more sophisticated. Today, mass media have evolved and expanded into a vast array of choices. In order to appreciate the evolution, it is important to study the history of publicity and its early practitioners, who defined many of the key principles used today. It is also key to understand the issues that are influencing media relations in the twenty-first century.

The Origins of the Mass Media

For more than two centuries before the introduction of radio and television, newspapers were the primary means of communicating information to the public. Starting in the 1700s, they became a major political force in North America—particularly in the US, where newspapers shaped public opinion leading up to the Revolutionary War. But it was not until the early part of the nineteenth century that advances in printing technology (as well as the growth of literacy) made newspapers a true mass medium. While they had previously been affordable only for the elite, newspapers became a cheap (typically a penny per copy) source of information and entertainment for everyone. The result was that from 1850, when just over 2,500 titles were published, the number of newspapers in America grew to more than 11,300 by 1880. Shortly thereafter, the larger daily papers were posting circulation figures in excess of 1 million copies.

Discovering the Power of the Press

With their unparalleled growth during the 1800s, newspapers made substantial fortunes—not only for their owners (such as William Randolph Hearst), but also for a number of enterprising individuals who recognized the power of the press to generate publicity. Among these was Phineas Taylor (P.T.) Barnum, perhaps best known for his circus, which he famously described as 'The Greatest Show on Earth'.

Barnum understood the importance of capturing the media's attention by staging newsworthy events. To promote one of his shows, he hitched an elephant to a plough and set to work on a field that just happened to be near a well-travelled railway line. It wasn't long before his publicity stunt gained nationwide attention from the press.

Barnum's genius for engaging the media helped to make him extremely rich. In a letter written shortly before his death in 1891, he acknowledged, 'I am indebted to the press of the United States for almost every dollar which I possess.'

P.T. Barnum: Patron Saint of Promoters

While best known for the circus, which still bears his name, P.T. Barnum was already famous when, at age 60, he entered the circus business in 1870. At the age of 25, he had paid $1,000 for Joice Heth, a black slave who was said to be 161 years old and the nurse of George Washington, and made about $1,500 a week exhibiting her in New York. (In later years, however, as a member of the state senate in Connecticut, he fought for the abolition of slavery.) In 1841, Barnum purchased the American Museum in New York City, which he promoted for its '500,000 natural and artificial curiosities from every corner of the globe'. During his lifetime, 40 million people paid 25 cents (half price for children) to enter the museum, making it the Disneyland of the 1800s—and making Barnum one of the richest men in the country. Although Barnum was skilled (some might say shameless) in using the press to promote his various enterprises, he also profited directly from the printed word. He started New York's first 'illustrated' newspaper in 1853 and, a year later, published his autobiography. The book sold over one million copies.

Publicity Enters the Modern Era

While P.T. Barnum relied upon his own talents for attracting media attention, others (including businesses and individuals) employed a press agent to get newspaper coverage. However, the excesses of press agentry were notorious; early practitioners wanted 'space at any price'. Variously known as 'flacks' and 'hucksters', press agents operated with few rules—no gimmick or stunt was too outrageous as long as it made the columns of the daily press.

It was not until the early 1900s that the ethically suspect practices of press agentry gave way to a more professional approach to media relations and publicity. One of the people who championed this transition was Ivy Ledbetter Lee, now considered to be a founding father of modern public relations. After working as a Wall Street newspaper reporter, he plunged into publicity work in 1903, and opened his own firm (with George Parker) in 1905. In an era when industrialists were regularly attacked by the popular press, Lee saw an opportunity for businesses to improve their public image by providing the press with as much factual information as possible.

'This is not a secret press bureau. All our work is done in the open. We aim to supply news. This is not an advertising agency; if you think any of our matter ought properly to go to your business office, do not use it. Our matter is accurate. Further details on any editor will be assisted most cheerfully in verifying directly any statement of fact. . . In brief, our plan is, frankly and openly, on behalf of business concerns and public institutions, to supply to the press and the public of the United States any prompt and accurate information concerning subjects which it is of value and interest to the public to know about.'

—Ivy Ledbetter Lee

Hired by the anthracite coal industry to represent mine owners during a coal strike in 1906, Lee used the occasion to issue a 'Declaration of Principles' on public information to newspaper editors. These principles were employed in the same year with the Pennsylvania Railroad, which had traditionally refused to allow reporters access to accident sites or to interview railroad personnel. As a result, both the press and the public regarded the railroad company with suspicion. Lee implemented a new policy, whereby reporters were provided with regular reports on the company's activities, as well as transportation to accident sites. This openness was revolutionary in its time and is a landmark in the evolution of public relations.

Dubbed the 'Prince of Puff' and the 'Baron of Ballyhoo', Edward L. Bernays (1891–1995) was arguably the most influential publicist of the twentieth century. The nephew of pioneering psychoanalyst Sigmund Freud, Bernays brought his own

astute grasp of human behaviour to the nascent field of public relations. He opened his own PR firm in 1919 and launched celebrated publicity campaigns for a variety of large companies and their products, as well as presidential election campaigns ranging from Coolidge to Eisenhower.

While Bernays remained active in the public relations field into his 90s, his most notable achievements date back to the years between the First and Second World War. In

1923, for example, he began working for Procter & Gamble to promote the company's Ivory Soap. The campaign was a model that any contemporary media relations practitioner would do well to study. Recognizing the news value of research, Bernays undertook a survey that showed the public preferred 'white unperfumed soap'. He then released these findings to the media, which duly reported them. What the media didn't report, but what everyone knew, was that Ivory Soap was the only white, unperfumed soap on the market.

Bernays obtained endorsements for Ivory that were also well publicized—one of the most notable being from the Ziegfeld Follies Girls, who pledged to use 'nothing but warm water and pure white, unscented, floating soap' on their faces.

Another Bernays triumph (although not in terms of public health) came with his work in 1929 for American Tobacco's Lucky Strike brand of cigarettes. At that time, cigarette smoking was widely accepted for men, but not for women. Those women who did smoke were not permitted (socially and, in some jurisdictions, legally) to do so in public. Bernays recognized that women, who had only recently won the right to vote, were ready to overturn this inequality and respond to his campaign to position cigarettes as 'torches of freedom'. By making public smoking a symbol of protest, cigarette sales among women increased significantly.

Public Relations in Canada Today

The history of public relations organizations in Canada dates back to the 1940s. Two professional associations were founded—the Canadian Public Relations Society (CPRS) and the International Association of Business Communications (IABC)—both of which have since contributed much to PR and communications education.

Over the past 70 years, the public- and media-relations profession has come a long way. Where its practitioners were once called everything from flacks and spin-doctors to snake oil salesmen, corporations, government agencies, small businesses, and non-profit organizations now recognize the value of their work. The public relations specialist is an advisor to management who acts as a mediator and interpreter, translating organizational goals into reasonable, publicly acceptable policies and actions. Public relations is also a means for the public to have its desires and interests heard by organizations.

Media relations professionals build and maintain relationships with clients, helping them to educate the public, enhance their reputations, launch products, raise funds, attract sponsorship, and a host of other activities. Media relations has helped companies to build on-going relationships with the media, as well as to deal with the media in a crisis.

In the twenty-first century

Today's CEOs and Executive Directors realize more and more that public relations is undervalued and that it can be more effective in building and keeping a reputation than all the advertising in the world.

Stay Tuned

There can be little doubt; the twentieth century belonged to broadcasting. And news has been central to the growth and success of the electronic era. By the time I was born in 1934, radio was well established across North America. My first memories are of the crackling sounds from the big box with the illuminated dial that sat in the corner as our family huddled around listening to the news about the Second World War.

There were the clipped tones of the CBC's Matthew Halton describing Nazi air raids over London and the stentorian presence of Lorne Greene, and on Toronto's CFRB the great Jim Hunter. They catalogued the progress of the fighting and the setbacks and the successes of Canadian troops.

The delivery of war news, so quickly and dramatically, established the importance to broadcasting of instantaneous information. Those who heard them will never forget the wartime broadcasts of Edward R. Murrow of CBS and the masterful way in which he weaved his commentary through the sounds of the sirens and the loud thunder of bomb explosions during and after the Battle of Britain. And, fittingly enough, it was radio that brought us the sounds of the glorious celebrations marking the end of the war in Europe from London, England and New York City.

But the laying down of arms brought a whirlwind of change to society as a whole and profoundly affected the future of radio. It had served us well, and would always have a place, but there was a new kid on the block demanding elbowroom in the fight for the public's attention.

No electronic innovation of the twentieth century would have an impact comparable to television. News on the tube was of scant importance at first. It wasn't given the pride of place it had won in radio with the hourly bulletins. Newscasts were 15 minutes in length, sometimes only 10. The CBC had a daily regional newscast at the peculiar time of 6:45 pm. Gradually, habit began to take hold with the 11 o'clock news, first with Larry Henderson and the avuncular Earl Cameron.

continued

In the US, John Cameron Swayze was holding forth with the 'Camel News Caravan', which presented the events of the day from a desk plastered with cigarette logos. When the networks began to take news more seriously, Douglas Edwards hosted a daily 15-minute spot on CBS in the days before Walter Cronkite arrived on the scene.

I made my first foray into the new medium at CBC Winnipeg in 1956. Having come out of radio, I was intimidated at first by the hot lights and sheer numbers of people who had to be available in the studio just to get a television broadcast to air. But all of us who were in on the ground floor were excited about television's possibilities and how pictures could enhance the daily news.

Still, in those times long before satellites, the pictures were usually a day or two behind the events. Since there were no teleprompters, viewers got to see the tops of a lot of newscasters' heads as some had trouble 'getting it off the page'. I would usually try, not always very successfully, to memorize the top few lines of the key stories. Even when prompters arrived, years later, it took a while for operators to get adjusted and the machines would often spin the copy backwards or sometimes simply die mid-sentence causing that 'deer in the headlights' stare to come over the faces of some broadcasters who had hopelessly lost their way.

On location, television was truly the '10 ton pencil'. Reporters were part of a crew that included, at minimum, a cameraman and a sound person. It always seemed to take forever to get the shots you needed, then send the film for processing and supervise the editing before you could get your story to air. Highly experienced print reporters, who had transferred to the new medium, often dissolved in paroxysms of anger and frustration. Lighter equipment and the ENG cameras would drastically improve news gathering methods down the road, even if they didn't do much to soothe the nerves of reporters who had to cope with increased pressures from tougher competition and tighter deadlines.

I had moved on from Winnipeg to Ottawa and then to Toronto when on a November day in 1963 I was tapped on the shoulder, while having lunch in the CBC canteen, and told to get to the studio quickly. President Kennedy had been shot in Dallas. There would be bulletins to do.

The next three days changed for all time the importance of television in the lives of a generation. Where were you on that day? It became the common question for years to come. Millions of people were glued to their black-and-white TV sets watching the live coverage, up to and including the funeral. The images of the poignant pictures are locked in our memories—Jacqueline Kennedy kissing her husband's coffin and John Jr, who died in a plane crash [in 1999], raising his tiny arm to salute as the funeral cortege passed in front of him.

continued

Through this searing tragedy, television had provided the forum for national and international mourning. It was a watershed event and the importance of TV was elevated as a meeting place for the shared experience through the presentation of 'live' news.

More 'live' broadcasting meant more challenges for on-camera people who would have to address the lens directly, in a wide range of situations, without benefit of scripts. Field prompters eventually became available, but for most events on location they simply weren't practical and the brute demands of TV saw many good reporters fall by the wayside because they couldn't master speaking extemporaneously.

Technology was constantly leading the way. Colour was introduced and became popular overnight. Videotape replaced film as the product of choice for news, and more satellites were launched to bring instant pictures from all over the world. The 'global village' had arrived through TV.

In July of 1969 I had to pinch myself to acknowledge that I was really part of the coverage that was bringing the moon landing to Canadians. Those pictures of astronauts Neil Armstrong and Buzz Aldrin bouncing, kangaroo-like, around the surface will survive as a marker of achievement for a century that was too often scarred by bloodshed and death.

Outlets for news and the time devoted to it continued to expand as stations and networks discovered that information programming could bring identity and credibility to their operations while making money at the same time. CBC and CTV added more minutes to their nightly broadcasts and all-news outlets on cable began broadcasting all day everyday. The golden age had arrived for TV news.

Through the years the general public has come to rely on television to cover and catalogue the major events of our times. And I have been among those privileged to tag along . . . through the glorious celebrations of centennial year to the night Canada came to the brink of breakup during the Quebec referendum of 1995.

While we are understandably in awe of the technology that has brought us this far, the fundamentals of what we do remain the same. They're about getting the story right as well as getting it first, being fair, and when warranted, honouring the tradition of 'comforting the afflicted and afflicting the comfortable'.

Article by Lloyd Robertson, chief anchor and senior editor of the CTV National News. Reprinted with permission from Press Review, *Sept. 1999.*

Resources

Media Organizations and Associations

American Journalism Review Database of Dailies by State   *www.newslink.org*
Academy of Canadian Film and Television   *www.academy.ca*
Advertising Standards Canada   *www.adstandards.com*
Associated Press   *http://customwire.ap.org/dynamic/fronts/HOME*
Broadcast Bureau of Measurement   *www.bbm.ca*
Canada NewsWire (CNW Group)   *www.newswire.ca*
Canadian Association of Broadcasters   *www.cab-acr.ca*
Canadian Association of Journalists   *www.caj.ca*
CARD Media   *www.cardmedia.com*
Canadian Business Press   *www.cbp.ca*
Canadian Community Newspaper Association   *www.communitynews.ca*
Canadian Magazine Publishers Association   *www.cmpa.ca*
Canadian Newspaper Association   *www.can-acj.ca*
The Canadian Press   *www.cp.org*
Canadian Public Relations Society   *www.cprs.ca*
Canadian Women in Communications   *www.cwc-afc.com*
CBC radio-Canada   *www.cbc.ca*
Cision Media Monitoring Limited   *http://ca.cision.com*
Editor & Publisher   *www.editorandpublisher.com*
Editor & Publisher Interactive   *www.mediainfo.com*
International Association of Broadcast Communicators   *www.iabc.com*
MediaBistro   *www.mediabistro.com*
News Voyager's Local Newspaper Listings   *www.newspaperlinks.com/home.cfm*
Poynter Institute   *www.poynter.org*
Print Measurement Bureau   *www.pmb.ca*
The Public Relations Society of America (PRSA)   *www.prsa.org*
The New York Times   *www.nytimes.com*

Reuters Newswire Service   *http://today.reuters.com/news/default.aspx*
Society of Professional Journalists   *www.spj.org*
Television Bureau of Canada   *www.tvb.ca*
USA Today   *www.usatoday.com*
Washington Post   *www.washingtonpost.com*
Women in Film and Television (WIFTA)   *www.wift.com*
US Newspapers by City   *www.newspapers.com*

Media Relations Online Resources

Writers.ca (Professional Writers Association of Canada)   Site to find a professional writer; maintained by Professional Writers Assocation of Canada (PWAC). See *www.writers.ca*.

Media Names & Numbers   Comprehensive directory of Canada's media, including television, radio, daily and weekly newspapers, and magazines. Available in print and online, cost is $109.95/year for print edition plus online access. Also available as a database. See *www.sources.com/MNN*.

MegaSources   Dean Tudor's list of gateways and information sites of interest to journalists, ranging from massive indexes and databases to specialized news beats. See *www.deantudor.com*.

National Public Relations Network   American site featuring directory of over 2,500 public relations agencies; information and articles on public relations issues, such as speech writing and trade shows. See *www.usprnet.com*.

Sources Calendar   Brief listings of events of interest to Canadian journalists, editors, researchers, publishers and others working in the media and in publishing. See *www.sources.com/SSOCal.htm*.

Sources Listings   Features more than 5,000 experts, contacts and spokespeople willing to be interviewed by the media. See *www.sources.com*.

Sources Select Links and Resources   Links to Internet sites and other electronic and print resources for journalists and researchers. See *www.sources.com/Links.htm*.

Sources Select Resources   Reviews and information about print and online resources for journalists and researchers. See *www.sources.com/SSR.htm*.

PR/Media Relations Blogs

BlinnPR Report   *http://www.blinnpr.com/blog*. Media relations perspectives from a boutique agency.

Corporate PR   *http://ringblog.typepad.com/corporatepr*. Commentary on the current and future practice of corporate public relations from Elizabeth Albrycht.

Edelman 6 A.M.   *http://edelman.com/speak_up/blog/*. Insight and analysis on PR and beyond from the president and CEO of the world's largest independent public relations firm.

For Immediate Release, The Hobson & Holz Report   *http://forimmediaterelease.biz*. Comments on PR and tech by Shel Holtz and Neville Hobson

The Flack   *http://theflack.blogspot.com*. Peter Himler's comments and analysis of politics, media, and culture geared toward shining a 'brighter light on PR's subtle influence over our lives'.

Force for Good   *http://jon8332.typepad.com/force_for_good/*. Jon Harmon's posts on 'aspirational PR'.

InfOpinions   *http://auburnmedia.com/wordpress*. Insight, wordplay, and analysis on marketing communications, PR, and technology.

Judy Cushman's Blog   *http://www.jc-a.com/blog/jcablog.htm*. Judith Cushman's Blog for senior communications professionals lists open VP positions (and above), candidly discusses human resource issues and identifies hiring trends.

Lubetkin's Other Blog   *http://lubetkinsotherblog.blogspot.com/*. Steve Lubetkin comments on news, journalism, and public relations issues.

Making News   *http://www.makingnews.typepad.com/*. Veteran PR exec David Henderson's new blog promoting greater understanding for practicing media relations to meet the needs of the news media as well as clients.

Media Guerrilla   *http://mmanuel.typepad.com/media_guerrilla*. Mike Manuel's inside look at tech PR.

MWW Straight Talk   *http://www.mwwstraighttalk.com/*. Michael Kempner, president and CEO of MWW Group, expounds upon his professional and personal experiences during the last 20 years.

NextFiftyYears   *http://www.NextFiftyYears.com*. Golin Harris's perspective on the future of communications.

Natterjack   *http://www.natterjackpr.com*. Tom Murphy's thoughts and opinions on the PR industry.

NewPR Wiki   *http://www.thenewpr.com/wiki/pmwiki.php*. Collaborate open source repository (wiki) of PR-related articles, information, and updates on how the industry is changing.

Phil's Blogservations   *http://www.philgomes.com/blog*. Posts on PR and media matters from Phil Gomes, senior counsel for online comms at Edelman.

POP! PR Jots   *http://pop-pr.blogspot.com*. Jeremy Pepper's commentary, opinions, and views on PR, publicity, and other things that strike his fancy.

PR Machine   *http://prmachine.blogspot.com*. Rob Hecht's blog featuring breaking PR blurbs and media news.

RepMan   *http://www.repmanblog.com*. One PR man's take (i.e., Steve Cody, CEO of Peppercom) on the importance of a good reputation in a world gone mad.

The Reputation Doctor   *http://www.TheReputationDoctor.com*. User-friendly reputation management advice and commentary regarding top leaders, celebrities, corporations, and organizations with reputations in crisis.

Reputation Management   *www.reputationxchange.blogspot.com*. Commentary on building, sustaining, and recovering reputation. Posted by Dr Gaines-Ross, Weber Shandwick's Chief Reputation Strategist.

Shel of My Former Self   *http://blog.holtz.com*. Meanderings on organizational communication and other issues by Shel Holtz.

SpeakCast   *http://www.speakcast.com*. Daily media training video and audio content from TJ Walker.

StraightTalk   *http://www.StraightTalkpr.com*. Douglass Davidoff offers PR insight from Indiana.

Strategic Public Relations   *http://prblog.typepad.com*. Kevin Dugan's blog on public relations strategy within integrated marketing communications.

TJ's Insights   *http://www.tjsights.com*. Commentary on media and speaking issues.

Canadian Public Relations Society Accreditation Reading List

Mike Beard, *Running a Public Relations Department*, 2nd ed. (London, UK: Kogan Page, 2001).

Thomas, Bivins, *Handbook for Public Relations Writing* (Chicago: NTC Business Books, 1995).

Thomas Bivins, *Mixed Media: Moral Distinctions in Advertising, Public Relations and Journalism* (Hillsdale, NJ: Lawrence Erlbaum, 2003).

Jeff Blyskal and Marie Blyskal, *PR: How the Public Relations Industry Writes the News* (New York: William Morrow, 1985).

Carl Botan, ed., *Public Relations Theory* (Hillsdale, NJ: Lawrence Erlbaum Associates, 2006).

Glen Broom and David Dozier, *Using Research in Public Relations: Applications to Program Management* (Englewood Cliffs, NJ: Prentice-Hall, 1990).

Cathie Burton and Alun Drake, *Hitting the Headlines in Europe. A Country-by-Country Guide to Effective Media Relations* (London, UK: Kogan Page, 2004).

William Wray Carney, *In the News—The Practice of Media Relations in Canada* (Edmonton, AB: University of Alberta Press, 2002).

Paula Marantz Cohen, *A Public Relations Primer: Thinking and Writing in Context* (Englewood Cliffs, NJ: Prentice-Hall, 1987).

John Cooper, *Crisis Communications in Canada* (Toronto: Centennial College Press, 2007).

Pamela, Creedon, ed., *Women in Mass Communication: Challenging Gender Values* (Newbury Park, CA: Sage Publications, 1989).

Scott Cutlip, Alan Center, and Glen Broom, *Effective Public Relations*, 8th ed. (Englewood Cliffs, NJ: Prentice-Hall, 2006).

Al Czarnecki, *Crisis Communications: A Primer for Teams* (Toronto: iUniverse, Inc., 2007).

Louis Day, *Ethics in Media Communications: Cases and Controversies* (Belmont, CA: Wadsworth Publishing Company, 2005).

Denise Deegan, *Managing Activism: A Guide to Dealing with Activists and Pressure Groups* (Dublin: Fitzwilliam Institute, 2001).

William Elwood, *Public Relations Inquiry as Rhetorical Criticism: Case Studies of Corporate Discourse and Social Influence* (Westport, CT: Greenwood, 1995).

Sherry Devereaux Ferguson, *Communication Planning* (New York: SAGE Publications, 1999).

Sherry Devereaux Ferguson, *Mastering the Public Opinion Challenge* (Toronto: Irwin Professional Publishing, 1994).

John Foster, *Effective Writing Skills for Public Relations*, 2nd ed. (London, UK: Kogan Page, 2006).

Jordan Goldman, *Public Relations and the Marketing Mix: Introducing Vulnerability Relations* (Chicago, Crain Books, 1984).

Anne Gregory, *Planning and Managing Public Relations Campaigns*, 2nd ed. (London: Kogan Page, 2000).

Anne Gregory, *Public Relations in Practice*, 2nd ed. (London, UK: Kogan Page, 2004).

James Grunig and Linda Hon, *Guidelines for Measuring Relationships in Public Relations* (Gainsville, FL: Institute for Public Relations, 1999).

James Grunig, *Excellence in Public Relations and Communication Management* (Hillsdale, NJ: Lawrence Erlbaum Associates, 1992).

James Grunig and Larisa Grunig, *Excellent Public Relations and Effective Organizations* (Hillsdale, NJ: Lawrence Erlbaum, 2002)

James Grunig and Todd Hunt, *Managing Public Relations* (New York: Holt, Rinehart and Winston, 1984).

Larissa Grunig and James Grunig, eds. *Public Relations Research Annual, Volumes 1 to 3* (Hillsdale, NJ: Lawrence Erlbaum, 1989, 1990, 1991).

Larissa Grunig and James Grunig, *Manager's Guide to Excellence in Public Relations and Communication Management* (Hillsdale, NJ: Lawrence Erlbaum, 1995).

T. Hagley, *Writing Winning Proposals: PR Cases* (Toronto: Pearson, 2005).

Seymour Hamilton, *A Communications Audit Handbook* (New York: Longman, 1987).

Jerry A. Hendrix, *Public Relations Cases* (Belmont, CA: Wadsworth Publishing Company, 2004).

Philip Henslowe, *Public Relations: A Practical Guide to the Basics*, 2nd ed. (London, UK: Kogan Page, 2003).

Helen Holmes and David Taras, eds, *Seeing Ourselves: Media Power and Policy in Canada*, 2nd ed. (Toronto: Harcourt Brace Canada, 1996).

Shel Holtz, *Public Relations on the Net* (Toronto: AMACOM, 1999).

Carole Howard and Wilma Matthews, *On Deadline: Managing Media Relations* (New York: Longman, 2000).

Robert Kendall, *Public Relations Campaign Strategies: Planning for Implementation* (Toronto: Harper Collins, 1997).

L. Lamb and K.B. Mckee, *Applied Public Relations: Cases in Stakeholder Management* (Mahwah, NJ: Lawrence Erlbaum, 2006).

Dan Lattimore, et al., *Public Relations: The Profession and the Practice* (Toronto: McGraw-Hill, 2003).

Mark Lavigne, *Making Ink and Airtime: How to Conduct Proactive Media Relations in Canada* (Aurora, ON: Hunter LaVigne Communications, Inc., 2007).

Philip Lesly, *Handbook of Public Relations and Communications*, 4th ed. (Toronto: McGraw-Hill Ryerson, 1998).

Walter Lindemann, *Guidelines and Standards for Measuring and Evaluating the Effectiveness of PR Programs and Activities* (Gainsville, FL: Institute for Public Relations, 2003).

Rowland Lorimer and Jean McNulty, *Mass Communications in Canada*, 2nd ed. (Toronto: McLelland & Stewart, 1996).

Mark MacElreath, *Managing Systematic and Ethical Public Relations* (Dubuque, IA: Wm. C. Brown Communications Inc., 1993).

Randall Marlin, *Propaganda and the Ethics of Persuasion* (Peterborough, ON: Broadview Press, 2002).

Craig McKie and Benjamin Singer, *Communications in Canadian Society*, 5th ed. (Toronto: Thomson Nelson, 2001).

Melvin Mencher, *Basic News Writing*, 4th ed. (Dubuque, IA: Wm. C. Brown, 1991).

Thomas Mickey, *Deconstructing Public Relations* (Hillsdale, NJ: Lawrence Erlbaum, 2002).

Norman Nager, *Public Relations Management by Objectives* (New York: Longman, 1984).

Norman Nager, *Strategic Public Relations Counselling* (New York: Longman, 1992).

Doug Newsom, et al., *This is PR: The Realities of Public Relations*, 4th ed. (Belmont, CA: Wadsworth, 2004).

Doug Newsom, et al., *Public Relations Writing: Form and Style*, 3rd ed. (Belmont, CA: Wadsworth, 2004).

David Olive, *Just Rewards/The Case for Ethical Reform in Business* (Toronto, Key Porter Books Limited, 1987).

Patricia Parsons, *Ethics in Public Relations: A Guide to Best Practice* (Gainsville, FL: Institute of Public Relations, 2004).

Patricia Parsons, *A Manager's Guide to PR Projects: A Practical Approach.* (Mahwah, NJ: Lawrence Erlbaum, 2003).

Philip Patterson and Lee Wilkins, *Media Ethics: Issues and Cases* (Dubuque, IA: Wm. C. Brown, 1991).

Deborah Poff and Wilfred Waluchow, *Business Ethics in Canada*, 2nd ed. (Toronto, Prentice-Hall, 1991).

Michael Regester and Judy Larkin, *Management in Public Relations*, 2nd ed. (London, UK: Kogan Page, 2002).

R. Reilly, *Public Relations in Action*, 2nd ed. (Toronto: Prentice-Hall, 1987).

Ed Schiller, *Managing the Media* (Toronto: Bedford House, 1994).

Peter Schwartz and Blair Gibb, *When Good Companies Do Bad Things* (Toronto: Wiley, 1999).

Fraser Seitel, *The Practice of Public Relations*, 6th ed. (Toronto: Prentice-Hall, 1995).

Gary Selnow, *Planning and Implementing Targeted Communications Programs* (New York: Quorum Books, 1987).

Raymond Simon, *Public Relations Management: A Casebook* (Columbus, OH: Publishing Horizons, 1986).

Benjamin D. Singer, ed., *Communications in Canadian Society* (Toronto: Nelson Canada, 1995).

Alvie Smith, *Innovative Employee Communications* (Englewood Cliffs, NJ: Prentice-Hall, 1991).

R.D. Smith, *Strategic Planning for Public Relations*, 2nd ed. (Mahwah, NJ: Lawrence Erlbaum, 2005).

Susan Sommers, *Building Media Relationships: How to Establish, Maintain, & Develop Long Term Relationships with the Media* (Toronto: Irwin Publishing, 2002).

David Taras, *The Newsmakers: The Media's Influence on Canadian Politics* (Toronto: Nelson, 1990).

Betteke Van Ruler, *Public Relations Metrics: Research and Evaluation* (London, UK: Taylor & Francis, 2008).

Austin E. Weintraub and B.E. Pinkleton, *Strategic Public Relations Management* (Hillsdale, NJ: Lawrence Erlbaum, 2006).

Dennis Wilcox, et al., *Public Relations Strategies and Tactics*, 8th ed. (Toronto: Addison Wesley Educational Publishers, 2006).

W. John Wright and Christopher J. DuVernet, *The Canadian Public Affairs Handbook: Maximizing Markets, Protecting Bottom Lines* (Toronto: Carswell, 1988).

Index

Access CNW, 20
accreditation reading list, CPRS, 235–8
'ad value', 177
advertising, 6, 11; media kits and, 114;
    v. publicity, 7
advertorial, 6, 11
AIDS Committee of Toronto (ACT), 24, 192;
    see also Fashion Cares
analysis, 22–3, 43–66; SWOT, 44
'angle', 18
Argyle Communications, 24, 27, 143
articles, contributed, 28–30
Assignment Editors, 71, 77, 80, 81
associations, media, 232–3
audience reach, 177–8
audiences, 77–81; defining, 37–40;
    internal, 41
audit: communications, 40–1, 174–9;
    media, 22, 41; risk assessment, 190
awards and recognition: media kits and,
    112–13

Bacon's Media Directories, 74
Barnum, P.T., 225–6
BC Housing, 115–16, 117, 118, 192–8
beat codes, 71
beat reporters, 78
Bednarski, Lisa, 24
Bergeron, S.L., and A.L. Sanchez, 222–3
Bernays, Edward L., 227–8
blogs, 49; media relations, 233–5
Blue Book: Matthews', 73; University of
    Toronto, 136
Blue Nose International Marathon, 217–22;
    Media Kit, 93–4, 99–100, 111–12, 113
Bowdens Media Directories, 73
Bowdens Media Monitoring Limited, 171
Broadcast Fax, 76
Broadcast News, 75

Broadcast-On-Demand, 76
broadcast personalities, 81
B-roll packages, 121
Bryden, Andrew, 25
budgets, 65–6
bulletins, 14–15
bureau chiefs, 71
bureau reporters/editors, 78
Burrelle's Information Services, 74
Burrelle's Media Monitoring, 172

calendar listings, 110
call-in shows, 80
Canada NewsWire, 19–20
Canadian Advertising Rates and Data
    (CARD), 73
Canadian Association of Broadcasters
    (CAB), 15
Canadian Association of Food Banks, 25
Canadian Broadcasting Corporation
    (CBC), 15
Canadian Community Newspaper
    Association, 74
Canadian Corporate News (CCN), 72–3
Canadian Football League, 25
Canadian Magazine Publishers Association
    (CMPA), 14
Canadian Press (CP), 13, 75, 124, 172
Canadian Public Relations Society (CPRS),
    5, 228; accreditation reading list, 235–8;
    Measurement Committee, 177–8
case studies, 23–5, 27–8; audiences and,
    39–40; crisis management, 204–9,
    217–22; evaluation phase, 180–2; goals
    and, 51–2; issues management, 192–8;
    media audit and, 42; media events, 164,
    166–7; research analysis and, 45–7;
    special events, 140–5; strategies and,
    53–5

celebrities, 167–8

CHIN, 16

Cision, 73; Media Monitoring, 171

City Editor, 78

CNW Group, 19–20, 74, 75–6, 128, 133–4, 170–1

columnists, 79

comment cards, 40

communications: elements of, 8; RACE process and, 23, 69–82

communications audit, 40–1, 42, 174–9

Community Media Canada, 74

consumer publications, 79

contract, sample, 61–3

corporations: as partners, 55

CP Command News, 172

CP Photo Assignment Services, 124

CP Television News Monitoring, 172

crisis, 199–209; audiences and, 200–1; definition of, 200; event-driven, 200; issues and, 191; issues-driven, 200; litigation-driven, 200; preparation for, 200; plan for, 201–4

crisis communication, 200, 202–3, 210–24; stages of, 213–16

Crisis Communications Team, 213

crisis management, 199–209, 210–24; plan for, 213

Crisis Media Kit, 203–4

critical path, sample, 64, 135–6

'dark site', 204

'data smog', 9

Daybook Summary, 133–4

deadlines: magazine, 79; newspaper, 78

Department Editors, 78

direct selling, 6

Donia, Teresa, 48–50

dress: media interviews and, 154–5

Editorial Boards, 132

Editorial Page Editor, 78

Editors: contributed articles and, 29; magazine, 79; needs of, 19; newspaper, 77–8

Edmonton Flood Prevention Strategy, 114, 116, 204–9

e-mail: broadcast, 76; media releases and, 133

embargo, 159

'encoding', 8

entertainment guides, 79

evaluation, 23, 169–83; reasons for, 173

eWatch™, 172–3

executive producers, 80, 81

expenses, 60–1

expert opinion, 136

e-zines, 14

Fact Sheets, 98–103

fanzines, 14

Fashion Cares, 24, 27, 140–2; audiences and, 39; budget for, 65; challenges and, 45; evaluation of, 180; goals of, 51; issues management and, 192; Key Messages and, 151–2; launch party, 164; media events and, 166–7; strategies and, 53

fax: broadcast, 76; media releases and, 133

fees, 60

filing system, 65

focus groups, 40

Freeman, Joe, 19–20

Friesen, Carl, 28–30

George, Alison, 24

ghost-writing, 29

Gill, Katrina, 212

goals: communications, 50–2, 70; issues management, 189–90; media relations program and, 50–2; research, 36

graphic designers, 123

Green Book, 73

'headline spin', 12

Hill & Knowlton, 25, 27–8, 144

Holland, Robert, 212

'hook', 18, 86, 130–1

'how-to' article, 30

Huybregts, Godfrey, 204, 205

Independently Healthy, 115–16, 117, 118, 192–8; *see also* BC Housing
information session, 131–2
inserts, 14–15
International Association of Business Communicators (IABC), 5, 212, 228
Internet, 17; crisis and, 204; media events and, 165; media relations plan and, 48–50; media releases and, 86, 122–3, 138; media room, 23, 48–9, 122–3; newswire services and, 19
issues, 187–98; definition of, 188; key markets and media for, 189; types of, 188–9
issues management, 188; goals of, 189–90; plan for, 190–1
issues statement, 188
Ivory Soap, 228

Kabalin, Romana, 205
Key Messages, 4, 22, 23, 52, 114, 151–2

Lash, Paula, 25
launch party, 164
Lee, Ivy Ledbetter, 227
'legs', 18
Levine, Michael, 9
Lions Foundation of Canada Dog Guides, 25
listings, calendar, 112
Lucky Strike, 228

M.A.C. Cosmetics, 24, 27; *see also* Fashion Cares
magazines, 13–14, 78–9
mail: media releases and, 133
Maloney, Tim, 25
Managing Editors, 77, 79
Marcomm Works, 204, 205
marketing: inbound/outbound, 4; media relations and, 4–7
marketing mix, 4–9
Matthews Media Directory, 72–3
matt story, 74, 85, 114
measuring: media campaign and, 177–8, 180–2

media, 10–20; broadcast, 15–17; calls from, 139–40; contacting, 77–81, 129–46; crisis and, 211, 213, 214–5; first contact, 130–1; follow-up and, 131, 134; history of, 225–32; local, 139; needs of, 18; as partners, 56, 57; pre-registration and, 158, 166; print, 11–15
media advisory, 95–7, 132–3, 134
media alerts, 95–7, 132–3, 134
media audit, 22, 41
Media Communication Centre, 213
media contact sheet, 140
media content analysis, 177
media database, 69–82; creating, 70–1; definition of, 70; sample entry, 71; sources for, 72–6; storing, 72
media directories, 72–6
media drop, 137–8
media events, 157–68; contact and follow-up for, 158–9, 163, 167; pre-registration for, 158, 166; types of, 158, 159–64
media interview form, 150
media interviews, 147–56; declining, 150; preparing for, 151, 152–5; problem, 155
Media Kit, 23, 83–128; components of, 84–5; crisis and, 203–4; definition of, 84; media events and, 159; other printed material and, 115–20; outside professionals and, 123–4; photography and, 124–8; reasons for, 84–5; use of, 121
media list tracker, 82
media monitoring services, 170–3
MediaNetCentral.ca, 74
media party, 163
media previews, 164
Media Ratings Points (MRP™), 177–8
media relations: communications process and, 8; definition of, 4; history of, 225–32; publicity and public relations and, 5–7; resources for, 233; role of, 3–9

media relations program, 23; debriefing and, 178–9; developing, 35–66; documenting, 179; goals of, 50–2; implementing, 129–46; monitoring and measuring, 169–83; planning for, 48–52; reasons for, 9; strategies of, 52–5

media relations specialists/firms, 31; roles and responsibilities of, 26–31

media releases, 85; broadcast, 121–2; optimized, 49–50, 86; results of, 95; samples of, 88–94; sending, 132–3; series of, 135–6; special events and, 132–3; video, 121–2; writing, 85–7

media report, 178

media room, 166; online, 23, 48–9, 122–3

MediaSource, 171

media tracking form, 171

MediaVantage, 170–1

Microsites, 76

mission statement, 85

monitoring, 169–73

'narrow casting', 15

Nestlé Purina PetCare, 25, 111; see also Purina Walk for Guide Dogs

News Canada, 76, 177–8

news conference, 159–63; online, 165; televised, 162–3

news engines, 49–50

news feeds, 80

newsletters, 14–15; media kits and, 114

news magazines, 79

newspapers, 11–13, 77–8, 225–6; community, 12

newswire services, 13, 19–20, 50, 76, 133–4

newsworthiness, 11, 18–19, 86, 160

Nielsen/Norman Group, 48

OMNI-TV, 16

organizations: media, 232–3; non-profit, 56

partnerships, 55–8

photo editors, 78

photography: media kits and, 85, 124–8

photo op, 95–7

PIER (Public Information Emergency Response) Ready Sites, 204

pitch, 85, 130–1; tips for, 71

press agentry, 226–7

producers, radio/television, 71, 80, 81

product launch, 164

product samples, 114

Professional Writers Association of Canada (PWAC), 75

program directors, 80, 81

promotion, 4–7

proposal, media relations, 59–61

public affairs directors, 80, 81

publicity, 5–7, 11; v. advertising, 7

publicity stunts, 165

public relations, 5–7; see also media relations

publics, 5

public service announcements (PSAs), 17, 80–1, 85, 110–12, 136

published works: media kits and, 112

'puff piece', 30

Purina Walk for Dog Guides, 24–5, 27, 42, 143; audiences and, 39; budget for, 66; challenges and, 46; evaluation of, 181; goals of, 51; Key Messages and, 152; Media Kit, 91–2, 97, 102–3, 104, 119; strategies and, 53–4

Purolator Tackle Hunger, 25, 47, 144–5; audiences and, 40; budget for, 66; evaluation of, 182; goals of, 52; Media Kit, 90, 96, 101; strategies and, 55

query letter, 29

RACE (Research, Analyze, Communication, and Evaluate), 21–3; analysis phase, 53–66; communication phase, 69–82; evaluation phase, 169–83; research phase, 35–42

radio, 16–17, 80–1; history of, 229; media releases and, 122; multicultural, 16

reading list, 233–5

Red Book, 73
reporters, 78; needs of, 19
research, 22, 35–42; goals of, 36; market, 4; post-campaign, 174–5; sources for, 36–7, 40
risk and threat analysis, 201
risk assessment audit, 190
Robertson, Lloyd, 229–31

sales promotion, 6
SARS (severe acute respiratory syndrome), 222–3
satellite media tour, 139
schedule: *see* critical path
social media, 86
special events, 132–6; fact sheets and, 105; non-profit, 136
speech therapy, 153
spokespeople, 148–9; crisis and, 203
sponsors, 55–8; contact form for, 58; in-kind, 57; media, 56, 57; principal, 57; title, 56
station managers, 80, 81
statistics: media kits and, 112
story ideas, 110
surveys, 40; post-campaign, 175, 176
SWOT (strengths, weaknesses, opportunities, threats) analysis, 44

'telephone tag', 131
television, 15–16; features, 79–80; history of, 229–31; media releases and, 121–2; multilingual, 16; news conferences and, 162–3; news, 80

testimonials, 110
Thom, Susan, 192
timetable: *see* critical path
Tisch, Daniel, 24
trade publications, 79
'trend article', 30
Trudeau, Elaine, 205

University of Toronto, 136, 155–6

video B-roll packages, 121
video news releases, 121–2
Virgin Mobile Canada Launch, 25, 27, 144; audiences and, 39; budget for, 66; challenges and, 46–7; evaluation of, 181–2; goals of, 52; Media Kit, 88–9, 105–9, 120; strategies and, 54–5
'voice', 37–8

webcast, 165
web conferencing, 165
Weber Shandwick Worldwide, 24, 27, 140–2
website, company, 138
wire service: media releases and, 133–4
writers, freelance, 123

Young, Sarah, 217

zines, 14